Hauntings: Psychoanalysis and Ghostly Transmissions

Studies in the Psychosocial

Edited by Peter Redman, The Open University, UK, Stephen Frosh, Birkbeck College, University of London, UK, and Wendy Hollway, The Open University, UK

Titles include:

Stephen Frosh
HAUNTINGS: PSYCHOANALYSIS AND GHOSTLY TRANSMISSIONS

Studies in the Psychosocial Series
Series Standing Order 978–0–230–30858–9 (hardback)
978–0–230–30859–6 (paperback)
(*outside North America only*)

You can receive future titles in this series as they are published by placing a standing order. Please contact your bookseller or, in case of difficulty, write to us at the address below with your name and address, the title of the series and the ISBN quoted above.

Customer Services Department, Macmillan Distribution Ltd, Houndmills, Basingstoke, Hampshire RG21 6XS, England

Hauntings: Psychoanalysis and Ghostly Transmissions

Stephen Frosh

Professor of Psychology and Pro-Vice-Master, Department of Psychosocial Studies, Birkbeck College, University of London, UK

palgrave
macmillan

Stephen Frosh © 2013

First published 2013 by
PALGRAVE MACMILLAN

Palgrave Macmillan in the UK is an imprint of Macmillan Publishers Limited, registered in England, company number 785998, of Houndmills, Basingstoke, Hampshire RG21 6XS.

Palgrave Macmillan in the US is a division of St Martin's Press LLC, 175 Fifth Avenue, New York, NY 10010.

Palgrave Macmillan is the global academic imprint of the above companies and has companies and representatives throughout the world.

Palgrave® and Macmillan® are registered trademarks in the United States, the United Kingdom, Europe and other countries.

ISBN 978–1–137–03124–2 hardback
ISBN 978–1–137–03127–3 paperback

This book is printed on paper suitable for recycling and made from fully managed and sustained forest sources. Logging, pulping and manufacturing processes are expected to conform to the environmental regulations of the country of origin.

A catalogue record for this book is available from the British Library.

A catalog record for this book is available from the Library of Congress.

10   9   8   7   6   5   4   3   2   1
22 21 20 19 18 17 16 15 14 13

Printed and bound in Great Britain by
CPI Antony Rowe, Chippenham and Eastbourne

In memory of my father, Sidney Frosh, 1923–2012.
May his memory be for a blessing.

Contents

Acknowledgements

The starting point for this book was an article called 'Hauntings: Psychoanalysis and Ghostly Transmission', © 2012 The Johns Hopkins University Press, that first appeared in *American Imago*, 69, 2 (2012): 241–64.

Part of the discussion of the Akedah in Chapter 6 was first published as 'Psychosocial Textuality: Religious Identities and Textual Constructions', *Subjectivity*, 3, 4 (2010): 426–41.

Translations of the commentary on Genesis by Rashi are from M. Rosenbaum and A. Silbermann, *Pentateuch with Rashi's Commentary: Genesis* (New York: Hebrew Publishing Company, published during the 1930s).

I would like to thank Derek Hook for his very helpful review of the first draft of this book. Thanks too to Angelina Baydala, Dov Lerner, Kate Loewenthal, Roger Luckhurst, Belinda Mandelbaum, Enrique Mandelbaum, Andrew Margolis, Rabbi David Mason, Jeremy Schonfield and Reina van der Wiel for various textual pointers. I would also like to thank the students of the Birkbeck Institute for the Humanities Critical Theory Summer School for their enthusiastic response to my ideas.

I am grateful to Birkbeck College for the gift of a period of study leave in 2011–12, during which this book was written.

1

Introduction: Psychoanalysis as a Ghostly System

Smoke gets in your eyes

Perhaps every generation has something that haunts it. Born in England within a decade of the end of the Second World War, my privileged generation of Jews was infected by the fragility of the times, by what had been lived through without enough opportunity for reflection, by awareness not only of immense loss, but also of the insecurity of being. If *that* happened *there*, what was the guarantee that it could not happen *here*? The postwar consensus on the unacceptability of antisemitism was never solid and has not proven durable, which meant that the optimistic view that the 'oldest hatred' had finally run its course was adopted more as a defence against the alternative belief that nothing ever changes than as a compelling consolation. And the things that people had gone through – what they had directly experienced, or heard about, or imagined or feared – were not fully known. Either they were hidden or they were spoken about in a way that was difficult to hear; or perhaps they were biding their time, wondering when a language would be invented in which they could be properly articulated. The 'people' that they affected were not abstract entities: they were the parents and aunts and uncles of the next generation; the teachers and writers. They all communicated that *something had happened*, but it was difficult ever to get a grip on what that something was.

This whole experience was not necessarily a dramatic one; it did not even have to give rise to the anxiety-laden explorative urge that David Grossman (1989) examines through his character Momik in *See Under: Love*. For many of us, it just meant that there was always something in the background that haunted the present, something not quite nameable even if we could give it an approximate name ('the War', 'the Nazis' or – later – 'the Holocaust'), something like a mist that slightly obscured

1

the details of everyday life, fading the colours a little, infiltrating the small nooks and crannies of our imagination. It keeps coming back, too, and it is very difficult to deal with: after all, we did not experience the trauma, so how can we lay claim to it? Those many of us who were not even 'second generation victims', the children of survivors, how could we speak of the Holocaust without falsifying it, without demanding an inheritance that was not actually our own? What kind of inauthenticity were we playing with there? Yet, something keeps cropping up, something that hovers a little in the background and cannot be put to rest, but that cannot be expressed without embarrassment, self-dramatisation, insufficiency and inaccuracy.

The imagery of ghosts and haunting is inescapable in contexts such as this, and is writ large not only in Jewish experience, but also in much of the cultural consciousness of the contemporary era. Indeed, it is starting to become a cliché, which presents difficulties for attempts like this one to mine it for new and productive insights. Its fullest exploration in the recent academic social science literature is that by Avery Gordon (1997), who has a clear idea that haunting is a social phenomenon, an index of oppression. She writes (p. xvi), 'I used the term haunting to describe those singular yet repetitive instances when home becomes unfamiliar, when your bearings on the world lose direction, when the over-and-done-with comes alive, when what's been in your blind spot comes into view. Haunting raises specters, and it alters the experience of being in time, the way we separate the past, the present, and the future.' The temporal disturbance produced by haunting is possibly its key feature, and one of the claims it has to critical usefulness: something that is supposed to be 'past' is experienced in the present as if it is both fantastic and real. This is especially the case with suffering. One of the things that Holocaust scholarship has demonstrated is how strongly a trauma lived through in one generation continues to have effects in later ones. Indeed, the question of how suffering is transmitted to those who 'come after' pervades discussions of memorialisation. In some respects it is no mystery: how surprising is it, after all, that people who live through terrible times should communicate to their children their own anxieties and grief? But like most apparently easily explicable phenomena, something else operates in the mix as well, making the response 'excessive' in the sense that it does not reduce easily to what might have been seen and heard. To be haunted is more than to be affected by what others tell us directly or do to us openly; it is to be influenced by a kind of inner voice that will not stop speaking and cannot be excised, that keeps cropping up to trouble us and stop us going peaceably on our way. It is to harbour a *presence* that we are aware of, sometimes overwhelmed by, that embodies elements of past experience and future anxiety and hope, and that *will not let us be*.

The language I am using here is openly psychoanalytic, reflecting my own intellectual concerns but also how psychoanalysis and haunting go together. To some extent this is simply due to the way in which psychoanalysis saturates Western culture to such a degree that it is hard to escape it. This is so even if we hate it, which is perhaps the only honest response one can ever have to it. Why is this? Because psychoanalysis intentionally stirs up demons, it refuses to stay silent about trouble and pain, it insists on talking about the things we would much rather hide or lay to rest. How can we do anything but hate it, especially as it is so evasive? If the unconscious exists, then whatever we say to avoid it, it always comes back at us, nipping at our heels as we try to outrun it. So there is this hateful thing, psychoanalysis, which refuses to allow its subjects to escape their ghostly remainders, the things that are left *over* from past happenings, or left *out* of conscious recognition. They are the peripheral things, sniping from the sidelines and the depths, harrying us as we go about our supposedly ordinary lives. We might think we are acting reasonably, but psychoanalysis *knows* that behind this rational façade there is something else lurking, waiting to mess things up, to make claims of its own.

The penetration of psychoanalysis in culture is not always easily visible. It crops up mostly in the background assumptions that many people hold about motives, desires, fantasies and blind spots. These are viewed not as accidents but as having causes, often unwitting ones; that is, we are willing to accept, in theory at least, that we know little of what we speak. Psychoanalysis is there particularly in the understanding we have of repetition and of certain kinds of memories – traumatic ones in particular. Strangely, it seems, the things we do not know trouble us more than the things we are aware of. They keep coming back, forcing us to return to the scenes of distress, enticing us to replay over and over again the disturbances that shape our lives. It is as if we think that we are seeing clearly, but smoke gets in our eyes. This is one source of the book's argument, expressed vividly in a quotation from Freud that I will deal with more thoroughly in Chapter 5. Defending his belief in telepathy from the criticism levelled at it by Ernest Jones, Freud says that Jones should reassure everyone that it is of little consequence for psychoanalysis. Tell anyone who asks, he writes (Freud, 1926: 597), that 'my acceptance of telepathy is my own affair, like my Judaism and my passion for smoking, etc., and that the subject of telepathy is not related to psychoanalysis'.

Judaism, smoking, telepathy – the occult in general – these are strange and somewhat disreputable things, personal to Freud. The personal, however, is central to psychoanalysis as a discipline, and the 'affairs' of Freud remain crucial to understanding how psychoanalysis has come about and what it might mean. What influenced him was *always* related to psychoanalysis; because of this, Freud's biography continues to haunt his invention and – through the transference that binds each generation of analysts with its predecessors – will inescapably do so. Judaism, smoking, telepathy: we have to admire the juxtaposition of these things that cloud the air, things we know about and can sometimes see, but can never quite pin down. Ghostly substances, indeed.

Psychoanalysis is one of Avery Gordon's base disciplines for her exploration, even though she has many criticisms of it. She credits psychoanalysis with being 'the only human science that has taken haunting seriously as an object of analysis' (Gordon, 1997: 27). But, she writes, 'psychoanalysis does not know as much about haunting as it might seem' (ibid.). This is because it (or at least Freud, with whom she deals) tries to reduce haunting to what comes from the unconscious and so tends to understand it as based on repression, which means that it can be exorcised through the usual analytic process of 'identifying the visible and disquieting symptoms of repression and bringing their origins and nature to light' (Gordon, 1997: 53). For Gordon, Freud's troubled awareness that there might be something real about ghosts, in the sense that one is haunted by things that actually exist, has been obscured here. This is what we have to get back to, she suggests that: 'The "reality-testing" that we might want to perform in the face of hauntings must first of all admit those hauntings as real' (ibid.). They are real because they are manifestations of actually existing, present-tense losses, resistances and suppressed wishes. They happen because there are people who are made ghostly by the silencing of their voices; and even if these people belong to the past, the effects of their silencing, of their writing out from history, can be felt today. Because of this, ghosts cannot be removed just by being spoken about; they can only be set free by some kind of action to bring them the justice they deserve. Haunting therefore demands a liberatory practice. One question is, to what extent can psychoanalysis be a basis for this?

Psychoanalytic baggage

Psychoanalysis itself is haunted by its overdetermined set of origins. These include the specific context of Jewish emancipation into which Freud was born; then-contemporary ideas on thought transmission and telepathy; and images of civilisation, scientific progress and primitivity. As a set of hauntings these origins produce something ghostly and melancholic. Spectrally troubled in this way, as several commentators have suggested, psychoanalysis draws into twenty-first-century culture material that is 'unworked through' yet still lively in its impact. The history of its engagement or non-engagement with its own Jewish origins is perhaps the most powerful example. Psychoanalysis never seems able to escape the ambivalence that comes from having a 'Jewish father' to whom one might feel in thrall, and against whom one might have to rebel, given the additional context of a culture of anti-semitism. Yet, psychoanalysis is also an active process of *using* the mechanisms of haunting, if we use the term to refer broadly to what is communicated at a spatial or temporal distance, whether between people who have no obvious physical connection to one another or across generations. From past to future, from subject to other, psycho-analysis disturbs rational communication. The dimensions here are both 'vertical' (time) and 'horizontal' (space). The *vertical* refers to what gets transmitted from one time period to another, from one generation to another, so that those who have no direct experience of an event may nevertheless be affected by it. Much of the scholarship and clinical writing that has attended to this vertical dimension of haunting has been concerned with the intergenerational transmission of trauma, and this of course is vital work. But it has other elements too, to which Freud was attuned, notably questions of the generational continuity of ethnic and religious identity. In more contemporary language, it is also what under-pins much postcolonial critique that considers the emergence of the active ghosts of previous times within the societies of today. How does this happen, how is something not-known-about nevertheless passed on, sometimes to the extent that it is obviously re-enacted? More myste-riously still, is there something in the 'it is' of the present that is already reaching forward to the 'it will be' to come?

The *horizontal* dimension refers to what passes between people whether or not they are in active conscious communication with one another. Psychoanalysis is the science that deals with the per-meability of personal boundaries in the face of unconscious events. As a practice of horizontal haunting, psychoanalysis may appear to seek clarity, as the analyst reflects on the patient's speech and tries to return it in a more rational, bounded form; but it is mired in an unconscious presence. Something moves across space from person to person, creating shivers of joy, recognition and anxiety. This has a professional vocabulary attached to it (for instance, 'transference' or 'projective identification'), but in truth it is close to occult ideas about thought-transmission or telepathy. Where it fits the rubric of *haunting* is in the sensations to which it gives rise. We each find ourselves troubled by the other, to a greater or lesser extent possessed by others who can get inside us and also read our mind. Telepathy and transference may be names for this mechanism, but the mechanism itself is a ghostly one. Otherness constitutes us as beings that can lose track of ourselves and of our boundaries; we can fade and flow as subjects, and be troubled and excited by such experiences at one and the same time.

There are of course many worries about adopting psychoanalysis as one's frame of reference. For this book, a major concern is the extent to which psychoanalysis is laden with baggage that prevents it from being the kind of emancipatory practice that is needed to free people from their ghosts. The key issue here is the location of psychoanalysis in a historical and cultural position that aligns it not with critical and progressive trends but rather with *repressive* factors that if anything maintain the presence of ghostly remainders of past – and continuing – oppression. Colonialism is the central problem. Psychoanalysis draws on colonialist thinking often and unreflectively, particularly in its use of the idea of the 'primitive' to refer to 'unreasoning' elements of people's psychic lives. Absolute hate is usually what is meant when psychoanalysts talk about primitive feelings, for example in formulations like a 'primitive fantasy of destruction' – though sometimes (but quite rarely) the metaphor is extended to mean unmitigated love. Why are these elements 'primitive'? Notionally, because they are 'basic', and 'fundamental', the building blocks of all mental functions. This does not seem so bad, but the term has too many associations – it is, to use the trope, *haunted* by too much history. For Freud, there were 'savages' and their way of thinking was contrasted to 'civilised' mentality; one could learn from them because their minds were like 'ours' in earlier times. At the beginning of *Totem and Taboo*, he writes, 'There are men still living who, as we believe, stand very near to primitive man, far nearer than we do, and whom we therefore regard as his direct heirs and representatives. Such is our view of those whom we describe as savages or half-savages; and their mental life must have a peculiar interest for us if we are right in seeing in it a well-preserved picture of an early stage of our own development' (Freud, 1913: 1). The repetitive first person plural pronoun is important here: 'we believe', 'we do', 'we regard', 'our view', 'we describe', 'us', 'our own development'. Over here, civilised 'us'; over there, the 'savage' and the 'primitive'. Freud also drew an association between 'savages' and children: 'It seems to me quite possible, however, that the same may be true of our attitude towards the psychology of those races that have remained at the animistic level as is true of our attitude towards the mental life of children, which we adults no longer understand and whose fullness and delicacy of feeling we have in consequence so greatly underestimated' (ibid.: 99). 'Our attitude', again; 'we adults', those who have not remained at the 'animistic' level. It is worth noting the ambivalence here: Freud recognises that something is lost in moving away from the 'savage' and the child, specifically, 'delicacy of feeling'. Nevertheless, this fits within a generally colonialist and patriarchal paradigm. The innocence of child and racialised other (and of the idealised woman, although she does not appear explicitly in this quotation) is also a way of legitimising domination: they cannot fend for themselves. It is clear where these associations come from – the prehistory of psychoanalysis and its foundation in a society that is grounded in racist ideology and a sense of itself as superior.

The relationship between psychoanalysis' Jewish origins and this colonialist mode of thinking is not straightforward. As has been documented very thoroughly (for example, Gilman, 1993; Frosh, 2005), the intense antisemitism of Freud's time was a highly significant backdrop, and maybe spur, to his achievement. Amongst the antisemitic discourses that were most prevalent were embedded ideas such as that Jews were castrated (hence, feminine), that they were 'oriental' and maybe even 'black', and that they were primitive both in the religious sense (Christianity having displaced Judaism, to which contemporary Jews clung) but also psychologically, socially and racially. Freud, in response, conjures up castration as a *universal* attribute, so that all people – including the most civilised – are in a sense Jews. But he also works on the conceit that the real primitives are the 'savages' of tribal societies, not the Jews of Europe; that is, as a riposte to antisemitism, Jews become lined up as 'same' (white) against the primitive, black 'other'. Celia Brickman (2003: 165) comments on Freud's 'universalizing reconfigurations' that turn the despised Jewish body into the model for humanity as a whole, writing that they 'were made at considerable expense', because 'the modalities of inferiority previously ascribed to the Jews did not simply disappear but were ambivalently displaced onto a series of abjected others: primitives, women and homosexuals'. Brickman notes especially the way in which the Jewish other comes to be displaced by the 'primitive' other of colonialism. Hence her critique of psychoanalysis' own racial politics:

The inclusion of the previously excluded Jew within the universal subject position of psychoanalysis not only repudiated femininity and homosexuality, it included Jews in the overarching, dominant cultural/racial category – civilization – which was defined by its excluded, constitutive opposite, the racialized other as primitive. Categorized as a member of a primitive race, Freud repudiated primitivity, locating himself and his work within European civilization, with both its scientific and colonizing enterprises, and replacing the opposition of Aryan/Jew with the opposition of civilized/primitive. (Brickman, 2003: 167)

This suggests that Freud responded to antisemitism by producing in psychoanalysis a theory that reconstructed human subjectivity according to the image of the disparaged Jew (we are all circumcised/castrated now). In so doing he also preserved the dynamics of racialised discourse, displacing it into his theorising on the 'dark continent' of femininity, and embedding in the idea of the 'primitive' – itself a powerful motif in nineteenth-century Western thought – the seeds for much of psychoanalysis' later racial blindness.

Despite all of this, psychoanalysis also influences contemporary postcolonial theory. This is because, speaking as it may from the heart of colonialism, it nevertheless offers a range of expressive ideas that can be used to unpick both the colonial mind and its legacy in the postcolonial world. Much of the work here was kick-started by the famous intervention of Frantz Fanon (1952), which deploys psychoanalytic ideas to examine the psychological effects of colonialism and in so doing draws a picture of a whole social world infiltrated by Freudian (and Lacanian) categories. More recently, this has been taken up energetically by a wide range of authors interested for example in the 'melancholic' aspects of the postcolonial state, meaning by that a cultural situation in which there is haunting of the present by the felt loss of a treasured past, which has been so comprehensively destroyed as to make even mourning it impossible. Psychoanalysis becomes available for use in two ways here. First, the fractures and lacunae noted above make it an exemplary instance of the way in which Western intellectual systems are infiltrated by racist and colonial ideas. Despite its potentially 'postcolonial' formation in Jewish responses to European antisemitism, psychoanalysis carries within it a history of racism and antisemitism that is still visible, not only in the fascination with the 'primitive' mentioned above, but even in quite explicit outbursts of antisemitism that refuse to go away (Frosh, 2011a, 2012b).

Second, psychoanalysis can be used as a tool to prise open the postcolonial setting and especially the impact of social oppression on psychosocial life. For example, Edward Said (2003) reads Freud's (1939) *Moses and Monotheism* (itself a provoking text for this book) as a meditation on otherness and on the instability of personal and national identity. This is constituted in 'Freud's profound exemplification of the insight that even for the most definable, the most identifiable, the most stubborn communal identity – for him, this was the Jewish identity – there are inherent limits that prevent it from being fully incorporated into one, and only one, Identity' (Said, 2003: 53). If Moses was an Egyptian as Freud claimed, then Jewish identity could not be fantasised as genetically or culturally homogeneous: at its source is an outsider, so claims for national or racial purity must always break down, in the specific case of Jews and in the general case of all cultures. What this does, therefore, is make a point that can be applied everywhere (that identities are always broken); and it also disputes claims for the fixedness and superiority of European colonial culture. There is no single identity, it is always open to the other; and so the European is infected from the start with the disruptive presence of the colonised, and psychoanalysis shows how this occurs.

This ambiguity inherent in psychoanalysis infects everything it comes into contact with. Both conformist and revolutionary, both racist and emancipatory, it shows how we are continuously infiltrated by things we know little about, or that we thought we had escaped. If the unspeakable experiences that people have are to be found hidden away in a safe or 'crypt' (a notion that will be explored particularly in Chapter 3), then psychoanalysis is both the lock that keeps it imprisoned there and the key that sets it free. This is because whatever it lets out it interprets in its own terms, and these are ready-made in the categories that operate within culture. We already know that we will find trauma there, that speaking about it should be therapeutic, that pain might be alleviated through interpretation. But psychoanalysis also teaches something else, which is that even once we are free – even when the secret has been opened up for inspection, the trauma for amelioration – there is no escaping the ghosts that come from elsewhere, from our own individual histories, from the lost cultures of the oppressed and (as we shall see in Chapter 2) from the future, from what we might become.

This book tries to unpack some of these associations in order to explore vertical and horizontal transmissions, focusing on and using psychoanalysis as its methodology. The book addresses the question of what passes through and between human subjects and of how these things structure psychosocial and psychopolitical life. Psychoanalysis is thus used as an object of study and as a framework for theorising transmission; it is placed ambiguously as a disturbing case history and also a source of radical psychosocial insight. The book works through a series of studies – of the uncanny and the death drive, melancholia, the gaze, inheritance and possession – to ask questions about what it is that haunts psychoanalysis and also what might be tangible in the vertical and horizontal dimensions of haunting with which psychoanalysis deals. It finds that something passes through psychoanalysis as a kind of *smoke*, material yet not quite graspable; and that this has some troubling effects. In particular, by engaging with a set of histories and conundrums in psychoanalysis, the book addresses one of the key questions facing psychosocial studies. The question is of how *transmission* occurs, with this referring both to the vertical transmission of identities, beliefs, intimacies and hatreds across generations, and the horizontal transmission of messages between and through subjects (a diachronic/synchronic distinction, to use the linguistic metaphor).

The puzzle here concerns transmission that appears to be 'nonmaterial', for example the preservation of ethnic and religious identities over time, the recrudescence of affiliations and hatreds in different generations, the 'pull' of the past; or the communication from one person to another of affects, thoughts and impulses. In crass shorthand, this can all be called 'transference' – although the notion of transference has to be both widened and sharpened in order to encompass the relevant phenomena. That the questions here might have importance is attested to by the large number of recent works on telepathy, melancholia and ghostly hauntings, some of which are discussed in later chapters. These works have not only reintroduced the kinds of 'occult' concerns that faced psychoanalysis when it first emerged, but have also shown how 'disreputable' elements of psychoanalysis' past might continue to inform its present, as a case history of how such pasts always haunt and disturb even the most placid of surfaces.

Structures and arguments

Much of this book draws on Jewish sources. This is for a variety of reasons. First, it follows a train of argument in which psychoanalysis is seen as heavily imbued with the residues of its Jewish origins and associations. These residues are to be found particularly in Freud and his historical period; but they have not gone away, and seem unlikely ever to do so. Judaism, Jewish identity and psychoanalysis are bound tightly together, which does not mean that no other cultures or traditions get a look-in, but rather that even when they do, the Jewish specificity of psychoanalysis still has to be dealt with. Second, Jewish sources mark out some of my own concerns and interests, and the historical and bio-graphical hauntings that come into play whenever I try to consider the kind of material covered here – material that includes repetition, vio-lence, intergenerational transmission, affective communication, trauma and forgiveness. There are plenty of other places from which one might come to address such issues; but the Jewish direction and the richness of certain Jewish assumptions and traditions is the one that constantly draws me in. So this book includes elements of Bible commentary and of Jewish folklore and it is tinged with an awareness of how Jewish inflec-tions in psychoanalysis intersect with traditional Jewish sensitivities. My hope is that rather than limit the reach of the book, this adds speci-ficity to it in a way that can be responded to by those who are working in other areas of psychosocial and postcolonial interest.

The six central chapters of the book deal in different ways with the vertical and horizontal dimensions of transmission described above, exploring particularly how temporality collapses under the weight of different sorts of haunting and how ghostliness spreads across and through people who might have contact with one another. Chapter 2 examines Freud's writings on the death drive and the uncanny. Freud was wary of attributing real existence to uncanny phenomena, but he conjured up this material in a very powerful way and in the process artic-ulated the wish for *dissolution* that is itself a classic mark of the ghost. What terrifies us, what do we run towards, what do we see coming in the future that scares us? For Freud, death is both desired and feared; we live continuously in its shadow and the experiences of doubling and disturbance that reach us from unconscious sources are premonitions of loss. For these reasons, whilst psychoanalysis is correctly presented as a discipline of repetition and hence of the *past*, its appreciation of haunt-ing is better understood as something that comes from the *future*: what ghosts intimate about us is what we are about to become.

Chapter 3 moves into a more formal exploration of haunting in psy-choanalysis and focuses especially on its social significance. Featuring especially strongly is the idea promoted by contemporary psychoanal-ysis that each of us is inhabited by the spectre of otherness – by a set of 'messages' that come from outside us and that are the subject of a lifelong effort at decoding. We do not know exactly what others want of us, what desire they put into us, what we mean to them. We know only that something is passed between people, that we inherit others' unconscious material and have to find our own ways of living with it. This is central to both modes of transmission – what is passed down intergenerationally and what is passed between people in the here and now – and it is the main cause of the sense that we are never free to be merely 'ourselves'. Others occupy us. When trauma is at the source of this, we are talking in terms of secrets, of 'encrypted' material that both attracts us to it and hides itself away. The chapter examines this idea in some detail from the perspective of Abraham and Torok's (1976) conceptualisation of 'crypts': spaces that give protection to unbearable secrets, but that also function as points of resistance and disturbance. This links up with the widely used trope of *melancholia* as a response to loss that falls short of completed grieving. There are some things that are so traumatic to lose that the loss itself is denied, even to the extent that knowledge of the existence of the lost object is itself repressed. This kind of melancholic object then remains as a psychic haunting: it is not known about, not recognised, therefore not grieved, and consequently its loss acts as a 'present absence' with continuing impact. Such melancholic objects exist as unconscious elements operating on individuals, often manifesting themselves in depression; but much current social theory also sees them in the lives of nations, especially where colonialism has stolen away cultural 'treasures' sometimes amounting to whole histories.

The next chapter, Chapter 4, balances an instance of compassion against penetration by the gaze, especially in the form of the evil eye. This is part of a longer discussion of communication across distance. There is a kind of gaze, especially a colonial one, that positions the other aggressively and enviously in a relationship of dispossession. It enters into the other to steal away what the other has, often destroying everything of value in the process. This is particularly clear in relation to racialised gazes. Here, Fanon (1952) is an important reference point, but it might be a broader truth: the look is both a communication and an action, the scrutinising eye can at times be comforting (as with the gaze of the lover or mother), but at other times it might feel inescapable, oppressive and even murderous. These operations of the gaze, refracted in psychoanalysis, colonialism, racism and sexuality, fill in the space between people that appears to be empty; actually, it is full of messages of the most material kind.

This becomes apparent more benignly in the discussion of telepathy in Chapter 5. Telepathy has a longstanding affinity with psychoanalysis, not only in that interest in occultism was one source of interest in psychoanalysis itself, but also because the question of how thoughts are transmitted is pervasive in psychoanalytic practice. What is transference if not a mechanism of telepathic communication of unconscious ideas, to which the receiver – usually the analyst – has to be alert? And if this is so, then telepathy indexes both the uncommunicativeness of unconscious life, in which repressed material is hidden away and consequently silenced, and its garrulousness – the way what is unconscious is also shared. It also alerts us to the question of intersubjectivity and the inmixing of subjecthood: what does it mean to be linked with another, to be absorbed in a space of connection in which communication is automatic, in which unconscious ideas are passed on? Such inmixing, referenced in some contemporary psychoanalytic ideas about 'thirdness' and transitional spaces, has great attractions but also dangers of a kind well understood by mystics who themselves are used to trying to lose their separateness and to absorb themselves in the divine.

Chapter 6 returns to intergenerational transmission, in this case examining some thinking about how trauma passes down through the generations. Violence is the main concern, initially in relation to the inheritance of the children of Nazi perpetrators but then to an examination of paternal violence and the fantasies that surround it. Following an exploration of this theme in the Biblical story of the Binding of Isaac and the rabbinic commentaries on it, my attention moves to Freud's commitment to Lamarckian mechanisms of transmission in *Moses and Monotheism* (1939). This can be understood as Freud's attempt to make sense of how Jewish identity is transmitted even to those like himself who reject Judaism. Despite this rejection, something calls to him, he says, and whilst he cannot explain it fully he thinks it has to do with a primal scene of father murder that is relived unconsciously by all later generations. This leads him to produce a very elaborate speculative theory of considerable generality. Turning psychoanalysis back on its founder, however, it also raises the question of why Freud adopts this extreme formulation when he could more easily have looked at the intimacy of his relationship with his own father, and thought carefully about how what is spoken and unspoken between generations passes things down. But perhaps it is the claim that this is 'easier' that is mistaken here. Perhaps rebuilding relationships with specific others – including fathers – is harder than imagining an impersonal cultural-historical process in which we all participate.

Chapter 7, finally, looks at the idea of forgiveness and redemption through some striking Jewish sources. The main one is S. An-sky's play, *The Dybbuk* (1920), and the classic film of it made in Poland in 1937. The play deals with spirit possession and ambiguously portrays it both as a revolt against an oppressive social order and an attempt to repair that order, which in an important way is failing to keep its promise to its subjects. The film, coming to us from the eve of the Holocaust, is not only a cinematic *representation* of possession and haunting; it is *itself* a haunted cultural artefact, full of the sounds and images of a destroyed culture and a murdered community. Despite this, and the pain it brings, it is a reconciliatory document in that it attests to certain tragic possibilities of forgiveness. The chapter draws on this thinking to explore briefly some ideas of the messianic in social thought, the relationship between violence and reparation, and the temptation that we seem all to be faced with of bringing the social order to chaos.

This book does not try to effect a theory of haunting, but rather to examine haunting and ghostly transmission as themes that recur in psychoanalysis and in culture. It deals with the return of the dead, as haunting always does, but it links them with other intimations of transmission, other ways in which we are possessed. Its ethical impulse is to find ways to listen to all of these different forms of ghostliness, not only to put them to rest, but also to keep them alive.

2
Facing the Truth about Ourselves

Running into danger

There is something about 'uncanny' experiences that arouses people and produces in them a mixture of shivering pleasure and anxiety. It is not completely clear why this is so, why for instance the appearance of something uncanny might be more disturbing than any other unexpected event, or why it might also exert a pull that draws people in. In some ways, an encounter with the uncanny ought to be unequivocally distressing, calling into question the assumptions we use to make ourselves secure. The uncanny suggests the existence of something odd that we have not noticed before, something that undermines the unattended-to foundations on which we stand. The uncanny is often particularly unnerving because it seems so close to home, so familiar, yet also fundamentally different – like the reversal of right and left in the mirror, or the way it might gradually dawn on us that a person we are talking to is not quite in her or his 'right mind'.

Perhaps a clue is offered through the contrast between what is uncanny because it is just slightly out of kilter, and what is completely different from anything we can possibly imagine. The absolute difference of the truly alien is strikingly disturbing and we tend to try to reduce it by various forms of anthropomorphism, as when we look into the eyes of an animal and think we see something reassuringly recognisable, rather than totally other. Thomas Nagel's (1974) famous paper, 'What is it Like to Be a Bat?', which is actually a subtle exploration of philosophical issues around subjectivity and consciousness, gains much of its rhetorical force from the starkness of the comparison it makes between humans and a closely related (bats are mammals) yet unreachable other. 'Even without the benefit of philosophical reflection', writes

Nagel (p. 438), 'anyone who has spent some time in an enclosed space with an excited bat knows what it is to encounter a fundamentally *alien* form of life.' Nagel argues that there is an unbridgeable gap between humans and bats – even if we picture what it is to be 'like' a bat, it will still be from the perspective of our own experience, not that of the bat itself:

> It will not help to try to imagine that one has webbing on one's arms, which enables one to fly around at dusk and dawn catching insects in one's mouth; that one has very poor vision, and perceives the surrounding world by a system of reflected high-frequency sound signals; and that one spends the day hanging upside down by one's feet in an attic. In so far as I can imagine this (which is not very far), it tells me only what it would be like for me to behave as a bat behaves. But that is not the question. I want to know what it is like for a *bat* to be a bat. (Nagel, 1974: 439)

We cannot understand an entity that comes from a totally different, and differently embodied, position. At best, trying to be empathic, we put *ourselves* in its place, but this is not the same as sharing the experience of *being that other*. The complete otherness of some other species, their illimitable wildness, invites our attempts at colonisation precisely because it so unbearable. It makes it clear that our embodied humanness is peculiar; it puts us in perspective as just one way of being, and we often try to deal with this by suffocating the otherness out of the creatures we meet. This applies to other humans as well, of course, and also to the ecosystem: in our rush to master it, we smother it with our fears.

The one who is almost the same, but not quite, presents another kind of problem. Whereas the absolutely alien is a clear threat, the almost-the-same is deceptive. It reassures us that it is a friend but then turns out to be on its own mission, connected up differently. It is only gradually that we realise something is wrong. This is what gives us goosebumps, as it removes the basis on which we relate to ourselves and others. It suggests that what we take for granted is not reliable, that there is some alternative perspective that can be brought to bear on reality and that in adopting it we might become dizzy and unsettled. To put it at its most general: if identity is a kind of illusion based on an assumption of psychological integrity and stability, then the small and unexpected difference that the almost-the-same brings to light is enough to open up a crack in identity, through which its emptiness and *in*stability can be perceived. It is this 'slightly different' other who we might consider to be uncanny, because there is something that we can relate to in it that is genuinely of ourselves and yet we cannot quite get there – there is always something a bit wrong. We should note that this might not be because of what is lacking in the disturbing other, but rather that there might be something *additional* there that is simply experienced as 'too much'.

This is certainly the Lacanian psychoanalytic view, which specifies that what makes it possible to be a human subject is to be split or separated from a small piece of otherness, enough to sustain a boundary between what can be symbolised and what cannot. Slavoj Žižek (1991) some time ago argued that the most terrifying thing about the postmodern condition is not just the gaps and absences in people's lives – a phenomenon perhaps most poignantly evoked by modernist visions of alienation – but the way in which everything is wrapped up together so closely that distance is disallowed. There is, in a sense, no space to breathe in. The problem of the uncanny – for instance when one comes face-to-face with one's double – is similarly that this otherness (termed the *object a*) engulfs the subject with its unexpected *presence*. Mladen Dolar (1996: 139) explains, 'The double is the same as me – *plus the object a*, that invisible part of being added to my image.' Imagine, he continues, 'that one could see one's mirror image close its eyes, or wink: that would make the object as the gaze appear in the mirror. This is what happens in the theme of the doubles.' Dolar goes on to note that it is here that the Lacanian account of anxiety is distinctive: rather than focusing on anxiety about loss (castration, birth anxiety, death), 'it is the anxiety of gaining something too much, of too close a presence of the object. What one loses with anxiety is precisely the loss – the loss that made it possible to deal with a coherent reality.'

We shall return to anxiety in a moment, but this vision of the uncanny also partly fuels the Lacanian idea of the *neighbour* as the one who embodies an alien 'Thing' that causes shivers to run down one's spine. It has often been pointed out how small the alienating distance might be – and how it is precisely the closeness-yet-difference from the expected norm that creates the shiver, the sense that this 'might be me but is not'. For example, Žižek (2006a) notes how the representation of the alien in popular culture is not always as something absolutely other and violent (though this is an important motif, as in Ridley Scott's *Alien*), but can focus on the one who seems exactly the same as the subject, yet is disturbingly different in the tiniest of ways. Žižek comments, linking this kind of alienness with the alien of racist fantasy:

> In contrast to Scott's alien, which is totally different from humans, the difference here is minimal, barely perceptible. Are we not dealing with the same in our everyday racism? Although we are ready to accept the Jewish, Arab, Oriental other, there is some detail that bothers us in the West: the way they accentuate a certain word, the way they count money, the way they laugh. This tiny feature renders them alien, no matter how much they try to behave like us. (Žižek, 2006a: 67)

There is a lot in this quotation that points towards the way 'slight' otherness can be the source or at least the stimulus for pervasive social violence, in this case that of racism. Žižek is a compelling writer on this topic (for example, Žižek, 2006b). In much of his work he also demonstrates something else, only hinted at in the passage above: how a complex layering of attraction and repulsion marks the relationship with the 'alien other', how racist repudiation and erotic excitement seem to run together. The disturbance that the uncanny generates is not always a source of aversion; quite frequently it generates interest, the thrill of something odd and troubling, even the excitement of being made anxious. What could it be that makes the unsettling so attractive? What makes us run towards danger?

In *Beyond the Pleasure Principle*, Freud distinguishes between different types of emotional response to danger. Discussing the various terms one might use to name these, he comments,

> 'Fright', 'fear' and 'anxiety' [in German, 'Schreck', 'Furcht' and 'Angst'] are improperly used as synonymous expressions; they are in fact capable of clear distinction in their relation to danger. 'Anxiety' describes a particular state of expecting the danger or preparing for it, even though it may be an unknown one. 'Fear' requires a definite object of which to be afraid. 'Fright', however, is the name we give to the state a person gets into when he has run into danger without being prepared for it; it emphasizes the factor of surprise. (Freud, 1920: 12)

Freud makes it clear that anxiety is an adaptive response to danger, mobilising the defences against it. Anxiety can get out of hand, but in principle it is necessary; without it, one would fall prey to the danger itself, with no preparation. Fear, too, is generally speaking adaptive: it knows what the danger is, and reacts to it. But *fright* is a different state altogether. Fright is what we get when we are unprepared for the danger we have encountered; and Freud's phrasing here ('run into danger') suggests not just neglect and carelessness, but *activity*. We have, consciously or unconsciously, sought the thrill of danger; we have avoided anxiety precisely in order to give ourselves a fright. Something is stirring here, the *frisson* that starts to suggest that there might be something in the way people behave that leads them *intentionally* to put themselves in danger. Sometimes this might be a form of self-therapy. For example, Freud (1920) suggests that certain unpleasant dreams might serve the function of raising anxiety in the dreamer precisely in order to make it possible for a danger to be recognised. If we are afflicted by a trauma, the difficulty we have is the failure to symbolise, the impossibility of articulating what it is we are troubled by. The dream points to the thing that cannot be said and finds a way to represent it. It repeats this representation until it is heard, until anxiety is generated – because once we feel anxious, it may become possible to defend ourselves against the frightening thing. So sometimes we seek out danger in order to clarify what we are afraid of, because once that happens – once the feared object can be symbolised – we might be able to survive it.

But fright does other things too. Applied to the thrill-seeking tendency, it is clearly a way of waking ourselves up out of a lethargy produced by living too much in the same. Running into danger not only tests our limits; it is also a way of loosening the self – losing the self – perhaps in order to give up normal constraints, or perhaps to bypass the inhibiting self-scrutiny that makes us too human, too self-conscious. The shiver produced by ghost stories, the shock of horror films, the giddiness of wild fairground rides, the 'adrenaline rush' of battle: these things all shake up the boundaries of the self so that we become more alive, less individuated and self-conscious. A thrill is a fright; in the moment of excitement we are not exactly afraid, even if we are frightened to the bone.

Running into danger without being prepared for it has at least one additional feature. It reveals how people create blind spots where anxiety fails to warn them of danger. These blind spots are neither casual nor ordinary. They tend to be central to the struggle that each of us has to make something of ourselves; more specifically, they tend to be precisely that place, that *spot*, which darkens our horizons just when we thought we were in the clear. There will be quite a lot to say about this later on, under the heading of the compulsion to repeat. However, what it points to here is not so much the suddenness of fright but a more general temptation to keep on doing the things that stop us settling; that is, whenever we think we might have got where we want to go, we run into danger, just to spoil it.

Doubling and death

Here is Freud's list of the kinds of things people do to upset themselves – a list that sounds ominously close to home. Describing 'normal', that is 'non-neurotic', people who nevertheless keep on repeating the same things, over and over, he states that:

> we have come across people all of whose human relationships have the same outcome: such as the benefactor who is abandoned in anger after a time by each of his protégés, however much they may otherwise differ from one another, and who thus seems doomed to taste all the bitterness of ingratitude; or the man whose friendships all end in betrayal by his friend; or the man who time after time in the course of his life raises someone else into a position of great private or public authority and then, after a certain interval, himself upsets that authority and replaces him by a new one; or, again, the lover each of whose love affairs with a woman passes through the same phases and reaches the same conclusion. (Freud, 1920: 22)

Most if not all of this list applies to Freud himself. We do not really know if each of his love affairs had the same outcome – he seems to have had hardly any, although there is evidence of a relationship with his sister-in-law (Maciejewski, 2006) – but all those men in whom he trusted abandoned him, split from him and resented his authority. This is perhaps a general truth of authority and leadership, but it is also a situation Freud continually recreated, first with Wilhelm Fliess, then Adler, Jung, Stekel, Tausk and others. These abandonments may have had plenty to do with the characters of the men concerned, but they were also produced by Freud's way of wielding authority, most importantly his inability to brook dissent. He needed followers and acolytes, but could not easily manage the sons who threatened to displace him. His own behaviour therefore enforced these repetitions. Freud comments that we might not be surprised about repetitions due to such 'active choices' on the part of the person concerned, especially if 'we can discern in him an essential character-trait which always remains the same and which is compelled to find expression in a repetition of the same experiences' (Freud, 1920: 22).

One might note, however, that this lack of surprise is only reasonable if we do not expect people to *learn* from experience. Having produced one self-harming state of affairs, why do we do it again and again? Why could Freud himself not learn? It is even stranger, Freud suggests, if there is no obvious way in which the person has constructed the repetition. He gives a peculiar example here: 'There is the case, for instance, of the woman who married three successive husbands each of whom fell ill soon afterwards and had to be nursed by her on their death-beds' (ibid.). Is there really 'no influence' that can be perceived here? Blatantly, the woman might have chosen sickly husbands who would need her to nurse them. Even more oddly, Freud is forced to produce a mythical example to clinch his argument that non-willed repetitions occur. 'The most moving poetic picture of a fate such as this', he writes, 'is given by Tasso in his romantic epic *Gerusalemme Liberata*. Its hero, Tancred, unwittingly kills his beloved Clorinda in a duel while she is disguised in the armour of an enemy knight. After her burial he makes his way into a strange magic forest which strikes the Crusaders' army with terror. He slashes with his sword at a tall tree; but blood streams from the cut and the voice of Clorinda, whose soul is imprisoned in the tree, is heard complaining that he has wounded his beloved once again' (ibid.). Freud comments, 'If we take into account observations such as these, based upon behaviour in the transference and upon the life-histories of men and women, we shall find courage to assume that there really does exist in the mind a compulsion to repeat which overrides the pleasure principle.' But why should we take into account examples such as these, which very obviously are not all based on the life histories of *real* men and women? In fact, Freud provides rather little evidence of non-'active' repetitions; one can usually see what it is that draws someone to keep on producing the same effects. However, looking more closely it becomes apparent that Freud is working on something else here, on what attracts us to this repetitious *destructiveness*, how people are eventually abandoned, betrayed or murdered – symbolically or actually – and the ways in which we kill the things we love.

There is a potential muddle here of different actions and motivations: it cannot be claimed that fright and the repetition compulsion are the same thing, only that in both cases we endanger ourselves. Nevertheless, something fairly transparent is involved in this mixture of fright and the uncanny, this repeated risk-taking with the things that are of value to us. What is common is an attraction to the disruptive and the deathly, a way in which we keep putting ourselves in the position of facing dissolution, even as we struggle to remain sane. We do not always obviously seek this out, but this does not stop us running into danger; so the repetition is something unconscious, recurring continually without hesitation or cease.

Freud's two most famous examples of uncanny repetitions are both comic, personal anecdotes included in his 1919 paper, 'The "Uncanny"'. One should note first the dating of this piece. Both *Beyond the Pleasure Principle* and 'The "Uncanny"' appeared soon after the end of the First World War and are perforce ruminations on what Wilfred Owen called 'war and the pity of war', on death and destructiveness, on revenants and ghosts. These are crucial texts for considering what psychoanalysis might say about the ways in which we are haunted by what we cannot bear. None of this should be a surprise; after that war, there were ghosts everywhere, living and dead. A good deal of both these papers is devoted to this, most explicitly in *Beyond the Pleasure Principle*, with its invention of the death drive as perhaps the primary motivating force in the human psyche; but also in 'The "Uncanny"', which is devoted to describing and exploring the shadow that fell, and falls, over all things. Freud's key example in the paper is Hoffman's story, *The Sandman*, but in the course of his theoretical analysis, he produces two personal stories, one of them in the text and one in a footnote. The footnote is the better known and appears when he is discussing the impact of the 'double':

> Since the uncanny effect of a 'double' also belongs to this same group it is interesting to observe what the effect is of meeting one's own image unbidden and unexpected. Ernst Mach has related two such observations in his *Analyse der Empfindungen*. On the first occasion he was not a little startled when he realized that the face before him was his own. The second time he formed a very unfavourable opinion about the supposed stranger who entered the omnibus, and thought 'What a shabby-looking school-master that man is who is getting in!' – I can report a similar adventure. I was sitting alone in my wagon-lit compartment when a more than usually violent jolt of the train swung back the door of the adjoining washing-cabinet, and an elderly gentleman in a dressing-gown and a travelling cap came in. I assumed that in leaving the washing-cabinet, which lay between the two compartments, he had taken the wrong direction and come into my compartment by mistake. Jumping up with the intention of putting him right, I at once realized to my dismay that the intruder was nothing but my own reflection in the looking-glass

on the open door. I can still recollect that I thoroughly disliked his appearance. Instead, therefore, of being frightened by our 'doubles', both Mach and I simply failed to recognize them as such. Is it not possible, though, that our dislike of them was a vestigial trace of the archaic reaction which feels the 'double' to be something uncanny? (Freud, 1919: 248n)

For Avery Gordon (1997) what is at stake here is the self made strange. She writes (p. 54), 'Freud's haunting experience consists of his looking into a mirror and seeing an alienating figure that turns out to be him too.' Freud's context is the uncanny feeling that is produced by an encounter with a double, a feeling that is not exactly that of fear, but more a kind of unhappy shiver, a dislike at being brought face to face with something slightly disreputable, the 'shabby-looking schoolmaster' or the 'elderly gentleman in a dressing-gown and a travelling cap'. Neither of these apparitions is attractive and both, when traced to their source, reflect back a truth about the perceiver that they would rather be without – the truth of getting old and shabby. Is this because the truth, reflected back, is always of something disreputable? Freud refers to projection in his discussion on the double, implying that the double is made up of unwanted elements of the self that have been expelled and put into the external object. If projection of this kind is a genuine psychic mechanism, then what the encounter with the double does is force one to see the projected material 'in the flesh'. We rid ourselves of what we dislike about ourselves, our envy, our hostility, our aggression, our shabbiness, only to find it coming back at us from the looking-glass. However much we attempt to disavow it we are occasionally brought up with a start, we have a fright: this nastiness is indeed part of our very own selves.

There is something still more abrasive here, however, something to set one's teeth on edge. Freud himself attributes the effect of the double not so much to the forced encounter with unwanted aspects of the self, but to the premonition of death. The background to this is complex, almost ironic. Drawing on Otto Rank's work, Freud suggests that the double begins as a way of staving off mortality by multiplying the ego in order to protect it from complete destruction; probably, he thinks (1919: 235), 'the "immortal" soul was the first "double" of the body'. However, once the primitive phase of such magical belief is over, the double becomes a reminder that death exists: 'From having been an assurance of immortality, it becomes the uncanny harbinger of death' (ibid.). So Freud's example is presented as illustrating how when we see ourselves unexpectedly – when we run into ourselves without preparation – we are unconsciously reminded of death, and shiver. This has some important implications with regard to temporality, upsetting the normal relationship between past, present and future. The double is in part what we dislike *now* about ourselves. It is also that which has been repressed and somehow encapsulated from the *past* yet never dealt with, coming back to haunt us until it can be laid to rest, operating in the way a trauma operates. Indeed, this latter function of the double is especially marked: the traumatic remainder exists in concrete reality precisely because it has never been turned into a symbol, which is exactly the reason traumatic experiences continue to plague us. That is, if a trauma is defined as an experience that cannot be absorbed and fully worked through until it is resolved, the very failure of symbolisation means that it is always present in its materiality, not broken down properly into digestible elements. This can make it unbearable if it is also pressing for expression, if for instance it is too close to what is going on for the person now, if too many reminders of the repressed lie all around. Under such circumstances, projection might be the most immediate and powerful defence available, with the effect that something appears in the external world that represents, in concrete form, the unbearable traumatic idea. All this – past and present – is bound up in the double, but there is also a message from the future, expressed in the notion of an 'uncanny harbinger of death'. The temporal movement is not just from the past to the present, but from the *future* to the present: the double is a reminder of what is to come. Not only does it announce that there once was a trauma that has not been laid to rest; it also promises a final unsymbolisable trauma that we will meet, and the premonitory shadow of that meeting weighs on us now. The other comes back to us from the future, beckoning; and we do not like what it shows us.

It is this *memento mori* effect of doubling that introduces the key concept developed by Freud in the wake of the First World War: that of the drive towards, or by, death. Funnily, perhaps defensively but certainly revealingly, the introduction to the 'compulsion to repeat' in 'The "Uncanny"' is again a personal vignette that does not seem to be about death at all, but rather its opposite; and that certainly registers on the scale of 'disreputable' impulses that Freud is willing to own up to. Referring to the 'factor of the repetition of the same thing,' Freud writes,

> From what I have observed, this phenomenon does undoubtedly, subject to certain conditions and combined with certain

circumstances, arouse an uncanny feeling, which, furthermore, recalls the sense of helplessness experienced in some dream-states. As I was walking, one hot summer afternoon, through the deserted streets of a provincial town in Italy which was unknown to me, I found myself in a quarter of whose character I could not long remain in doubt. Nothing but painted women were to be seen at the windows of the small houses, and I hastened to leave the narrow street at the next turning. But after having wandered about for a time without enquiring my way, I suddenly found myself back in the same street, where my presence was now beginning to excite attention. I hurried away once more, only to arrive by another détour at the same place yet a third time. Now, however, a feeling overcame me which I can only describe as uncanny, and I was glad enough to find myself back at the piazza I had left a short while before, without any further voyages of discovery. (Freud, 1919: 237)

One hardly needs psychoanalysis to enable one to interpret this. Freud says nothing revealing about it, adding to it some apparently innocuous incidents of being caught in a mist or bumping into the furniture in a dark room, and noting merely that, 'it is only this factor of involuntary repetition which surrounds what would otherwise be innocent enough with an uncanny atmosphere, and forces upon us the idea of something fateful and inescapable when otherwise we should have spoken only of "chance" ' (ibid.: 237). But it is not solely the 'factor of involuntary repetition' that is at work here. It is also the lure of sex, 'disreputable' sex at that, which keeps bringing Freud back to the same spot until his presence 'excites attention'. It is not any old place that he keeps bumping into, but one full of 'painted women'; this may be embarrassing, but it hardly seems a good example of what is genuinely uncanny.

Freud refers to the 'detour' that leads him constantly back to the same place. This place is that of sex, but as we shall see the 'detour' also refers to the work of the life drives, staving off death. Sex and death go together in Freud's theory as they do in popular culture. It is obvious that the unconscious is at work in Freud's behaviour, and in terms of his text that is part of the point. But what *is* the unconscious here? Is it the past, back to haunt us, or the future, threatening us with what we might become? Fear is, after all, usually directed towards what may happen, not what has already come to pass – that is more likely to be a matter for *regret*. Though the fear that one may discover something about the past that will put the future in jeopardy is, surely enough, a haunting fear. In the future Freud might become what he had always been, but had never been able to see: the one who frequents 'painted women'; the one whose appearance is 'thoroughly disliked'. The repetition here is consequently not only an expression of an underlying wish, another nail in the coffin of his self-esteem to match the 'thorough dislike' Freud has of his own image. For sure, he is fascinated by the painted ladies and cannot tear himself away; there is little that seems 'uncanny' about this. Something more poignant comes into play at this point in Freud's text, with the apparently random example of how, faced with the unexpected recurrence of a number ('addresses, hotel rooms, compartments in railway trains'), 'a man' can get superstitious and even 'take it, perhaps, as an indication of the span of life allotted to him' (ibid.: 238). Freud chooses the number 62 as his instance. This is no random choice, though whether it was consciously intended or not is an open question. Freud was at that age when he wrote 'The "Uncanny"' (the paper was published in the autumn of 1919, but he was completing it in March, before his sixty-third birthday in May of that year) and 62 was one of the three ages at which Freud was convinced he would die. Peter Gay describes Freud's superstition as follows:

> For years he harboured the haunting belief that he was destined to die at the age of fifty-one, and later, at sixty-one or sixty-two; he felt pursued by these fateful ciphers as reminders of his own mortality. Even the telephone number he was assigned in 1899 – 14362 – became confirmation: he had published *The Interpretation of Dreams* at forty-three, and the last two digits, he was convinced, were an ominous monition that sixty-two was indeed to be his life's span. Freud once analyzed superstition as a cover for hostile, murderous wishes, and his own superstitions as a suppressed desire for immortality. But his self-analysis did not completely free Freud from this bit of irrationality, and this residue of what he called his 'specifically Jewish mysticism' made him susceptible to Fliess's wildest speculation. (Gay, 1988: 58)

The reference at the end of this quotation is to Wilhelm Fliess' numerological speculations; the 'specifically Jewish mysticism' will recur later in this book. But what this revelation about Freud's death-fixation suggests is that the examples in 'The "Uncanny"' are all to be read similarly, as a shiver produced in Freud by the intimations of mortality that he finds all around him. What is uncanny, he tells us, is what we already know but refuse to recognise, come back to haunt us: 'an uncanny experience occurs either when infantile complexes which have been repressed are once more revived by some impression, or when primitive beliefs which have been surmounted seem once more to be confirmed' (Freud, 1919: 249). This seems true enough, but not the whole story of Freud's text. What sends shivers down *his* spine, it seems, is not the return of the infantile repressed, but the beckoning from the *future*; that is, it is the *future* that haunts the present, and not the past. This future is one in which Freud is an old man, in which he will regret what he comes to be; in which death calls him, and daily reminds him of its threat.

Daemonic returns

Along the road to death, the path is paved by expectations, superstitions and residuals. Things return all the time, and the question is what kinds of recurrences are we dealing with? Freud is not innocent of his apparently hidden conflicts. Whilst not writing specifically about his own dread of death, he makes it a central element in his account of why some things turn out not to be merely frightening but uncanny as well. Three elements apply here. The first is that the uncanny is to be linked to the idea of recurrence – the return of the repressed, the compulsion to repeat, the sense of having been there before. 'The uncanny', Freud (1919: 220) writes, 'is that class of the frightening which leads back to what is known of old and long familiar.' The second is animism, the failure to completely overcome the belief that 'the world was peopled with the spirits of human beings; by the subject's narcissistic overvaluation of his own mental processes; by the belief in the omnipotence of thoughts and the technique of magic based on that belief; by the attribution to various outside persons and things of carefully graded magical powers' and so on (ibid.: 240). The third is specifically the encounter with death:

There is scarcely any other matter ... upon which our thoughts and feelings have changed so little since the very earliest times, and in which discarded forms have been so completely preserved under a thin disguise, as our relation to death. Two things account for our conservatism: the strength of our original emotional reaction to death and the insufficiency of our scientific knowledge about it ... Since almost all of us still think as savages do on this topic, it is no matter for surprise that the primitive fear of the dead is still so strong within us and always ready to come to the surface on any provocation. Most likely our fear still implies the old belief that the dead man becomes the enemy of his survivor and seeks to carry him off to share his new life with him. (Freud, 1919: 241–2)

This last idea, of the living being carried away by the dead, is one staple of ghost stories. Freud goes on to examine what has happened to this basic fear in the light of changes in belief, suggesting that it is repressed and then partially expressed as piety towards the dead. But he also suggests that in such things as the 'uncanny effect of epilepsy and of madness' and the 'idea of being buried alive by mistake' we can see not only vestiges of ancient beliefs, but fear produced by the continuing inability of people to distinguish clearly between fantasy and reality, between the goings-on in their minds and what the world really does to them. This has uncanny effects, as when we see manifested in reality something that we had previously only imagined.

In response to this, thinking about the way in which psychoanalysis acknowledges the experience of being haunted but then seems to reduce it to something psychological, Avery Gordon asserts,

> But it is precisely the experience of being haunted in the 'world of common reality,' the unexpected arrival of ghosts or wolves or eerie photographs, that troubles or even ruins our ability to distinguish reality and fiction, magic and science, savage and civilized, self and other, and in those ways gives to reality a different coloring. The 'reality-testing' that we might want to perform in the face of hauntings must first of all admit those hauntings as real. (Gordon, 1997: 53)

This idea that there really is something to be haunted by, which Gordon places in the realm of the social, will also be returned to later. However, the reading of 'The "Uncanny"' that has Freud neglecting the materiality of the ghostly, chaining it instead to the activity of the personal unconscious, is not quite alert to everything going on in his text. Clearly it is part of Freud's explanation to regard the uncanny as a return of the repressed that draws on the kinds of vestigial thinking that make people such unreliable judges of what is real and what is not. This certainly has its rationalistic and reductionist element: the uncanny exists only in one's head. But whilst maintaining this stance, Freud characteristically does something else as well. It should be remembered that there is always a kind of double-dealing tension in psychoanalysis. It treats 'madness' seriously, giving it a voice and a place as psychologically meaningful; and it also tries to 'conquer' it in the interests of science, so that it can be better understood. Yet the act of making the unconscious conscious, which is principally what is going on here, never fully displaces the unconscious itself. That is, psychoanalysis really does stir up the depths, creating the phenomena that it then tries to account for. In the consulting room, the unconscious is produced in the talk between the patient and the analyst; the more it is talked about, the more powerfully it is felt. It is a material force, something to be looked at and revolved, inspected from all angles, but never quite encompassed or fully put in its place. The situation is similar with these intimations of uncanniness. Even as they are pronounced to be features of a fantasy life that has not yet fully escaped animism and omnipotence of thought, they also reverberate and trouble the writer who has not died at 62, but might have done; or who has not frequented the painted women, but finds himself the kind of person who might be remembered for the impulse to do so.

The compulsion to repeat is not, for Freud, vestigial and easily analysed away. It is rather an absolutely central element of his thinking in this period after the First World War and perhaps it can be seen as the quintessential defining motif of psychoanalysis itself. Even the future, with all its fright-inducing messages, is a mode of repetition: it is what I will become given what I have always and already been. Lacan identified the tense of psychoanalysis as the 'future anterior': whatever happens 'will have been': 'What is realized in my history is not the past definite of what was, since it is no more, or even the present perfect of what has been in what I am, but the future anterior of what I shall have been for what I am in the process of becoming' (Lacan, 1953: 86). The sense of movement in this is important, the 'process of becoming'; we are running into danger again. There is something unknown, but this does not make it new. Indeed, Freud returns again and again to the idea that at the core of the uncanny is the oldest thing of all, the most basic of 'returns', which he sees as both daemonic and completely, biologically rational: that of the drive towards death. 'What I shall be for what I am in the process of becoming' has many resonances, but in the end there is one irreducible 'what I shall be', and that is, 'no more'.

It is hardly a surprise to find the death drive materialising in a piece written so soon after the war as *Beyond the Pleasure Principle*. This link is explicit in Freud's writing, in that he deals with the puzzle of war-induced traumatic dreams that seem to be disturbing to the dreamer, and hence to be exceptions to the general rule that dreams are wish fulfilments. But he also takes as a starting point for his argument a very famous set of observations that seem to have no necessary connection either to trauma or to the introduction of the idea of the death drive, even though they too centre on repetition. These observations are of his grandson, whose play has gone down in psychoanalytic history as an early empirical demonstration of the value of infant observation, now a major plank in the training of many analysts around the world. What seems strange here is that Freud offers a range of possible explanations for the child's actions, all of which are plausible and do not really require the heavy-handed metapsychology that he later introduces into his article. The well-known story is the 'fort-da game' in which the child is observed throwing a wooden reel out of his cot and then pulling it back in again, accompanying these actions with sounds interpreted as the German words 'fort' ('gone') and 'a joyful "da" ("there")' (Freud, 1920: 15). Having been puzzled by the child's repeated act of throwing away his toys, Freud now realises that the game needs its two parts and suggests that, 'It was related to the child's great cultural achievement – the instinctual renunciation (that is, the renunciation of instinctual satisfaction) which he had made in allowing his mother to go away without protesting. He compensated himself for this, as it were, by himself staging the disappearance and return of the objects within his reach' (ibid.).

Freud suggests some interpretations of the game. First, it changes a passive situation into an active one, so that the boy is mastering his distress at his mother's disappearance by controlling her symbolic reappearance. Second, he might be taking a pleasurable revenge on her: 'In that case it would have a defiant meaning: "All right, then, go away! I don't need you. I'm sending you away myself"' (ibid.: 16). Freud comments, 'We know of other children who liked to express similar hostile impulses by throwing away objects instead of persons' (ibid.). This is more or less where he leaves it: that whilst it might seem odd that a child should engage in the repetition of something unpleasant (symbolically re-enacting his mother's disappearance), in fact it serves functions that in at least some respects are pleasurable, helping him to master the anxiety-producing situation by making him feel less helpless, or enabling him to take symbolic revenge. There seems nothing wrong with these explanations, and Freud even offers further support for them from elsewhere, for instance from the 'pleasurable' effects of tragic art; so why does he link this observation of playful repetition with the kinds of traumatic repetitions that reveal the existence of the death drive?

A deathly reference perhaps opens up a way into this. In a footnote, Freud comments, 'When this child was five and three-quarters, his mother died. Now that she was really "gone" ("o-o-o"), the little boy showed no signs of grief. It is true that in the interval a second child had been born and had roused him to violent jealousy' (ibid.: 16n). What is slightly strange about this is its *coolness* on the part of the child and of

Freud. Perhaps the suggestion is that the premonitory 'mourning' carried out by the child in his game, added to by the Oedipal issues indexed by Freud (rivalry with the brother), has inured him to grief. This seems unlikely, however, because a child who had successfully dealt with separation anxiety would be expected to show *more* grief – that is, to be better able to mourn – than one who had blocked it off. What we do know is that when this child's mother died, *Freud* was devastated. The woman in question was his daughter Sophie, his 'Sunday child', who died in the postwar influenza epidemic early in 1920. From Peter Gay's biography, it is clear that Freud tried to manage his grief in a way consistent with his own general stoicism; as he wrote to Sophie's husband, 'One must bow one's head under the blow, as a helpless, poor human being with whom higher powers are playing' (1988: 392). But his feelings were clearly deeply stirred and never fully settled thereafter. Gay quotes Freud's encounter with a famous patient over a decade later:

in 1933, when the imagist poet Hilda Doolittle – H.D. – mentioned the last year of the Great War during an analytic hour with Freud, 'he said he had reason to remember the epidemic, as he lost his favourite daughter. "She is here," he said, and he showed me a tiny locket that he wore, fastened to his watch-chain. (Gay, 1988: 392)

Freud's little footnote perhaps does more than simply link his grandson's preemptive mastery of loss with his apparent indifference to his mother's death. It does not even just suggest Freud's own distancing; rather, it sets a hare running that, when we follow it, evokes a very deep melancholia, something that cannot be recovered from, an unspoken haunting. *Beyond the Pleasure Principle* was not written in response to Sophie's death, but that death is also not absent from it; and death itself, stalking Freud and the whole European continent, is the prime topic even where it seems to be life (the little boy's play) that is being celebrated.

When death does come, it is as an answer to the question of what it is that can explain unpleasant repetitions, what it is that is genuinely 'beyond the pleasure principle'. Freud's argument is consistent with his longstanding idea that satisfaction of a drive depends on reduction in tension. His model here is explicitly sexual (Freud, 1920: 62): 'We have all experienced how the greatest pleasure attainable by us, that of the sexual act, is associated with a momentary extinction of a highly intensified excitation. The binding of an instinctual impulse would be a preliminary function designed to prepare the excitation for its final elimination in the pleasure of discharge.' Increase in tension due to stimulation raises excitation, but the actual fulfilment of the pleasure principle occurs when that tension dissipates, and the organism – the human body and mind – returns to rest. This idea is coupled with Freud's equally longstanding commitment to the duality of drives: 'Our views have from the very first been dualistic, and to-day they are even more definitely dualistic than before – now that we describe the opposition as being, not between ego instincts and sexual instincts but between life instincts and death instincts' (ibid.: 53). One question here is whether both sets of drives follow the pleasure principle, or whether that urge towards reduction of tension is encased in only one set, so the duality is between an urge towards multiplication, complication and increased stimulation – the life drive – and the counter-urge towards release, destruction and quiescence – the death drive. If this is so, we might really be talking about one drive broken into two parts: one that increases tension (akin to 'the binding of an instinctual impulse') and the other that releases it ('extinction').

The key uncertainty here is in the 'beyond' of *Beyond the Pleasure Principle*. If all drives aim to reduce the organism to rest, which is supposed to be the essence of pleasure, then there is no drive that is 'beyond'. But Freud astutely recognises that whilst in theory this might be the case, the phenomenology of life is such that there is a complication around the nature of pleasure. Sometimes pleasure does indeed seem to be the 'momentary extinction of a highly intensified excitation'. Sometimes, however, it resides in the *increase* of complexity, in the *postponement* of the discharge – something that can serve pleasure in the longer term by increasing tension (unpleasure) in the here and now. And sometimes what we find is an addiction not to pleasure, but to something else – to attempts to remove excitation to such a degree that no more discharge is possible. For Freud, the 'conservatism' of the drives is such as to programme the organism towards *return* in the sense of seeking an earlier state of affairs; rest is something that comes when one gets back to the situation before there was any disruption, any need to do anything at all. This is what makes it 'beyond' pleasure: pleasure comes from the reduction in tension, but what is beyond that is the static position of complete rest. This is true for the individual but also for the species:

> [It] is possible to specify this final goal of all organic striving. It would
> be in contradiction to the conservative nature of the instincts if the
> goal of life were a state of things which had never yet been attained.
> On the contrary, it must be an old state of things, an initial state

from which the living entity has at one time or other departed and to which it is striving to return by the circuitous paths along which its development leads. If we are to take it as a truth that knows no exception that everything living dies for internal reasons – becomes inorganic once again – then we shall be compelled to say that '*the aim of all life is death*' and, looking backwards, that '*inanimate things existed before living ones.*' (Freud, 1920: 37)

We are forced to participate in life by 'the history of the earth we live in and of its relation to the sun' (ibid.: 37), and the drives accept this as they must, building the adaptations required into their own programme. But this is not an enthusiastic embracing of life; it is rather a way of seeking out the 'circuitous paths' that will enable the organism – the human one included – to find its own way towards death. 'For a long time', writes Freud, 'living substance was thus being constantly created afresh and easily dying, till decisive external influences altered in such a way as to oblige the still surviving substance to diverge ever more widely from its original course of life and to make ever more complicated détours before reaching its aim of death' (ibid.: 38–9) It is these 'circuitous paths to death' that we mistakenly classify as the phenomena of life; actually they are exactly a detour, something that takes us away from the straightest line of extinction and rest, but nevertheless always brings us back to the same place, as in Freud's 'painted women' example. Peter Brooks (1982) reads all this as having the structure of narrative: beginning and end could be quickly told, but life inheres in the complications of the narrative middle, the point of which is to lead to an end that makes some kind of sense. 'We emerge from reading *Beyond the Pleasure Principle*', he writes, 'with a dynamic model which effectively structures ends (death, quiescence, non-narratability) against beginnings (Eros, stimulation into tension, the desire of narrative) in a manner that necessitates the middle as *detour*, as struggle toward the end under the compulsion of imposed delay, as arabesque in the dilatory space of the text' (ibid.: 295).

An arabesque is an ornamentation; something is dilatory when it is slow. Life is a mode of ornamentation that helps make some sense of death, but it is not really the opposite of death. Rather, it is the path to it. Žižek (2011: 305) comments, referencing Deleuze, 'Eros and Thanatos are not two opposing drives that compete and combine their forces (as in eroticized masochism); there is only one drive, the libido, striving for enjoyment, and the "death drive" is the curved space of its formal structure.' Perhaps, however, it is the other way around: not that there is only libido that acts within the framework of death, though this makes sense; but rather that there is one primary drive, the *death drive*, and Eros is a temporary light, flickering for a while before it goes out. Freud is himself struck by the ironies here: 'Another striking fact', he writes, 'is that the life instincts have so much more contact with our internal perception – emerging as breakers of the peace and constantly producing tensions whose release is felt as pleasure – while the death instincts seem to do their work unobtrusively. The pleasure principle seems actually to serve the death instincts' (Freud, 1920: 63). Life interferes with the progress towards death, but death is the more potent and permanent force, and the more mature one, working without fuss, yet always there in the background, ready to act. Every time we meet ourselves coming back from somewhere, in every return of the repressed, in every compelled act of repetition, whenever we are absorbed in melancholy or made to shiver by some uncanny encounter, the primary drive is at work, and the evanescent displays of life are punctured by reminders that we are on the way to somewhere, that something solid lies in the background, but that it is not recognisable as 'us'.

Meeting oneself on the way back

The shiver we feel when encountering something uncanny is a shiver of recognition and of premonition. The crucial thing is that what should be the present is in fact infected both by the past and by the future. These two tenses, however, are themselves not distinct: the future has the structure of a return; the 'curved space' of which Žižek writes is one in which the end matches the beginning. The *now* of the present is a temporary movement away from something that continues without change in the background; Freud calls it the death drive, and makes it responsible for destruction (the projection of the death drive onto the world). The destruction is, however, not of the basic principle of being, but of the vain project of immortality; all that the death drive does is create the conditions for returning in the future to the nothingness (the state of 'nirvana', as Freud (1920: 56) calls it in passing) out of which each of us emerged.

If past and future haunt the present in the same way, as reminders and harbingers of death, then the double is both what we have been and what we will become. In this sense, the double is truer of us than we are of ourselves; more formally, the double, as an externalised projection of death, shocks the ego into recognition of its fragility. Lacan's (1949) over-used idea of the mirror phase is often drawn on to illustrate the manner in which the ego is built as a way of using external images to cover over the internal experience of dissolution. The idea is that as the infant is directed by the mother to see itself in the mirror, it gratefully accepts the fantasy that it can become an integrated being and survive the fragmenting drives to which it has previously felt itself to be prey. Instructively, Lacan (1949) locates the effect of this in the *future*:

> The fact is that the total form of the body by which the subject antic-ipates in a mirage the maturation of his power is given to him only as a *Gestalt*, that is to say, in an exteriority in which this form is cer-tainly more constituent than constituted, but in which it appears to him above all in a contrasting size that fixes it and in a symmetry that inverts it, in contrast with the turbulent movements that the subject feels are animating him. (Lacan, 1949: 2)

Lacan is arguing that the subject gains relief from the intensity of fragmenting internal impulses through the boundedness and apparent stability of the mirror image – something external but connected to the subject, holding a promise of future 'power'. Seeing oneself in the mir-ror, one sees what one might come to be. However, the mirror image is specious because it covers over the internal 'lack' that drives the infant to seek consolation in that image; and the future on which it is based is one of fantasy and imagination. Freud (1920: 15n) offers another ver-sion of this story in a footnote supplementing the fort-da game: 'One day the child's mother had been away for several hours and on her return was met with the words "Baby o-o-o-o!" which was at first incom-prehensible. It soon turned out, however, that during this long period of solitude the child had found a method of making himself disappear. He had discovered his reflection in a full-length mirror which did not quite reach to the ground, so that by crouching down he could make his mirror-image "gone".' In many ways, Freud's mirror story is more revealing than Lacan's, or perhaps it can be seen as its complement. The Lacanian mirror phase emphasises the false sense of security that the child gets from propping up its ego with the external account given to it by the mirror and the mother: 'you are whole, you will be all right'. The Freudian mirror is one of disappearance: the infant discovers that it too can disappear, just like the mother. The implication is that the second part of the game is also important – the reappearance of the self – but this is not stated in the text. What we are actually given is a child who learns how to make his ego disappear, who can fall into the abyss below the mirror and shares a fundamental human experience by so doing.

Just as the mother disappeared, so did the child; we all fall out of sight, and this is what we most profoundly share with other human beings. Discussing the way in which trauma is conceptualised in *Beyond the Pleasure Principle*, Cathy Caruth (1996) adds something significant to the relationship between fright and return. For her, fright is not generated by the danger we run into, but by the fact of *survival* – the question of what it is we come back with. She writes,

> If *fright* is the term by which Freud defines the traumatic effect of not having been prepared in time, then the trauma of the nightmare does not simply consist in the experience *within* the dream, but in *the experience of waking from it* ... What is enigmatically suggested, that is, is that the trauma consists not only in having confronted death, but in *having survived, precisely, without knowing it* ... Repetition, in other words, is not simply the attempt to grasp that one has almost died but, more fundamentally and enigmatically, the very attempt to *claim one's own survival*. If history is to be understood as the history of a trauma, it is a history that is experienced as the endless attempt to assume one's survival as one's own. (Caruth, 1996: 64)

The question of how one survives trauma will recur later in this book. Flagging up the link between fright and survival raises another issue: once one has experienced a trauma, for example the trauma of encountering the ghost of oneself coming back from the future, what can it mean to find oneself again? What has changed and what can remain the same? Caruth implies that all later history becomes a recurrent process, something 'endless' and hence impossible, always incomplete: 'the endless attempt to assume one's survival as one's own'. The one who passes through trauma never finally succeeds in assuming the state of 'survivor'; something remains 'unassumed', outside the experience of going-on-being, irretrievably alien. Caruth locates the trauma 'not simply' in having 'confronted death', but also in '*having survived, precisely, without knowing it*'. This parallels exactly the fort-da game, and suggests a reason why the child does not cry at the tragedy of the actual 'o-o-o' of his mother when she dies. The child may have brought himself back from the brink by drawing in the wooden reel; but his encounter with loss leaves him scarred, already incomplete, a 'survivor' who carries death inside. Waking from the nightmare is in itself a fright; it plunges us into the disturbing reality that dreams can come true.

When Freud meets himself in the mirror, he does not feel relieved like the Lacanian infant. Instead, he gets a nasty shock: he sees what he has become and what he will come to be. The mirror-double is a harbinger of death; it pops up, having fallen away for a while, with the reminder of the abyss from which it came and to which it will return.

Dolar (1996: 140) comments, 'The double is the initial repetition, the first repetition of the same, but also what keeps repeating itself, emerging in the same place (one of the Lacanian definitions of the Real), springing up at the most awkward times, both as an irruption of the unexpected and with clockwork precision, totally unpredictable and predictable in one.' The double is clearly a representative of the death drive, however homely the form that it takes. It does not exactly give Freud a fright to see himself, but it makes him shiver with dislike. More fully, what haunts us is this reminder of something beneath the mirror that cannot be symbolised in or by the ego; it is genuinely 'beyond' what can be categorised under the heading of identity, yet it is deeply personal and very well known. The double, in its concreteness, makes us see it again, but it is always there in the background, always marking the present with the future and the past.

3
Ghostly Psychoanalysis

Unlaid ghosts

There is a lot in psychoanalysis that falls under the heading of 'haunting'. Perhaps it even makes sense to think of its whole project that way – as a practice of exorcism. In a famous formulation, Freud (1909: 123) writes, 'In an analysis...a thing which has not been understood inevitably reappears; like an unlaid ghost, it cannot rest until the mystery has been solved and the spell broken.' What troubles us now is laid at the feet of a ghost; that ghost must be identified, appeased and put to rest. This is not just a matter of naming it but also of understanding it in a very particular and comprehensive way, offering it something that acknowledges it and that makes reparation for the damage done to it. There are rituals attached to this: free association, interpretation, working through. During analysis, the ghost grows in substance and certainty precisely in order that it can be later dissolved. This might be a loving process in which something lost is recognised and mourned. Or it could be a traumatic experience in which something we never knew we had comes back to plague us, a repetitive and destructive inheritance that holds tight with its talons and can only be released with violence and pain. It may be a ghost from individual history, something we have done or has been done to us. It may also be a transgenerational one, haunting us because of events that took place in earlier times.

In a strange article that adds a sixth act to *Hamlet*, Nicolas Abraham (1988) writes psychoanalytically about ghosts. He identifies them with *shameful* secrets (p. 3): 'Yes, the shameful and therefore concealed secret always does return to haunt. To exorcise it one must express it in words. But how are we to accomplish this when the phantoms who inhabit our minds do so without our knowledge, embodying the unspeakable secret of...an other? This other, of course, is a loved one.' There are some important strands in this statement that recur throughout the consideration of how psychoanalysis operates in the domain of haunting. The secret comes from the *other*, whatever and whoever that might be, and this is a reason for protecting the secret. In other words, it is not only that certain kinds of knowledge are difficult to face – the usual, trauma-based explanation for the desymbolisation that is communicated through haunting – but also that there is a *protective* factor at work. Something is being preserved, some precious idealisation or maintenance of a bond, or a lost object that cannot be let go of by allowing grief to come to an end. This sounds like a melancholic object, one that is never fully acknowledged and consequently can never be properly mourned, which means that it is somehow preserved in a kind of half-life or living death. Moreover, it is not only the object itself that is both lost and preserved, it is also *awareness* of that object – we seek it, driven by an inner sense of something missing, but only under the condition that we will not actually find it. 'The gaps and impediments in our communication with the loved one,' writes Abraham (1988: 3), 'wrought by the secret, produce a twofold and contrary effect: the prohibition of knowledge coupled with an unconscious investigation.' The consequence of this is that secret knowledge, often referred to using Bollas' (1987) terminology of the 'unthought known' to signify a memory that cannot be openly recalled yet is also never lost, keeps finding its way through into consciousness only to be rejected by the subject. Something speaks, but even as we hear it we pretend that we do not know what it is. Abraham continues (1988: 3), 'This twofold movement is manifest in symptoms and gives rise to "gratuitous" or uncalled-for acts and words, creating eerie effects: hallucinations and delirium, showing and hiding that which, in the depths of the unconscious, dwells as the living-dead knowledge of someone else's secret.' Ghosts are the product of this show-and-hide ambivalence: something is let through but also denied, so it cannot be symbolised but only experienced as a concrete reality that comes from outside.

One thing to note is that we should probably be cautious about how much we can understand. Lacan's stricture on this functions importantly as a warning not just to analysts, but to everyone:

How many times have I said to those under my supervision, when they say to me – *I had the impression he meant this or that* – that one of the things we must guard most against is to understand too much, to understand more than what is in the discourse of the subject.

> To interpret and to imagine one understands are not the same things. It is precisely the opposite. I would go so far as to say that it is on the basis of a kind of refusal of understanding that we push open the door to analytic understanding. (Lacan, 1975: 73)

This is contrary to most people's vision of psychoanalysis, which places it as an interpretive science committed to the possibility of finding meaning in everything. If a man keeps repeating an obsessional act, it is *because* he is warding off disturbing sexual thoughts. If a woman dreams of a lost child, it points to her own inner sense of abandonment and rejection. Lacan's warning is very precise here: it is not possible to understand more than 'what is in the discourse of the subject'. What the analyst has to cultivate is a capacity to stay ignorant, to avoid leaping in with the kind of understanding that will close down the possibilities for something to happen. Knowing too much, knowing it too soon, stops what is unknown from coming into being. In this sense, psychoanalysis is a practice of *not* knowing, of refusing to understand what cannot be known.

None of this is aimed at promoting mysticism, but rather at avoiding the assumption that everything that happens is already foreshadowed by theory and by the experience of the interpreter. It aims to promote a practice of listening where that which is not available to awareness is also that which is appreciated most – appreciated, but not bound, not restricted to the elementary principles of sense making. All this is to say: we cannot know everything and it is a necessary if painful attack on our narcissism to accept this limitation as a fact. What happens, however, if it is exactly that which we do *not* know that recurs as a concrete object, if it is *only* in the figure of the ghost that otherwise unknowable reality can be found? For example, it is a commonplace that some things are very difficult to speak about and that there may even be things that can never be said. This may be because they are too subtle, too ephemeral or marginal to experience, and consequently cannot be pinned down sufficiently. But such things can at least be evoked, and much of art and literature is dedicated to precisely this activity. These are not lost and repressed things; they are simply so precious that one is wary of destroying them by giving them too clumsy and crude a name.

Indeed, it is possible to argue that these things are not 'pathological' ghosts that have to be exorcised, but are rather a kind of haunting that is *necessary* for ordinary psychic life. The present cannot exist on its own, as a separate point in time uninformed by past and future: it is always transient, in process, so always saturated with the sounds and sights of memory and expectation. This means that without a certain degree and kind of haunting, there is no possibility of a present. In a review of an earlier draft of this chapter, Derek Hook commented that, 'one problem with the notion of haunting as it is often utilised is that it all too often seems to imply that the past's disturbance of the present is unusual, if not in fact necessarily frightening, disturbing, when "haunting" may be a necessary condition of possibility for "the present" – which is never really a distinct or separable segment of history – to exist. Haunting then, certainly understood in terms of the repetition of certain signifiers or cultural modes, or in terms of the inheritance of parental or generational desires, may not only be the norm, but quite ordinary. By this logic, a lack of haunting would seem the truly precarious and disturbing condition.' The normality of this kind of haunting is important to hold in mind when faced with the ubiquity of exorcism; without ghosts, our minds might be emptied of content.

Other things, however, cannot be spoken because they are too 'crude' in a different sense. They resist symbolisation because of the pain it causes to allow them existence; so, to put it simply, they are repressed, rejected or 'abjected' as objects of destruction and death. Their presence cannot be tolerated, their loss cannot be borne. The experience surrounding them generally goes under the name of 'trauma', as if this is a way of explaining it; but in fact all this terminology does is gesture towards the unbearableness of being in such circumstances. These things cannot be spoken of either because the pain of their presence is so overwhelming, or because the tragedy of their loss is of such terrible proportions that even recognising that they were once ours is too much to cope with. So they are left unspoken and unspeakable, but psychically crucial and real. Abraham (1988) codes this through a riff on truth and lies that locates the source of each in the other, implying that the existence of a certain kind of intolerable truth ('Truth') is only indicated through the lies used to circumvent it. The analytic task is to peel away these lies to gain glimpses of the truth, in the hope that something less deceitful will subsequently arise. Abraham writes (1988: 3–4), 'One senses that this Truth, the final cause of so many lies, is supremely abominable and as such is intolerable to the gaze. Nonetheless, thanks to this idea, a certain wisdom is acquired. The dissipation of even a single phantom cannot but indirectly touch the clandestine core of the ultimate abomination. Consequently, its offspring will be modified; some of its partial "truths" will acquire the right to exist openly.'

Cryptic truths

That which we cannot understand is precisely that which we need to look at most closely, with respect and care, and without trying to place it into a network of meanings that will reduce its sting and distort its significance. This is one sense in which ghosts have to be granted their reality, which in turn is a source of criticism of psychoanalysis for being too quick to write off the occult as a solely psychological phenomenon. Avery Gordon (1997: 57), for instance, states that: 'I think Freud was afraid of what he saw. Sometimes this is necessary in the face of ghosts. But he gave it up too quickly. If you let it, the ghost can lead you toward what has been missing, which is sometimes everything.' She has in mind the social sources of haunting, to which we will return; but she is also noting something else, that in reducing ghosts to fantastic expressions of the unconscious one runs the risk of not appreciating how their reality stretches further than the psychological alone. That is to say, we are not dealing with psychology here, but with the way psychology falls apart when confronted with the real.

Derrida is more appreciative of Freud:

> It is known that Freud did everything possible to not neglect the experience of haunting, spectrality, phantoms, ghosts. He tried to account for them. Courageously, in as scientific, critical and positive fashion as possible. But by doing that, he also tried to conjure them. Like Marx. His scientific positivism was put to the service of his declared hauntedness and his unavowed fear. (Derrida, 1996: 85)

Whilst psychoanalysis might be dedicated to removing ghosts, it is also the case that, as a theory and as a practice, it would not exist without them. It conjures up and tries to find a way to deal with spectres that keep bubbling up, and at the root of this activity is 'unavowed fear'. Facing this fear is immensely difficult; Freud's own strategy of 'scientific positivism' allows him to do this but also somehow keeps it at bay. Yet Freud did not simply turn away from haunting, for his whole procedure is based on the idea that facing the apparently un-faceable is a necessary act. Why should this be? Because at the heart of the kind of 'good life' that Freud seeks there is the unfaltering search for truth, in the sense of the reality of one's emotional response to the world in all its bareness as it has its various rationalisations and defences stripped away. This mode of being is a way of becoming more fully alive. Derrida follows in this tradition when he argues that what is at stake in psychoanalysis is not just a therapeutic release, but an act of truth. The truth, however, is 'spectral', it can never be fully tracked down, it is never quite there. He writes:

> we should not forget that if the psychoanalytic explanation of haunt-edness, of hallucination, if the psychoanalytic theory of spectres, in sum, leaves a part, a share of nonverisimilitude unexplained or rather *verisimilar*, carrying truth, this is because ... there is a *truth of delusion*, a truth of insanity or of hauntedness. Analogous to that 'historical truth' which Freud distinguishes, notably in *Moses*, from the 'material truth', this truth is repressed or suppressed. But it resists and *returns*, as such, as the spectral truth of delusion or of hauntedness. It *returns*, it belongs, it comes down to spectral truth. (Derrida, 1996: 87)

If the truth is spectral, then there is something true about what has been repressed, lost, maybe murdered too. These lost truths keep coming back to haunt us, and demand recompense. They are unwanted apparitions, troubling us; we often wish they would let us alone. Yet as well as shivering the calmness that we seek, these spectral truths give psychic life its depths. 'The truth is spectral', writes Derrida (1996: 87), 'and this is its part of truth which is irreducible by explanation.' Something is left over whenever we try to account for ourselves, some area of 'opacity' as Butler (2005) terms it. It is towards this leftover, this hidden remainder, that we need to look if we are to find the thing we seek in life, whether it goes by the name of the unconscious or not. Royle (1995: 361) suggests that, 'All of Derrida's work can be read as an attempt to respond to this question of "remains".' Explanation leaves a remnant, that which is irreducible. At other times one might refer to this as the 'things that can't be said' (Frosh, 2002), either because putting things into particular words means that some other possible ways of articulating them are closed down, or because some things, being intolerable, are violently abjected. Whichever the case, there is an elemental level of the residual, that which stays behind; and it is often here that a certain kind of psychic but non-psychological 'truth' resides.

What we have so far is an amalgam of issues around otherness (the secret of the other), abjection and spectral truth. These come together psychoanalytically in the notion that what is most fundamental to each of us is also most 'other'. Gordon's (1997) understanding of ghosts as social events is articulated in the context of 'The "Uncanny"' as a statement about how each subject is inhabited by social others. 'The uncanny', she writes, 'is the return, in psychoanalytic terms, of what the concept of the unconscious represses: the reality of being haunted by worldly contacts' (ibid.: 54). In Gordon's elaboration, ghosts are sociological events, traced to the social order and especially to the traumatic instances of oppression that are pushed to the margins of history, yet continue to infiltrate the imagination of later generations:

> The ghost is not simply a dead or a missing person, but a social figure, and investigating it can lead to that dense site where history and subjectivity make social life. The ghost or the apparition is one form by which something lost, or barely visible, or seemingly not there to our supposedly well-trained eyes, makes itself known or apparent to us, in its own way, of course. The way of the ghost is haunting, and haunting is a very particular way of knowing what has happened or is happening. (Gordon, 1997: 8)

What is a ghost? It is a 'social figure' that if we follow its trail will lead us to 'a dense site' of social life. 'What's distinctive about haunting', Gordon claims (ibid.: xvi), 'is that it is an animated state in which a repressed or unresolved social violence is making itself known, sometimes very directly, sometimes more obliquely.' This rendering of haunting as social enables her to call on powerful articulations of political oppression as representations of the kinds of living death associated with ghosts: for instance, the 'disappeared' of Argentina and the generational chains of slavery in Toni Morrison's (1987) *Beloved*. In each case, what is left unresolved in history works its way into the present as a traumatic haunting that is profoundly social, yet is lived out in the deepest recesses of individuals' lives. This stance also fuels her idea that ghosts have to be thought of as *real*: they actually exist, because what haunts us is the denied reality of oppressed lives, lives demoralised or cut short, lives marginalised and written out of history, precarious lives treated as dispensable but impossible fully to forget precisely because their effects linger on.

Ghosts come from somewhere, and if one treats them seriously it becomes apparent that this somewhere is not located within the individual's mind. It is instead to be found in the fabric of history and culture, embedded in the symbolic structures of society that maintain the liveliness of some memories whilst marginalising others. The materiality of the social is perhaps never more apparent than when considering this apparently mystical haunting; which is to say, what appears unannounced in consciousness is derived from the routines and practices of the symbolic order, constantly reproducing its history. What haunts us psychically is, in this rendering, some *injustice*, something that has not been dealt with rightly. This is one of the oldest views of ghosts, that they wander the world and cannot find rest because they have been mistreated, displaced and left unrecognised. An injustice has been done: they have been murdered, a memorial has not been set up for them, someone has forgotten to say the memorial prayer. 'I have suggested', writes Gordon (1997: 62), 'that the ghost is alive, so to speak. We are in relation to it and it has designs on us such that we must reckon with it graciously, attempting to offer it a hospitable memory out of a concern for justice. Out of a concern for justice would be the only reason one would bother.'

Gordon sees Freud as having subtly, perhaps uncomfortably, recognised the social origins of the modes of haunting with which he was concerned. 'Freud cannot quite get away from the possibility that the unconscious derives its characteristic force from its role as the place where all the others out there in the world and their life come inside me and unhinge my sense of self as they make me what I am, as they live within me' (Gordon, 1997: 47). The Freudian unconscious is not exactly a 'social unconscious' in the sense of a shared space bought into by all social subjects – we do not all have the same unconscious lives. Its sociality resides rather in how, for each person, it is constituted by the incorporation of external figures, those who look after us in infancy, those who impact upon us in the immediacy of their dependable or violent presence, those who pass on to us their own wishes or desires, their own specific 'message' about what it is to be present in the world as we find it. If one is to seek theoretical leverage on this from within psychoanalysis, it is possibly to be found in Jean Laplanche's (1999) idea that what enters into every human subject from the other does so as an untranslatable message of excitement, an arousal that is troublingly enigmatic. Whilst some elements of the parental message are successfully understood by the infant, others are not. They are a 'remainder' that cannot be integrated into the subject but rather inhabits the subject as something alien yet constitutive. But even if they are not so specifically linked to the other, if unconscious impulses are merely Freudianly repressed ghosts, each such impulse 'proliferates in the dark, as it were, and takes on extreme forms of expression, which when they are translated and presented to the neurotic are not only bound to seem alien to him, but frighten him by giving him the picture of an extraordinary and dangerous strength of instinct' (Freud, 1915: 149).

There is nothing novel about seeing psychoanalysis as concerned with internal, psychic foreignness. For example, Julia Kristeva's meditation on otherness, *Strangers to Ourselves* (1988), is premised on exactly this idea, that the existence of an unconscious 'inside' each one of us means the haunting of the individual human subject by something else, strange, foreign, and yet real. 'Uncanny', she writes (p. 181), 'foreignness is within us: we are our own foreigners, we are divided.' It is the link between this foreignness and the *disturbing* nature of the uncanny that helps explain why we end up dealing with it in ways that are ambivalent and at times nasty. We do not very often *welcome* the foreigner within, even if we should. 'The "Uncanny"' might attract readers, but the uncanny is – as Freud (1939: 91) put it in relation to circumcision – 'disagreeable', giving rise to antagonism.

The other is what founds us, creating those enigmatic strands that link what is most central in the psyche to what is extrinsic to it. Through the dependency each infant has on someone to care for it, and through the continuing impact of other people's desires and demands, something secret comes in and troubles the subject, manifesting itself as an unconscious message that is resistant to translation and to full symbolisation. This is a kind of trauma, by definition, and hence the kind of thing that leads to haunting. The routine understanding of what it means to call something 'unconscious' is that each one of us becomes *subjected to* forces that are not controllable and also not speakable. What is added by the Laplanchian paradigm is that the specific message around which unconscious life is organised is a message from the other; and that this is a secret in part because it is not conscious to the other either. For example, it is not known to the mother how much her erotic life is pressed into action by her contact with the child, but this is nevertheless passed on by her to her infant as an unconscious message, an indigestible piece of psychic activity. Thus, when Laplanche talks about the enigmatic signifier he may be indexing something very similar to Abraham when the latter writes (1988: 3), as mentioned above, 'the phantoms who inhabit our minds do so without our knowledge, embodying the unspeakable secret of...an other'. The secret of the other, what can that be? Is it a statement about sexual desire; or maybe something more profound and widespread, an elemental secret, a kind of name that can never be pronounced?

According to a now famous formulation by Abraham and Torok (1976), elaborated by Derrida (1986), the deepest secrets are hidden away in a 'crypt'. It is first worth noting that there is something pleasurable at work here, a disturbing pleasure it is true and one that forces the radical excision of certain ideas – of specific *words* – from consciousness. But a disregarded pleasure is nevertheless there, as Abraham and Torok make clear when they describe the different layers of secrecy that the crypt might hold:

> Beneath the fetish, the occult love for a word-object remains concealed, beneath this love, the taboo-forming experience of a catastrophe, and finally beneath the catastrophe, the perennial memory of a hoarded pleasure with the ineducable wish that one day it shall return. (Abraham and Torok, 1976: 22)

This 'hoarded pleasure' is not in any way straightforward, but it registers something surprising that is located in the place of a trauma. Words are key here: words that become 'cryptonyms', coded locations of material that is preserved in a hidden-away, never even whispered-about form. Many writers see cryptonyms and particularly cryptographs (written versions of these codes) as ways of breaking through to the crypts in which feared or traumatic memories are held, enabling them to see the light and be released and hence allowing the necessary psychic work to be done for healing to begin. Abraham and Torok, however, stress how the cryptonym is itself the hidden thing, lying at the source of the trauma and of the repression or foreclosure to which it is subjected:

> It is not a situation *including* words that become repressed: the words are not dragged into repression by a situation. Rather, *the words themselves, expressing desire, are deemed to be generators of a situation that must be avoided and voided retroactively.* In this case, and only in this case, can we understand that repression may be carried out on the word, as if it were the representation of a thing, and that the return of the repressed cannot have at its disposal even the tortuous paths of metonymic displacement. For this to occur, a catastrophic situation must have been created precisely by words. (Abraham and Torok, 1976: 20)

What kind of catastrophic situation could this be? For Gabriele Schwab (2010: 2), perhaps simplifying unduly, a crypt 'buries a lost person or object or even a disavowed part of oneself or one's history, while keeping it psychically alive'. This begins to sound again like a melancholic object, that which is kept alive even in death. Schwab locates the key element of secrecy in the way in which a traumatic narrative is covered over. In her study, she considers the position of being the child of Nazi perpetrators. She asserts, 'Remaining frozen in guilt not only sustains a culture of silence but also induces defenses that prevent working through the past' (ibid.: 13). Janine Chasseguet-Smirgel (1987: 437) was more direct in her day, in the aftermath of the 1985 Hamburg Congress of the International Psychoanalytic Association, the first to be held in Germany after the Nazi period. Here is her summary, which takes as its starting point the address to the psychoanalysts by the mayor of Hamburg, Klaus von Dohnanyi, and tracks just how hard it is to rise to the challenge of dealing fully with the malevolent past:

> When opening the Congress, Klaus von Dohnanyi exclaimed: 'If we say "our Beethoven, our Bach", we must also say "our Hitler"'. Thomas Mann entitled one of his articles 'Bruder Hitler'. After all, the problem is one of identification... *What is one to do with a Nazi father?* Apparently, the only solution is to reject him. If you speak of the need to integrate your identification with that father, you are immediately treated as a Nazi yourself... In order to become a human being in the full sense of the term, we have to be able to discover, confront and own, the *Hitler in uns*, otherwise the repressed will return and the disavowed will come back in various guises. (Ibid.)

'*What is one to do with a Nazi father?*' is certainly a question to be hidden away, as explosive and damaging to all concerned, yet without facing it – without giving it its *proper name* – the damage caused by the perpetrator generation continues. The problem is that the repressed and the disavowed never go away; it is precisely the fact that they always come back that lies at the heart of haunting. The worst of it is when what is passed down from generation to generation is something unspeakable, pinned to a hidden word ('the *Hitler in uns*') so that we are burdened by the secret of those who have come before, unacknowledged victims or perpetrators leaving their unworked-through heritage to their children and children's children. The crypt is something that contains these unspeakables, a word-place that locks them up, a code so hard to break that even the code-master does not know it.

Derrida makes it clear that this is a complex and elaborate process of building partitions and warded off places resulting in a space that is not part of anything, that is a real 'no place':

> Constructing a system of partitions, with their inner and outer surfaces, the cryptic enclave produces a cleft in space, in the assembled system of various places, in the architectonics of the open square within space, itself delimited by a generalized closure, in the *forum*. Within this forum, a place where the free circulation and

exchange of objects and speeches can occur, the crypt constructs another, more inward forum like a closed rostrum or speaker's box, a *safe*: sealed, and thus internal to itself, a secret interior within the public square, but, by the same token, outside it, external to the interior. (Derrida, 1986: xiv)

The crypt hides something alien: 'the *crypt* as a foreign body included through incorporation in the Self, and the *ghost* effect, more radically heterogeneous insofar as it implies the topography of an *other*, of a "corpse buried in the other"' (ibid.: xxx). Moreover, the crypt is itself *hidden away* by an act of violence that does not announce 'here is the safe', but rather buries it behind one wall and then another, until only a ghost who can pass through walls could possibly get out. This all sounds hopeless, unforgiving in the impossibility of release; and this is often how it is experienced, perhaps just as strongly by the guilt-ridden children of perpetrators as by those of victims. If there is no actual external place for grief and mourning, then we try to build one inside. But secrecy is also the invitation to action and also to psychoanalysis: find the place, the crypt, release the dead body from its limbo, and bury it properly, in its rightful place. Far from the usual idea that psychoanalysis is an inward-looking process, in fact it aims to create a shared awareness of something that actually exists, an *objective* phenomenon that can then be properly mourned. Derrida makes of this an exhumation that arises from suffering and references again the pleasure, which he codes as 'an exquisite corpse':

The very thing that provokes the worst suffering must be kept alive. The outpouring of the libido at the moment of loss...is repressed, not in and of itself, as such, but in its ties with the dead...The 'conservative' repression installs in the Unconscious what takes on for the Self the appearance of an exquisite corpse: apparently illegible and devoid of meaning, blurring the records by the segmented accumulation of pieces of folded sentences...but also infallibly designating...the corpse of an exquisite pleasure, disguised by repression as an exquisite pain, the singular, precise, chosen (exquisite) spot where the repressed is to be exhumed...(Derrida, 1986: xxxv)

As Derrida notes, there is 'self-torture' involved in this process. We return something to life precisely in order to kill it off, or perhaps it would state it more fully if we said we are constantly fascinated by what seems to have been killed off, but continues to exist. 'The very thing that provokes the worst suffering must be kept alive'; 'ties with the dead'; 'the corpse of an exquisite pleasure'; 'the repressed is to be exhumed'. These are terms not only of remainder but also of a mode of enjoyment in which what is most painfully lost is secretly fed even without the knowledge of the feeder. We are compelled to keep the encrypted other alive, but we do it blindfolded, without knowing exactly what it is we are in contact with.

Insisting on the materiality of ghosts, Gordon (1997) also insists on the hope that is bound up in them. 'When you touch the ghost or the ghostly matter (or when it touches you)', she writes, 'a force that combines the injurious and the utopian, you get something different than you might have expected' (ibid.: 134) There is a great deal of complexity involved in working out what it is that ghosts keep alive. On the one hand, they have suffered injustice and are demanding recompense. When we come up against this aspect of a ghost, action is demanded of us, ranging from acknowledgement to reparation. A prayer may not be enough, nor might be an apology of the kind given decades or centuries too late to the victims of colonial oppression, thievery and genocide. The necessary act could involve digging up the 'exquisite corpse' and reinterring it according to the proper rituals – and these may involve not just ceremonials, but political action. How else does one free the next generations, whether they be descendants of victims or indeed, as Schwab tries to think it, of perpetrators? In a talk on acknowledgement and reparation, Jessica Benjamin (2009) ventriloquised one version of the issue like this: 'Humanising the perpetrator becomes the challenge that the victim can make: "You are a human being who is capable of taking responsibility, now please do this for me."' On the other hand, we who carry on may be maintaining the ghost for our own needs, because it is too painful to acknowledge the fact of loss or even the existence of the loved object in the first place. What we desire most is hardest to give up, so it is maintained by denying that it is lost – and this can go so far as to deny that it ever existed. 'I never loved, I never lost,' to adapt the formula Butler (1997) uses for gender melancholy. The haunting presence then becomes something to which we are too strongly attached; it will not let us alone because we cannot find a way to allow it to leave. And bringing these two hands together: the reason we might fail to grieve and let the lost one go might be precisely because of the injustice that we still feel attaches to them, and the responsibility that we continue to feel but cannot face. If this is not a melancholic state to be in, what is?

Melancholic returns

There are various psychic expressions for this kind of maintaining death-in-life, but melancholia is the one that has recently gained the greatest currency. Melancholia is receiving a surprisingly good press in some academic circles, so it is worth reminding ourselves first of how, psychoanalytically, it has traditionally been referenced as a mode of pathology, of unworked-through mourning that leaves the subject depressed and out in the cold. Against this unpromising backdrop, melancholia has been resurfacing as a paradigm of subversion, an instance of how what is written off as a profound negative can be reinterpreted as a call to arms, even a messianic call in some renderings. The key element in this rereading of the productive possibilities of melancholia is the idea of the *preservation of the object.* Mourning, we are told, is a process whereby we recognise a loss and grieve it; it results, however painfully, in coming to terms with that object's demise and introjecting it into the ego so that life can go on. The object loss fades because it is dealt with; the thing that is lost no longer has existence, even if it is recalled with pleasure and sorrow. The life of the grieving subject is even expanded through the way the introjected object fuels psychic growth: we learn from and identify with aspects of those we have loved and lost.

In melancholia, however, there is no recognition of the loss of the object, which instead becomes an unconscious spur to continuing psychic trouble. It exists 'in' the unconscious as something that cannot be grieved because it is never acknowledged. Derrida explains this in relation to *incorporation.* The object is taken in whole, but it is never finished off: 'by resisting introjection, it prevents the loving, appropriating assimilation of the other, and thus seems to preserve the other *as* other (foreign), but it also does the opposite. It is not the *other* that the process of incorporation preserves, but a certain topography it keeps safe, intact, untouched by the very relationship with the other to which, paradoxically enough, introjection is more open' (Derrida, 1986: xxi–xxii). Schwab (2010: 55) reads the crypt similarly: incorporation 'severs the processes of vital exchange between self and world and forecloses transformation and emergence'. Introjection is dynamic, allowing movement; incorporation is the process of the crypt, keeping the object whole, in a certain sense, but also locked away, unavailable and stagnant, but lurking behind as a potential threat.

This has some contradictory effects. One the one hand, the object is not recognised so cannot be seen for what it is, and therefore cannot be let go of; it continues to trouble the ongoing life of the subject, it causes depression of a kind that cannot be escaped because its source is not known. On the other hand – and this is what is leading to a revaluation of the melancholic motif – it in some sense preserves the object precisely because the object is never grieved. That is, whereas mourning deals with object loss and integrates the object into the subject's psychic life, dissolving it so that it becomes a part of the subject, melancholia can be read as an act of refusal on the part of the object to being taken up and destroyed in this way. From a failure of the subject to a refusal by the object – this is an important shift in perspective that gives space for a rereading of the 'lost' object as now no longer lost. Butler, using a more generic term for the taking in of lost objects ('internalisation'), describes the psychoanalytic mechanism at work as follows:

> If in melancholia a loss is refused, it is not for that reason abolished. Internalization preserves loss in the psyche; more precisely the internalization of loss is part of the mechanism of its refusal. If the object can no longer exist in the external world, it will then exist internally, and that internalization will be a way to disavow the loss, to keep it at bay, to stay or postpone the recognition and suffering of loss. (Butler, 1997: 134)

Because it is undigested, still present in psychic space as something that is neither recognised nor disposed of, it still exists. It lies in wait for that moment in which, as Butler (2011: 102) describes it (drawing on Walter Benjamin), it can 'flash up' as a moment of reminder, a breaking through of that which was occluded in history, but can now be recovered as a potentially revolutionary agent. 'One time breaks into another precisely when that former time was to remain forgotten for all time,' writes Butler (2011: 88), describing this as a mode of 'messianic secularism'. In the life of the individual, melancholia signals that something important is still there, waiting to be recognised; in the life of the collective, the same thing applies.

At the heart of much of this discussion is a dynamic of regret and potential. The object is lost, but unrecognised as such, so there is an unlocated sense of 'something lost' that cannot be pinned down and hence saturates the subject with a regret that shades into melancholia. At the same time, there is an augury of potential ghostly re-emergence of the lost object that perhaps threateningly, perhaps promisingly, can radically reshape the contemporary psychosocial and political scene. How the latter trend might triumph over the former is never clear, but the model here seems in many ways to be a conventional 'depth to surface' one in which – like the unconscious – there is always something pressing for release, and at some point it cannot be held back any more. The anti-apartheid struggle might be one instance of this; so too, however, might be the resurgence of nationalistic myth-making and violence subsequent to the breakdown of the Eastern European Soviet states (Žižek, 1990). No wonder then that contemporary subjectivity falls under the shadow of melancholia: something is coming back to haunt us, which was not recognised before, and perhaps we are uncertain both of its provenance and its direction of change.

Melancholic postcoloniality

It will probably be obvious why so much of the reinstating of melancholia has been linked with postcolonial studies. Lisa Baraitser (2012) summarises the field, connecting it to the melancholia present in psychoanalysis itself as a discipline that is always somehow out of time, out of date, embracing lost objects without accepting that they have really gone. Part of her thinking here is that in the context of twenty-first-century time pressures, psychoanalysis is at odds with the buzz and pace of Western urban life that gives so much of the hectic 'feel' to contemporary culture. Standing against the thrust towards constant productivity that dominates economic thinking, psychoanalysis is one of those sets of practices that are clearly 'redundant', demanding too much time and money, too much commitment – a space in which nothing happens, for ages. She suggests that 'we might usefully think of both psychoanalysis and particular inflections of performance...as "redundant" forms of human contact, deliberately "useless" and "stupid" forms that nevertheless continue to stage the possibility for something to happen' (Bayly and Baraitser, 2008: 353). Baraitser comments on how this 'out-of-timeness' is intrinsic to psychoanalysis not only because of its preservation of a peculiar treatment space, but also because of its conceptualisation of how present time is always embroiled with resurrecting the past. The trope here is that of anachronism, which is opposed to what might seem its close cousin, nostalgia, because it challenges rather than just laments the here and now:

> One way, then, that psychoanalysis is linked to anachronism is through its theorization of chronological misplacement – the way, as Lacan would have it, that future events control the meaning of events in the past, and through après-coup, give rise to the past

itself. But more importantly, psychoanalysis is also an anachronistic and melancholic profession due to an unacknowledged 'othering' constantly at work in its theoretical antecedents, and which we must make visible, but not entirely work through. The 'work of melancholia' (as distinct from the work of mourning) requires a stubborn attachment to a traumatic historical past that is important for both the colonized and the colonizer, as forgetting constitutes a denial of this shared, though unequal history. (Baraitser, 2012: 224–5)

Melancholia is being used here to express the attachment to the past that refuses forgetting and therefore opposes the 'colonising' act of appropriating history that makes it the 'history of the victors'. The quotation also emphasises how the past is always a work in progress: the notion of 'après-coup' referenced in it relates to 'Nachträglichkeit' or 'afterwardsness', understandable as the reinvention of the past in the light not only of the present, but also of the future – of what we might hope or fear to become. This operates for individuals, as each of us seeks some reconciliation with the unmourned objects of past losses, hauntingly continuous in their effects. It operates too at the level of collectives, as the unspeakable events of the past – experienced by people as victims or perpetrators – become the conscious and unconscious sources of contemporary struggle and regret. Ranjana Khanna (2004), in her influential text on postcolonial melancholy and psychoanalysis, is another author to make the link explicit:

Whereas Freud wrote of the work of mourning as the work of assimilating the lost object, the work of melancholia has a critical relation to the lost and to the buried. It manifests, sometimes in paralysis, stasis, or demetaphorization, loss, and it thus calls upon the inassimilable remainder. It does not merely call for inclusion, assimilation, reparation, or retribution. It calls for a response to the critical work of incorporation, and the ethical demand that such incorporation makes on the future. (Ibid.: 25)

And more of this is present in the work particularly of Homi Bhabha (2004) and Paul Gilroy (2004) drawing backwards towards Fanon (1952) as the recognised psychoanalytically informed precursor of postcolonial studies. Colonialism not only oppressed its victims; it also stole their past, making it unmournable. The consequence is an encrypted thing that acts as a hole in history; something imagined and felt as absent, but denied being, a never-having-been that continues to haunt the present.

This has powerful material effects. Partly, it offers a prospect for radical rethinking of what might now occur, in ostensibly postcolonial times: what lies in the past could be recuperated and reworked to become something new. But partly this melancholic political state produces a continuing re-enactment in which the loss of history is covered over by an embrace of colonial values themselves, these being all that is left of the fantasy of wholeness and rationalistic utopianism held out by the coloniser as the benefit of being taken over.

There is much to be said about this, and there are several important studies of the modes of racialisation and indeed of racism that can be teased out of the nexus of colonialism and psychoanalysis (for example, Brickman, 2003; Hook, 2012; Seshadri-Crooks, 2000). From within the history of oppression, what comes across most urgently is the idea that in emerging into a postcolonial space something from the unremembered past raises its head, unacknowledged and unwanted yet having intensely ambivalent effects on contemporary subjectivities. The ambivalence can perhaps be spelt out along two dimensions, as one might predict. First, colonialism so comprehensively destroyed the sources of value within the cultures that it conquered – left those subjects so unrecognised, one might say – that whilst there might be powerful *sensations* of loss at work in those cultures, there is little access to the actual things that were lost. What might have constituted the subjugated culture as living and substantial was wiped out so thoroughly that even its loss cannot be known. This could also forge a psychic response in which the unbearable nature of this loss is denied and replaced by a manic rush towards the *coloniser's* mode of being, for example in aping the structures of the colonial nation state. To adapt Butler's (1997) version of melancholic loss from the context of gender and sexual formation, 'I never loved, I never lost' becomes the condition under which the colonised nation is formed, with melancholia as its characteristic 'state of mind'. This unrecognised loss has powerful effects. As it breaks through to postcolonial nationhood, the colonised culture is haunted precisely by the lost object that it cannot name, which has become somehow incorporated and kept alive yet is neither integrated nor acknowledged, is truly in this sense melancholic. Khanna (2004: 25) implies that the whole concept of nation-statehood as an unrecognised construction of colonialism needs to be 'radically reshaped' if new nations are to survive 'without colonies'. More specifically, melancholic subjectivity is something that produces a kind of restlessness in which it becomes known, or at least felt, that something has gone missing – that something, indeed, has been *stolen*, to use a trope familiar from Lacanian accounts of racism (Žižek, 2006b). Because it is impossible to trace what this is, the subject is haunted by a kind of empty rage and odd deference towards those who possess something to which they can point as having value. Perhaps envy, perhaps internecine destructiveness arise from this, a kind of violence in which loss is covered over in a devotion to death.

What stands out here is that in refusing to nominate an object of loss, but rather instead preferring to delineate an empty space in which loss is felt but not remedied, there is an invitation to violence that turns inwards on the subject, and on the society in which the new postcolonial subject is formed. Youth violence is given by Margarita Palacios (2013) as an instance here: acting as if death does not matter, or is somehow not real, subcultures dominated by melancholic violence deny themselves the possibility of active, outward-directed revolt. Despite its contemporary language, this idea would not have been unimaginable by Freud, who after all made the distinguishing characteristic of melancholia its inwardness, its 'self-reproaches and self-revilings' (Freud, 1917: 244). Schwab (2010: 45) comments, 'If the lost object is the self, melancholia resembles an act of self-cannibalization: the encrypted self eats away at the traumatized surviving self from inside, trying to kill it off by severing its ties to the world outside.' Violence here is attested to in the idea of 'self-cannibalizing'; what is fed on by the melancholic ghost is the self that it also needs to survive.

Kelly Oliver (2004) similarly draws attention to the production of violence through the way in which the postcolonial situation externalises the violence of colonialism itself. Paraphrasing Fanon, she states, 'Fanon's work suggests that there is a transfer of affect in the colonial situation, that the white colonizers *inject* or *deposit* their anger into the colonized, who are then forced to expel it in self-destructive ways, secreting the waste-product *race* that perpetuates and justifies racism, or doing violence against themselves either individually or in tribal or gang wars' (Oliver, 2004: 50). The colonialist enterprise involves projecting anxiety and guilt into the colonised other, where it takes root and becomes an organising principle of psychosocial life. 'The success of the colonization of psychic space', she writes, 'can be measured by the extent to which the colonized internalize – or become infected by – the cruel superego that abjects them and substitutes anger against their oppressors with an obsessive need to gain their approval' (ibid.: 54). The values of the coloniser – particularly, the values of *whiteness* – are taken over as the values to be aspired to by all. They are the fantasy object, the Imaginary as Lacanians might have it; that which will bring completeness:

'whiteness becomes an ethical good impossible to attain; and the phobic object must be excluded to sustain the good or clean and proper body image' (ibid.: 55). The phobic object here is specifically the black body; but it can be generalised to mean the colonised. The colonised thus become phobic to themselves, their history and specificity occluded and foreclosed from history.

There is a great deal of ethical and political ambiguity in the psychoanalytic engagement (or lack of it) with postcolonialism. After all, as noted in Chapter 1, psychoanalysis participates in the perpetuation of colonial and even racist discourses through its historical investment in distinctions between 'civilised' and 'savage' societies (Freud, 1913) and its continuing adoption of the trope of the 'primitive' to reference the most deeply destructive unconscious urges. On the other hand, psychoanalysis reveals the presence of these 'primitive' states in the heart of the supposedly 'civilised', universalising them and consequently breaking down the distinction it also promotes. 'Cilvilised' rationality may be a Freudian aspiration, but it can never withstand the existence of an irrational power that is ubiquitous – as both psychoanalysis and the history of twentieth-century violence attest. However, what is important in the current context, in the light of melancholia, is a different kind of ambiguity: how the melancholic object is desired and preserved, but also denied and repudiated. The effect of this is to create an encrypted object that has been incorporated but not introjected, which means that it has been left 'whole' in the psyche rather than integrated with other fantasmatic objects. And the effect of *this* is that the melancholic object retains some of its integrity, even a kind of 'purity'; but it is also always out of time and out of place, *displaced*, so that even its revolutionary potential as an excluded other is infected by violence and pain.

The second face of the ambivalence of melancholy is however the potentially resistive 'messianic' one produced, as described above, by the internalisation of the lost object without breaking it down into digestible, colonisable bits. Because it is internalised (incorporated) whole rather than assimilated, it remains to trouble the colonising subject, ready at some point to burst out so that it can challenge the myth that *nothing existed there*. That is, the failure to mourn the lost object means it continues to press for recognition; and the revolutionary postcolonial and queer act is that of acknowledging this lost object and drawing from it the voices of oppressed people who previously did not have a place, who could not be mourned because their very existence was denied. From these voices a new dynamic can be produced, shaming the colonial rewriting of history; the past therefore 'flashes up', disturbing the present, radicalising the vision of what once was and therefore could be built anew. Before arguing against this position and insisting 'on the need to denounce the objective cynicism that such a rehabilitation of melancholy enacts', Slavoj Žižek describes it comprehensively:

> Against Freud, one should assert the conceptual and ethical primacy of melancholy. In the process of the loss, there is always a remainder that cannot be integrated through the work of mourning, and the ultimate fidelity is the fidelity to this remainder. Mourning is a kind of betrayal, the second killing of the (lost) object, while the melancholic subject remains faithful to the lost object, refusing to renounce his or her attachment to it. This story can be given a multitude of twists, from the queer one, which holds that homosexuals are those who retain fidelity to the lost or repressed identification with the same-sex libidinal object, to the postcolonial/ethnic one, which holds that when ethnic groups enter capitalist processes of modernization and are under the threat that their specific legacy will be swallowed up by the new global culture, they should not renounce their tradition through mourning, but retain the melancholic attachment to their lost roots. (Žižek, 2000: 658)

Žižek recognises the power of this argument, but denounces it as used, in practice, to legitimise the continuation of precisely the oppressive social conditions that it is meant to challenge: 'The melancholic link to the lost ethnic Object allows us to claim that we remain faithful to our ethnic roots while fully participating in the global capitalist game' (ibid.: 659). Indeed, he claims that this might mean that postcolonial studies itself is sustained by a logic he calls that of 'objective cynicism'. 'To make things absolutely clear', he writes, 'what is wrong with the postcolonial nostalgia is not the utopian dream of a world they never had (such a utopia can be thoroughly liberating) but the way this dream is used to legitimize the actuality of its very opposite, of the full and unconstrained participation in global capitalism' (ibid.).

Lost lacks

One can see some of the potential problems here as melancholic attachments to imagined lost goods come to stand in for progressive attempts to respond to contemporary conditions of the actually existing

Symbolic. Of course, the Imaginary domain can in principle be a source of utopian and hence radical hope: this is what Žižek is referencing when he comments that 'such a utopia can be thoroughly liberating'. It can be a way of reimagining boundaries and challenging constraints, for example in relation to gender divisions assumed under the order of patriarchy to be 'natural' and immutable. But there are two weak links. One is utopianism itself: it characteristically underestimates the power of the actually existing social order to take hold of its dissidents and either to crush them or, precisely, to colonise them, to appropriate them to its own tastes and concerns. Before the advent of melancholic nostalgia in its current form (though at a time when 'roots' were being uncovered as a source of ethnic pride, particularly in America), Hélène Cixous (1976: 255) noted, using the notion of the 'Symbolic' to refer to the patriarchal order of language and the law, 'Their "Symbolic" exists, it holds power – we, the sowers of disorder, know it only too well.' This remains a realistic statement of the limits to which it might be possible to challenge the structures of power and violence by purely cultural means: the force is not necessarily with us.

The second weakness, perhaps more relevant here, is that in imagining the existence of a lost object that can or must be 'recovered', a mythology is created that has a number of potentially nefarious effects. It is, by definition, backward-looking to a supposed time when there was a pure culture of the now-oppressed, a kind of romance of origin that can be called on to establish the distinctiveness and perhaps purity to which the group can return. Particularly in the context of ethnic and postcolonial challenge, this is a dangerous strategy in that it sets up a division between the 'authentic' culture of the oppressed group – a fetish of the lost object, in psychoanalytic terms – and the reality that one still lives with the effects of colonialism even after its apparent demise. The postcolonial world is not the same as the precolonial one; *Nachträglichkeit* applies here as well as in the individual psyche, because what might or might not have actually existed at one time can be recovered and read only from the specific position in which one now finds oneself. Allowing the lost object to 'flash up' as if it has not changed may disturb the present, but there is a danger that what is produced is something fantasmagoric and potentially reactionary, the lost object becoming a call back to a neverland of imagined time.

As Derek Hook (2012) has shown, Edward Said (2003) provides a useful parallel concept to *Nachträglichkeit* with some of the same resonance – something taken out of time to disturb the present – providing a way of thinking through past challenge and present being that acknowledges the irreducibility of each to the other, yet still allows them both to be shaken up by their encounter. Said's concept is that of the 'contrapuntal', reading or hearing different lines of thought against one another, keeping them in tension without it being a case of restoring the past in the present or harking back to a better time. He writes about those figures from the past who should be read 'out of context' in this way:

> I see them contrapuntally, that is, as figures whose writings travel across temporal, cultural and ideological boundaries in unforeseen ways to emerge as part of a new ensemble *along with* later history and subsequent art. (Said, 2003: 24)

Out-of-time reading of this kind (which does not mean to say that Said neglects historical context in his work) leads to a radical form of 'reading against the grain' that operates in two directions – to unsettle the present, for sure, but also to reopen the past in the light of present concerns, exploring how it changes as one reads it differently. This is again similar to the way in which psychoanalysis makes it impossible ever to find a pure lost object uncontaminated by the accretion of later fantasies around it, as well as repositioned by the context within which the memory of it arises. Said comments:

> Thus later history reopens and challenges what seems to have been the finality of an earlier figure of thought, bringing it into contact with cultural, political and epistemological formations undreamed of by – albeit affiliated by historical circumstances with – its author. (Said, 2003: 25)

There is no fixed original form of the primary object, trauma or wish that can be recaptured in the present, that can flash up as if it has been preserved unchanged for centuries. It was never like that. One can go back to the texts and stories, the reconstructed memories and cultural myths, and make use of them in the present for purposes for which they were not intended, to shake up and challenge the present, to offer new ways through. But this is still not a way of allowing something *real* to speak its truth; and the danger of insisting that it is so is that of creating a present that is essentialist and reactionary. What is at stake here is the importance both of tracing the history out of which the present has emerged, so that there is recognition and acknowledgement of oppression as well as restitution and liberatory action, but without fetishising the past so that its constructed character is denied.

The question arises here of whether valorising melancholy as a structure of loss is actually a way of covering up something else, more profound and more pervasive – which from the Lacanian position occupied by Žižek can only be that of *lack*:

> In short, what melancholy obfuscates is that the object is lacking from the very beginning, that its emergence coincides with its lack, that this object is nothing but the positivization of a void or lack, a purely anamorphic entity that does not exist in itself. The paradox, of course, is that this deceitful translation of lack into loss enables us to assert our possession of the object; what we never possessed can also never be lost, so the melancholic, in his unconditional fixation on the lost object, in a way possesses it in its very loss. (Žižek, 2000: 660)

The lack versus loss argument might seem unnecessarily arid even for Lacanian theorists, although it has some interesting resonances with Derrida's idea that the 'remains' with which one deals are 'remains of remains' rather than remains of some actual, substantive object (Royle, 1995). In any case, one can see its implications in the postcolonial space of contemporary subjectivity. If melancholia is organised around a lost object that can later be recovered it fixes the subject in the past; like the Jewish prayer to 'restore our days as of old', it is premised on the idea that there is a truth-trauma to be uncovered and mourned and that there has been a kind of degeneration since those days. Something has been stolen from us (which may of course be the case), and its absence haunts us until it is restored. Žižek's claim, however, is that this is a kind of fakery, in which two related things occur. First, there is no lost object as such, but rather a constitutional and universal experience of lack, of an impossible gap that can never be fully bridged; and second, a way develops of dealing with this lack by pretending that it is actually a loss – that is, by inventing an object that can be lamented, even though it has never been necessary to mourn it at all. 'Therein resides the melancholic's stratagem', Žižek writes (2000: 661), 'the only way to possess an object that we never had, that was from the very outset lost, is to treat an object that we still fully possess as if this object is already lost. The melancholic's refusal to accomplish the work of mourning thus takes the form of its very opposite, a faked spectacle of the excessive, superfluous mourning for an object even before this object is lost.' It is not the object that is lost, but rather it is desire that is always disappointed: we may find the object (the postcolonial nation state, for instance) and then experience that finding as a lack, because it can never satisfy the desire around which it was constructed. Politically, what we have here is a possible opposition between closure and openness. The melancholic attitude is to look back for the thing that once recovered will bring history to an end, the thing that replaces what was lost, destroyed or stolen; the alternative is an approach to history that sees it as constantly unfolding in its modes of newness, never satisfied and complete, and because of that always seeking something else, restlessly alive with possibilities as well as threats.

There are many problems with the Lacanian and Žižekian presentation of lack as constitutive of the political as well as the psychic arena, not least that it can produce a nihilistic account in which nothing can be done to induce change (Robinson, 2004). Even without this contested point (Lacanians argue, for example, that incompleteness and 'lack' in the system is precisely what allows human creativity to emerge), there is the question of exactly what it is that is always and fundamentally lacking. Is it something beyond history, a secularised Fall? Lacanians would have it to be a necessary failure that is constitutive of human subjectivity: there is always something that escapes symbolisation, termed by Lacanians the Real, theorised as a potential for breakthrough or breakdown. Conjuring up the Real in the realm of the political, for instance, Stavrakakis (2007: 54) comments that it 'refers to the moment of failure of a given identity or social construction; a failure that not only dislocates the identity in question but also creates a lack, stimulating the desire for a rearticulation of the dislocated structure, stimulating, in other words, human creativity, becoming the condition of possibility for human freedom'. That is, the fact of lack creates the desire for change – an idea that drives Stavrakakis' belief in and commitment to radical democracy.

It is perhaps in this context that Butler's (2011) reassertion of Walter Benjamin's take on Jewish messianism is most alluring. For her, drawing from but opposing Gershom Scholem (1941), the Kabbalistic imagery of the breaking of the ten *sefirot* (the vessels set aside to hold God's holiness) during creation is an important image. In Jewish mystical tradition, as described more fully in Chapter 7, the breaking of the vessels is seen as a cataclysm: they were meant to hold the divine light and their loss scatters this light everywhere, producing an exile of the divine that forces history into motion as a process of suffering and searching until the scattered sparks can be redeemed. For Butler, however, the divine scattering of light across all peoples creates the prospect for diversity and what she calls 'co-habitation'. The messianic gathering-in of these holy sparks is not then a metaphor for the end of history, but for its continued creativity. Butler comments (2011: 83), 'The Messiah is neither a person nor a historical event; it can be understood neither as anthropomorphism nor as teleology; rather, it is a memory of suffering from another time that interrupts and reorients the politics of this time.' This secular messianism is therefore a powerfully political form of haunting.

Butler (ibid.) notes that the 'flashing up' of the lights of the *sefirot* is read by Benjamin not as a final gathering in of Jewish exiles, but as ' "a revolutionary chance in the fight for the oppressed past" '. As with Gordon's (1997) assertion that the reason to engage with ghosts is to put right injustice, so this focus on fighting 'for' the oppressed past is the reason to be interested in what flashes up from there. Butler (2011: 83) wants this to allow a kind of breaking-apart of the 'surface of time' that then transposes 'the memory of suffering into the future of justice, not as revenge but as the figuring of a time in which the history that covers over the history of oppression might cease'. This means that there is no actual lost object simply to be recovered, a presence that will return to lead everything to its satisfactory, integrated conclusion – the traditional view of the reunification of the sparks, which sees the fragmentation of society (the 'breaking of the vessels') as a degraded system that needs to be put right, demanding a reparative response that is itself the marker of the messianic. By contrast, Butler's use of Benjamin advances the cause of continuing 'flashing up' of the hidden sparks, in which those who have lost most and who are written out of humanity have the chance to return, to make their presence felt. This kind of 'melancholia' understands the recovery of the lost object not as something that refers only to the past, but as a ghostly act troubling the present because of its *continuing* suffering. So the mode of subjectivity that is open to this announces itself as one that is always toppling over, is never capable of a satisfied balance; it is a radical subjectivity exactly because it has no option but to hear the voices of the oppressed as they continue in their resistance. Not solely melancholic now, but somehow assertive too. Žižek (2000: 665) notes, with reference to Derrida, 'on account of its very radicalism, the messianic promise forever remains a promise, cannot ever be translated into a set of determinate economic and political measures'. This is troubling subjectivity at its most poignant: something speaks from the other that cannot ever be fully answered, some demand, threat or promise that the subject knows it can never contain.

Benjamin himself (1940) asserts the necessity of haunting in the form of recognition of the past in the present; without such recognition, the past disappears. 'For every image of the past which is not recognized by the present as one of its own concerns threatens to disappear irretrievably,' he writes (ibid.: 247). The melancholic strand here is clear, as is the political argument for disinterring the past and ensuring that it can indeed, as Butler stresses, 'flash up' to inform the present. But Benjamin has something else to say too about how haunting can be future oriented, and how ghosts might still take hold of that future and force it to radicalise:

> We know that the Jews were prohibited from investigating the future. The Torah and the prayers instruct them in remembrance, however. This stripped the future of its magic, to which all those succumb who turn to the soothsayers for enlightenment. This does not imply, however, that for the Jews the future turned into homogeneous, empty time. For every second of time was the strait gate through which the Messiah might enter. (Benjamin, 1940: 255)

There is no magic in the future, but this does not mean that it cannot be envisaged as holding potential for messianic transformation. There is a long way to go to achieve this, however. Benjamin draws explicitly on the Jewish consciousness of time, the refusal of soothsaying and the significance of remembrance. This has a certain cultural specificity – Jewish histories will be quite distinct from those of colonised peoples – and carries the implication that different ghosts will have particular kinds of identities and mechanisms of haunting that arise from repeated and specific modes of trauma. But it also speaks to something quite universal. The incitement to remembrance that Benjamin references directs us to continually re-examine the past, to keep it in the present as a living entity, not only as a memorial to something lost. What happened, what was done, what is the legacy? Especially, what injustice does it speak of that penetrates the present in barely visible streams of dust and smoke? The dust of historical oppression; the smoke and fumes of past destruction; these vapours drift across time and are breathed in by every generation – ghostly emanations that infiltrate the present, structuring it and giving it meaning, and sometimes poisoning it too. And the future? Benjamin writes that 'every second of time was the strait gate through which the Messiah might enter'. Kafka (1961: 45) famously claims that 'The Messiah will come only when he is no longer necessary; he will come only on the day after his arrival; he will come, not on the last day, but on the very last.' There is, it seems, no way to know what will happen. The future should not be imagined as a repetition, though that is how we mostly think of it and relate to it. The future is only sustainable in the present as an openness, with no trace of ghostliness in it; but this might mean that something has to be forsaken, or perhaps forgiven, something has to be let go of, some melancholia overcome, before we can learn to move on.

4
The Evil Eye

Compassionate yet burning tears (The Blinding of Isaac)

In the vast psychoanalytic literature on the Biblical story of the binding of Isaac (the 'Akedah' in Hebrew), one traditional element gets very little mention. What is the connection between the Akedah and Isaac's later blindness, both physical and spiritual? For Isaac goes blind, and the destiny of the Jewish people depends on this blindness. It is because of this blindness that he cannot tell the difference between his two sons, Esau and Jacob, and so is deceived when it comes to giving them a blessing. Jacob, the smooth-skinned son, is lured by his mother to dress up in his brother's clothes, rough animal skins, and pass himself off as Esau in order to claim the firstborn's blessing from his father. The ruse works, and Esau is left howling in rage, demanding a blessing of his own and plotting Jacob's death. Jacob has to flee, and he runs away – into the arms of his future wives. The Children of Israel derive from this trick, this manipulation of a blind man, this easily fooled supposed-sage.

Isaac is regarded in Jewish literature as exceptionally pure, but also as passive and lifeless. His one active moment post-Akedah is when he passes his wife Rebeccah off as his sister and is spotted 'sporting' with her (Genesis 26, 8). Otherwise, he is a holy man who allows things to happen to him, who meditates in the field. Yet he is not empty of emotion: he can love. Indeed, it is love that brings light into his life and love's fading that makes things darken. We are told that his grief after the death of his mother Sarah was intense and lasted until he learnt to love Rebeccah, and the exact words matter. Isaac has been meditating, or maybe he has been somewhere else; he wanders homewards and comes across Rebeccah, who is being brought to marry him. When she sees him, she falls off her camel. Why does she experience such a shock when she sees her future husband? What is it about his appearance that scares her so? Bracketing that question for a moment, along with the related query about where Isaac was coming from, the text states:

> And Isaac brought her into his mother Sarah's tent, and took Rebeccah, and she became his wife, and he loved her. And Isaac was comforted for his mother. (Genesis 24, 67)

According to the mediaeval commentator Rashi, 'As long as Sarah lived, a lamp burned from the eve of the Sabbath to the eve of the following Sabbath, the dough was blessed and a divine cloud hung over the tent. When she died, it all ceased; but on Rebeccah's arrival it was resumed.' The theme here is of love, comforting and light: the lamp that burns is the one that overcomes trauma through human closeness. It is a specifically feminine light that attaches itself to the mother and the wife. Indeed, it is a kind of feminine *principle* in which mother and wife are one and the same as bringers of light. Rashi adds this to his interpretation of the verse: 'he brought her into the tent and behold she was his mother Sarah!' We should recall too that Sarah is said to have died as a consequence of the Akedah: the news of it could not be borne, 'the shock of learning that [Isaac] had nearly been sacrificed was too much for her' (Rashi on Genesis 23, 2). Trauma overwhelms compassion, but it is through love and compassion that trauma itself is overcome.

But trauma is never *fully* overcome, and perhaps the compassionate side of it is as hard to deal with as the trauma itself. Isaac's blindness is said to stem from the Akedah. When he is lying there, bound to the wooden altar, looking up as his father lifts his hand and the knife glints in the sun, about to fall, the legend is that 'at that very moment the heavens opened, the ministering angels saw it and wept, and their tears flowed and fell upon Isaac's eyes which thus became dim' (Rashi on Genesis 27, 1). The angels' tears are what lead to later blindness, but what are they if not tears of compassion and perhaps also of shame? Isaac's eyes receive the tears of angels, and are blinded by them. Why is this? Isaac is from this moment set apart. There is also a tradition that he actually died and was brought back to life, that he had to be cared for in Paradise for three years to heal him from the marks of the knife, and that it is from there – that is, from Heaven – that he is returning when he meets Rebeccah:

> No wonder Rebeccah lost her equilibrium 'and she fell from the camel' – for what she perceived was Isaac coming down from

Paradise, and he walked the way the dead walk, head down and feet up. And what was he doing all that time in Paradise? 'They were healing him there.' When was that? After the incident on Mount Moriah: 'And the angels bore him to Paradise, where he tarried three years, to be healed from the wound inflicted upon him by Abraham on the occasion of the Akedah.' . . . Support for this legend was found in the Song of Songs, as R. Joshua ibn Shuaib of that generation testifies: 'In the opinion of the Midrash, Isaac was not in that city [Hebron] at the time [of his mother's funeral], because he was in Paradise to recover from the effects on his neck of what his father did to him during the Akedah, which left a mark in the shape of a bead. And that is why it is written, "With one bead of thy necklace." ' (Spiegel, 1967: 6–7).

The trauma is an absolute one; the lover's bead is that of the knife. Whether literally dead or not, Isaac is *as* one who has died and come back to life, and is never the same again. He is dipped in deathliness and is made unworldly by it. His blindness is to the way of the world, to the deceptions of wives and sons; he is bathed in the tears of compassion and that is what brings light, but with these tears darkness also grows.

The maternal, compassionate theme has been very little emphasised in the literature on the Akedah, which deals primarily with the issue of paternal law-giving and violence. There is much to say about this too, but it belongs to a discussion of transgenerational identity and trauma and will appear later in this book. However, the notion that the theme of the Akedah is not the paternal but is rather something maternal has been raised by Bracha Ettinger (2006) in a meditation on the limitations of Levinasian ethics. Her general idea is that there is something she terms 'com-passion' that arises in the 'matrixial' embrace experienced in, and symbolised by, the womb. Com-passion is a connectedness that is also a kind of border-crossing, and it is the source of responsibility and care. Ettinger asks (ibid.: 100), 'Can you imagine Isaac's compassion for his father?' This is a big ask; his father is seeking to murder him, so why should Isaac have compassion for him? Jewish sources dwell on Isaac's *respect* for his father – he does what Abraham requires of him, with no more challenge than Abraham himself makes of God – and also Isaac's willingness to subject himself to God's command. He was, after all, no small boy, but a man of 37 who could have overcome his 137-year-old father and run away if he had so wished. One might call this piety and honouring of a parent, but not compassion. Yet Ettinger insists that something else is at stake:

> We have to imagine Isaac's compassion for his father, Abraham. This compassion is primary; it starts before, and always also beyond, any possibility of empathy that entails understanding, before any economy of exchange, before any cognition or recognition, before any reactive forgiveness or integrative reparation. It is woven with-in primordial trans-sensitivity and co-re-naissance. (Ettinger, 2006: 100)

We have to imagine Isaac's compassion for his father. Let us put the stress on the word 'imagine'; that is, it is not in the text, but is something we might wish for. Ettinger is perhaps thinking of the way the text stresses the togetherness of father and son on their journey: 'and they went both of them together' (Genesis 22, 6) and again, 'So they went both of them together' (verse 8). This might be paternal or maternal, it hardly matters. But she may be right in seeing it as 'matrixial' in her specific sense of pressing a connection that is based on a community of spirit, a compassion that each might have for the other and that goes beyond, or lies before, words. 'Isaac's compassion toward his father', writes Ettinger (2006: 109–10), 'what for Freud could have been standing for a direct identificatory love link, is based upon the infant's primary compassion toward the m/Other. This has been arising into life in com-passionate co-response-ability with the m/Other inside her compassionate hospitality toward the infant. Passing through the matrixial horizon where the father is included after birth, this compassion spreads toward the father. *In that sense Isaac is every-infant in innocent youth in passive vulnerability.*' We know for sure how bound up Isaac's old mother was with him, how unexpected and miraculous a joy he was to her, how she was willing to be murderous on his behalf, expelling his half-brother Ishmael into the wilderness in order to protect him. Before being bound to the wood-pyre, he was bound to her 'in passive vulnerability'. Now he accepts the yoke of that com-passion and extends it to his father.

Com-passion and co-response; the neologistic breaking-up of these words stresses that they are intense and active, that there is nothing soft in them. Com-passion is the passion one has alongside or with another; co-response is the active recognition and interlacing of one's own consciousness inside and with that of another. Abraham and Isaac are united in their going 'both of them together'; their togetherness is passionate and responsive, which means that it has effects. Isaac looks up from his bindings and is blinded not so much by what he sees – the heavens opening – but by what he *receives*, the angels' tears dripping into his eyes. At the moment that vision is replaced by touch, sight is overcome. If it is reasonable to associate sight with masculinity and touch with femininity – the father's gaze, the mother's embrace – then the loving compassion of the angels feminises Isaac and burns him to the core.

The gaze

The psychoanalytic gaze is a reminder of all this. The gaze is a central element in psychoanalytic thinking. This is particularly so for Lacan (1949), who builds around it the 'mirror phase' in development and hence makes it the foundation of that element of experience that he calls the Imaginary – that which centres on the fantasy image, and consequently on sight and visual illusion. Lacan emphasises the deceptiveness of vision, how it lures the subject into a set of false beliefs about the nature of the ego and the possibility of integrity and meaning. 'In this matter of the visible, everything is a trap,' he writes (1973: 93). 'There is not a single one of the divisions, a single one of the double sides that the function of vision presents, that is not manifested to us as a labyrinth' (ibid.). The key point is that the gaze is not the subject's; the psychoanalytic concern is not so much with looking as with being looked *at*, and with the question of what happens when the subject becomes aware of this look. We are born into the gaze of the other, always watched (over) before we do any systematic gazing ourselves. Later, we look into the mirror and the image looks back; this is what makes it so uncanny and disturbing. The human subject is *subjected to* the gaze, the object of sight: 'in the scopic field, the gaze is outside, I am looked at, that is to say, I am a picture' (ibid.: 106). For Lacan, gaze, like voice, is a partial object; this means that it is not 'on the side of the looking/hearing subject but on the side of what the subject sees or hears' (Žižek, 1996: 90). The gaze is always something more than the subject; it comes at us from outside and produces a sense of strangeness, it is once again uncanny; and as we shall see, it is by no means always either pitying or benevolent.

Let us accept the stereotype of the patient on the couch, perhaps looking out of the window or at the bound volumes of Freud's collected works (the psychoanalyst's equivalent of Paradise), and the analyst sitting behind the couch, out of the patient's vision. Whatever the analyst is actually looking at, the patient imagines the gaze as directed at her or himself. 'I am looked at, that is to say, I am a picture.' This gaze that comes from the analyst is imaginary in that the patient cannot see it and can only piece together its possible meaning in a 'speculative' way, building it up from what the analyst says and does not say, from the moments of speech and silence that accompany the gaze but cannot ever be exactly the same thing. The gaze might be experienced, therefore, as anything, reflecting the fantasy of the patient and – if we use the frame of psychoanalysis itself – the state of the transference. Nevertheless, there might be some systematic ways of reading this gaze. Here is a speculative list, a meditation on how the analytic gaze can manifest itself in the consulting room. One might say, even, that it is a way of trying to pin down the spectral nature of the analytic gaze, which always escapes full symbolisation:

- *As alienation.* The 'subject' is turned into an 'object'. Such a gaze ensures that nothing that happens can be reduced to the status of an ordinary relationship. The refusal of the face-to-face in analysis signifies that there is no straightforward intersubjectivity in which the realistic to-and-fro between people produces a bond of reciprocal dependency and perhaps of liking. In an important way, this kind of gaze signifies the *absence* of a relationship, or at least the production of a very peculiar kind of non-relationship, something that makes a person struggle with the idea of relationship itself. Žižek (2005: 148) presents this as a kind of encounter with a barren landscape: '*no* face-to-face between the subject-patient and the analyst; instead, the subject lying and the analyst sitting behind him, both staring into the same void in front of them. There is no "intersubjectivity" here, only the two without face-to-face, the First and the Third.' This is an especially ascetic rendering of what happens in psychoanalysis, neglecting how a shared project can emerge between analyst and patient; nevertheless, it registers the blankness of the analytic stare and the refusal to participate in a comforting gesture of support.

- *As boredom.* Perhaps this is one of the greatest fears a patient can have, that the analyst will be too bored to care, that the needs of the patient will not be looked at, but *overlooked*. The analyst is not gazing at the patient at all, is barely awake enough to do so; or if the analyst is looking, it is without understanding what she or he sees. 'Notice me' is often the child's demand, and the adult's too: 'don't be distracted, don't be on the lookout for someone more interesting, find something in me that I cannot find in myself'. Human subjectivity relies on the response of the other, on being envisioned; each of us wishes to be seen as a real and valuable centre of consciousness and we gain our subjecthood only in this way. This is why the all-seeing eye of totalitarianism is not destructive only because of its persecutory aspect, though this is real. It is also because people are not seen as separate subjects but are amalgamated interchangeably into the whole. Seen in this way – as another boring patient – we cease to exist.

- *As frustration and non-recognition.* The analyst resists engaging, but watches and thinks. The patient wonders if there is anyone there at all, and who or what it is that she or he has come to for help. Every one of the patient's attempts to make sense of the analyst is disrupted by this gaze, in which what is traced is the failure to achieve the object of one's desires. That which we hope for the most is exactly what is refused. We could also give a more normative account from within object relational psychoanalysis, where the misrecognising other, the one who fails to see us as we are, is held responsible for the troubles that can come to befall us. The child who seeks recognition but finds unresponsiveness is faced with the difficult task of waking the parent up, theorised in a variety of ways by different analysts. For André Green (1983) it is the 'dead mother' complex; for Donald Winnicott (1956) what might develop is a 'false self' conforming to the child's idea of what the mother wants, rather than to the child's own needs. There are many questions about this, not least those relating to gender assumptions, but perhaps the point holds: without recognition, we do not know if we are alive.

- *As a lure, an enticement or seduction.* Being looked at can make a person feel admired and desired too; and if the looker gives no particular signs but simply and archly looks, it can be experienced as an invitation, a come-on. Do we imagine the other as one who lacks and wants, as desiring, as calling us in to fill a gap? What *provocation* is in place when we are looked at in this inscrutable way? 'What does the other want of me?' is meant to be the most insistent question that the subject asks of the social order (the Big Other) in which it finds itself. Lacan says about this:

> In the intervals of the discourse of the Other, there emerges in the experience of the child something...namely, *He is saying this to me, but what does he want?* ...The desire of the Other is apprehended by the subject in that which does not work, in the lacks of the discourse of the Other, and all the child's *whys* reveal not so much an avidity for the reason of things, as a testing of the adult,

a *Why are you telling me this?* ever-resuscitated from its base, which is the enigma of the adult's desire. (Lacan, 1973: 214)

Amongst the various things picked up in this quotation, which in truth is about the speech rather than the gaze of the Other, there is the issue of the enigmatic nature of the adult's desire, implanted in the child as a source of confusion and wonder. This idea is taken furthest by Laplanche (1999) with his concept of the enigmatic signifier. Unintentionally, unbidden, the adult implants in the infant a disturbance that cannot be fully interpreted, but that remains encrypted as the kernel of the unconscious. This is a *seduction*, exciting the child in an enlivening way but also producing the continuing pressure for interpretation and enlightenment that every human subject feels. The analyst's gaze can evoke this and result in the kind of 'testing' to which Lacan refers and which might be coded, 'are you really there, what are you thinking, *what do you want of me?*'

- As persecution. Traditionally evoked by the concept of the superego, the analyst's gaze can be judgemental, bearing downwards until all the patient's foibles and infidelities, lies and imaginings, are revealed. This is not a matter of asking questions or indeed of speaking at all; it is there in the mere gaze, which enters into the patient's mind and rummages around its contents. But in addition to the judgemental superego, always finding fault, there is the jealous or envious gaze, to which we shall return; something that poisons at a distance. The look here is not distant, it is supercilious and wicked; it tries to penetrate in order to destroy what is inside.

- As pity. This is where we started. The maternal gaze, if for a moment it can be gendered, in which there is sympathy and compassion, in which the analyst is imagined as watching over the patient, seeing what is wrong and sorrowing for it. This is the most regressive fantasy of all, because it imagines being gathered up in the gaze and cared for. It is perhaps what patients most wish for – that the analyst will look on them compassionately and help them. And it is what is most feared, because in the look of pity there is a kind of condescension, and maybe even a loss of hope: 'you have really gone through something terrible, no-one should go through this; I can't see how you will ever recover'.

If the story of Isaac is anything to go by, one might wish for anything but this last possibility, for if the analytic gaze is a pitying one, then there must be something very wrong indeed. Lying on the couch, looking up and out from the consulting room, being watched and imagining being watched – what response would we want? In this regressed and potentially vulnerable state, the equivalent perhaps of being bound to the pyre, the pitying, compassionate glance could be what saves the patient's life, staying the hand of violence. But it might also be too painful to bear, because it responds to the patient's neediness and dependency. It would feel better to be subjected to an admiring glance, feeding one's narcissism. It might even be better to receive a gaze that is full of aggression and envious hostility: at least we can then believe that we might be in possession of something worth envying. But *compassion* is a very hard thing to call forth in another.

Looking

This is all about the *receipt* of the gaze, but there is another angle on things to consider. What about the act of looking itself? There is first a question about why we might resort to gaze, to staring, as a way of dealing with relational tensions. John Steiner (2006) takes the line that the 'proximity senses', by which he seems to mean touch and smell, are absorbing and in a way *too close* to the object. Reading this negatively, in comparison with Ettinger's imagined matrixial, he argues that, 'A reliance on the proximity senses favours a part object relationship because a degree of separateness and distance is necessary for both object and self to be seen as a whole' (Steiner, 2006: 947). Vision allows this sense of distance, and is reverted to with some relief even though the proximity senses remain important 'especially in our relationship with basic elements of life such as food, faeces, illness, death and sex'. But there are things that can go wrong here: vision can itself become blurred, can destroy the separateness that it was made to engender. One could say that disturbance of looking results from the difficulty a person might have in tolerating what they are made to see. Under such circumstances, 'If humiliation is too painful and separateness becomes unbearable' (ibid.), the eyes might start to function as a proximity sense *in order not to see clearly.* 'In particular', writes Steiner (ibid.), 'projection and introjection now come to be mediated by the eyes, and gaze becomes capable of penetrating and can be used not only to observe the object as a whole but also to enter the object and identify with it.' The subject's position is transformed from observer to voyeur 'and the identification can lead to a further transformation in phantasy from a watcher at a distance to that of a participator in bodily contact'.

Freud himself tells us something of what might happen next in his paper on 'Psychogenic Disturbance of Vision' (1910). Wrapped up in a guilty voyeurism that sexualises the gaze and makes it equivalent to sensual touch, repression acts not only on the specific voyeuristic gaze, but on all sight in a kind of 'talion' punishment. 'The beautiful legend of Lady Godiva', he writes (ibid.: 217), 'tells how all the town's inhabitants hid behind their shuttered windows, so as to make easier the lady's task of riding naked through the streets in broad daylight, and how the only man who peeped through the shutters at her revealed loveliness was punished by going blind.' This is the realm of gaze as something compulsive and material; distance is lost and the subject and object are linked by sight, binding them to one another. Under such conditions, looking can become compulsive and can bring with it a kind of poison that is very hard to resist. The angels' tears are the material medium through which Isaac is blinded; gaze becomes something that works along a channel, transferring the contents of one subject's mind into that of another.

In a classic paper, Otto Fenichel (1937) explores the 'scopophilic instinct', the impulse to look. Immersed in the psychoanalytic orthodoxy of the time, which now looks reductive and formulaic, this paper is still vivid in its description of the potential eroticism and destructiveness of the gaze. The key notion is 'the symbolic equation to look at = to devour' (ibid.: 6). Fenichel argues that 'the idea of devouring, which in the unconscious underlies that of reading, actually represents a form of sadistic incorporation' (ibid.). The destructive element in looking can be seen in the many myths of turning to stone – the basilisk, the Medusa and Lot's wife. But before we address this, there is also an identificatory element to looking, a process of taking something in and becoming like it. 'What is the aim of the scopophilic instinct?' asks Fenichel (ibid.: 10), before answering as follows: 'I think that there can be no possible doubt that it is *to look at* the sexual object. Freud adds: to look at the genitals of the desired person or to watch him or her performing the functions of excretion ... one looks at an object in order *to share in* its experience.'

The scopophilic instinct is a dual one, aiming to share and to devour. Looking involves appropriation; conversely, being looked at means to risk having something taken away. 'It seems then that there are two tendencies which always or often determine the goal of the scopophilic instinct: (a) the impulse to injure the object seen, and (b) the desire to share by means of empathy in its experience' (Fenichel, 1937: 11). The gaze is castrating – hence, he says, 'the compulsion so frequently met with in women to look in the region of a man's genitals' – but also internalising, the main theme being 'I wish what I see to enter into me.' The eye itself is phallic, its stare equivalent to an erection; being blinded is the same as castration, so eye, look and desire are all bound up together, the seer and the seen (and, indeed, the primal scene, the witnessing of which is central to the libidification and repression of sight) shifting in their roles. The scopophilic gaze is active, going out to meet the object. It is this active look that is so phallicly penetrating, so disturbingly assaultive; yet, in its incorporating capacity it is feminine, biting and devouring. The look is 'magical' when through looking one takes on or over the attributes of the other, as does the camera, taking (away) the likeness; witness how disturbing it is to see pins put in one's pictorial image. Fenichel (ibid.: 32) writes, 'when a primitive or superstitious person is looked at (has his likeness taken), he feels that something is taken away from him. Once again the eye is conceived of as an organ which robs or bites.'

As with many writers on the gaze, Fenichel is interested in the myth of Medusa and in the general notion of a basilisk – something that has fatal power over one who looks at it. Fenichel is sure that such entities are castrating, that what is being symbolised here is loss of the penis. The attribution is to the assaulting female: 'When we reflect that the object which turns people into stone is very often a glaring eye (basilisk, snake, hypnotist), it is natural to conclude that such an eye is another symbol for the terrible, devouring, female genital... To be turned into rigid stone symbolizes not only erection but also castration, just as the eye symbolizes not only a penis but a vagina (and a mouth)' (ibid.: 25–6). The symbolism overflows: stone equals penis equals mouth equals vagina; the vagina is to be entered but it also devours. Most tellingly, this mode of sight shows just how fragile the boundaries of selfhood are when faced with the power of identifications based on intense terror and desire:

'To be turned into stone' by the sight of something means to be fascinated by it. The primary basis of this phantasy must have been the recollection of the physical feeling of actual inability to move and rigidity which comes over a person who suddenly sees something terrifying. This fascination represents the child's helplessness in face of the enormous masses of excitation experienced when he witnesses the primal scene. Further, it has something to do with the adult genitals which he observes – with both erection and absence of the penis – and indicates his identification of his own condition with both of these, and especially his expectation of castration. (Fenichel, 1937: 26)

Sympathetic magic operates here, activated, writes Fenichel (ibid.: 27), 'by looking at the object: he who looks at that which has been castrated (the head of Medusa) himself undergoes castration. He who looks at the dead is himself struck dead. Therefore the counterpart to the dread of being turned into stone is that of being forced in some uncanny way to look at a stone (dead) man.' Fascination occurs: we cannot tear our eyes away, we are fixed in some way on the object that scares us, the event that we are implicated in, the thing we already know but cannot escape. This sounds like the death drive again, but it is also something more specific, 'identification which is at one and the same time a wish-fulfilment and a punishment' (ibid.: 28). The gaze draws us in and makes us one with the thing we fear; we look (scopophilia), and the punishment for looking is shame, castration and death:

> Thus we arrive at the conclusion that the rigidity of a person turned into stone stands for the fixed gaze and the rigidity of the whole muscular system of a person fascinated by something he sees, and that it signifies erection or (death and) castration. In this train of thought the essential point is that looking is conceived of as a means of identification. If we pursue it, it leads us finally to the problems of the effect of shock and of traumas in general, i.e. the victim's sudden inability to master the outside world, a reaction which is a mode of defence against excessive masses of excitation. (Fenichel, 1937: 29)

Perhaps we are back here to the fright described by Freud and discussed in Chapter 2: turning a corner, we see something that frightens us. We stare at it and become absorbed in it; but we are also devoured by it. Or maybe, we look upwards into the heavens and a channel opens whereby we look in terror at a knife whilst angels look back at us with compassion and pity, dripping tears that are too fierce to be managed, that are indeed 'excessive masses of excitation'. Moreover, the staring has to do with the 'primal scene', the parents' sexual intimacy, the thing that cannot actually be seen because it is the cause of our conception and so predates us. We look out for all the later instances of this primal scene, fascinated by it, terrified too – what birth might it lead to, to what other subject will it give rise who might displace us, who might push us aside?

The stare of the basilisk is what terrifies us; the psychological process through which it works is identification with the gaze that opens up the crypt holding the most fundamental fears of being annihilated through the desire of another. The primal scene *excludes* us even if we were once the consequence of it. Along these paths of sex, castration and death flows an intensity of poisonous affect that infects us as we are looked at. That is to say, the persecutory, hate-filled gaze is one with which we are prone to identify, because it stirs up what has been long buried and hidden away. The fear is of having the life sucked out of one, of losing blood, of becoming the living-dead, under the sway of another's desire, turned to stone, unable to get away. Fixed and fascinated; put crudely and brutally, at the mercy of envy.

The evil eye

There is general agreement that envy enters the field of vision in the form of the 'evil eye'. In her book on S. An-sky, the author of *The Dybbuk*, to which we shall return in Chapter 7, Gabrielle Safran quotes the following story:

> One day when his mood was especially bad, he remembered a time when he was in the woods with a little girl. 'She picked a berry and said happily, "A berry, a berry!" I said, "Throw it away, it's nasty!" She looked at me and at the berry and said calmly, "It's you, brother. You have nasty eyes." ' (Safran, 2010: 69)

Nasty eyes are eyes of cynicism and destructive envy, the kind that turn anything beautiful into dust. Fortunately for An-sky and for the little girl in the story, the child shows great resilience and a kind of innocent capacity to understand what is true and what is not. But the nastiness of eyes is still redoubtable and the source of fear throughout the world. Lacan is particularly assertive about this. The Other gazes at the subject, and does so with 'some appetite of the eye on the part of the person looking' (Lacan, 1973: 115); that is, the gaze is a desiring one, and its desire is to *consume* the subject. Lacan (ibid.) makes this one of the central functions of the gaze: 'This appetite of the eye that must be fed produces the hypnotic value of painting. For me, this value is to be sought on a much less elevated plane than might be supposed, namely, in that which is the true function of the organ of the eye, the eye filled with voracity, the evil eye.'

The eye filled with voracity: this is a compelling phrase with which to conjure the simple malevolence of the gaze turned against things that people treasure. Lacan comments that there is 'no trace anywhere of a good eye, of an eye that blesses' (ibid.), which seems wrong given the gaze of pity – the angels' tears – described above. Nevertheless, his emphasis on the destructive component of the gaze matches the centrality of this idea in an extraordinarily wide range of cultures; and as Lacan notes, the predominant interpretation of this destructiveness is in terms of what he calls *'invidia'*, that is, envy:

> The most exemplary *invidia*, for us analysts, is the one I found long ago in Augustine, in which he sums up his entire fate, namely, that of the little child seeing his brother at his mother's breast, looking at him *amare conspectu*, with a bitter look, which seems to tear him to pieces and has on himself the effect of a poison. (Lacan, 1973: 115–16)

A bitter look, tearing the rival to pieces, having the effect of a poison: these are indeed widespread renderings of the functioning of the evil eye and have all the resonance of envy. And as Lacan goes on to say, what is perhaps most characteristic of such an envious state of being is that it is not even interested in possessing what the hated rival has; the child, for instance, does not necessarily even wish still to be at the breast. What the envious eye seeks to do is not to gain something for itself, but simply to destroy what seems beautiful in the other; it is the other's *contentedness*, its *blessedness* that it cannot bear. 'Such is true envy', he writes (ibid.: 116), 'the envy that makes the subject pale before the image of a completeness closed upon itself, before the idea that the *petit a*, the separated *a* from which he is hanging, may be for another the possession that gives satisfaction.' We are of course back in the realm of the death drive here, but this time in its most projected form, the vicious attack on the enjoyment (imagined as) experienced by the other.

Lacan's understanding of the evil eye is consistent with most psychoanalytic accounts, beginning with Freud himself. Coming from a Jewish culture in which belief in the evil eye was a widespread phenomenon, Freud included it in his litany of uncanny experiences, naturalising it as an expression of envy:

> Whoever possesses something that is at once valuable and fragile is afraid of other people's envy, in so far as he projects on to them the envy he would have felt in their place. A feeling like this betrays itself by a look even though it is not put into words; and when a man is prominent owing to noticeable, and particularly owing to unattractive, attributes, other people are ready to believe that his envy is rising to a more than usual degree of intensity and that this intensity will convert it into effective action. What is feared is thus a secret intention of doing harm, and certain signs are taken to mean

that that intention has the necessary power at its command. (Freud, 1919: 240)

It is noteworthy that Freud attributes envy to the person who actually possesses the thing of value; the evil eye is a projection of what the subject 'would have felt' in the place of the other. Destructiveness is therefore self-inflicted; we look for it because we cannot believe our good luck. Or perhaps, more in tune with the death drive, whenever we have something that is genuinely 'valuable and fragile' we take steps to wreck it ourselves. Why should this be? What is so unbearable about beauty?

Didier Anzieu (1986), in his book on Freud's self-analysis, notes one of Freud's dream presentations, known as the dream of 'Company at table d'hôte'. It runs as follows:

> Company at table or table d'hôte... spinach was being eaten... Frau E. L. was sitting beside me; she was turning her whole attention to me and laid her hand on my knee in an intimate manner. I removed her hand unresponsively. She then said: 'But you've always had such beautiful eyes.'... I then had an indistinct picture of two eyes, as though it were a drawing or like the outline of a pair of spectacles. (Freud, 1901a: 636–7)

Freud's various associations to this dream lead him to issues of debt and repayment in relation to a friend who is an eye surgeon, and he comments (ibid.: 639), 'Incidentally, the friend whose guests we were yesterday has often put me in his debt. Only recently I allowed an opportunity of repaying him to slip by. He has had only one present from me – an antique bowl, round which there are eyes painted: what is known as an "occkiale", to avert the evil eye.' Anzieu (1986: 547) explicates, 'The manifest content emphasises the declaration of love: "You've always had such beautiful eyes." Conversely, the latent content (the occhiale, with its painted eyes, given to an oculist) stresses what might be called a declaration of hatred: "You have the evil eye." The increasing importance of the evil eye can be sensed from a gradual deterioration in the representation of the beautiful eyes.' Deterioration in the eyes (the indistinct picture) is a representation of them turning from good to bad, from love to hate. Anzieu locates this in a developmental matrix, as founded on early infantile experience. 'For the infant,' he writes (ibid.), 'the mother is at once a breast that suckles, a mouth that speaks, and eyes that look: the dream of "Company at table d'hôte" visualises those three functions successively.' The infant sucks at the gratifying breast, but the breast also 'disciplines' him; it is there one moment and not there the next. The mother speaks to the infant lovingly, but the infant also has to deal with the seductiveness of her incestuous approach – a reference back to Laplanche's (1999) idea of a primary unconscious seduction. And the eyes of the mother look at the child, who sees in them her or his own deep ambivalence.

Perhaps putting this more strongly than does Anzieu himself, the deterioration in sight expresses an assault on the gaze. Freud's friend is an 'eye surgeon'; Freud has referred a woman patient to him for spectacles and then has a sexual dream about a woman 'with whom I have hardly at any time been on friendly terms, nor, so far as I know, have I ever wished to have any closer relations with her' (Freud, 1901a: 637). Is Freud fleeing his own desire? Is this why he removes the woman's hand 'unresponsively'? There is some latent aggression in the dream, it seems, attached to the eyes; the beautiful eyes are envied and then taken away, covered over by spectacles, abstracted as something indistinct. Freud gives his friend a defence against the evil eye, necessary perhaps because his patients will be constantly looking at him; it is the looking that does it, and anything with beauty is particularly at risk. To be told one has beautiful eyes, as Freud is in the dream, is to become the object of envy and thence at risk from the evil eye. Or perhaps there is envy of the friend himself, the one who works directly on the eyes, when Freud has to struggle constantly with his patients and himself to gain any 'in-sight' at all. Mahlendorf (2000: 392), by the way, points out that Freud 'had good reason' to be envious of his friend, whose name was Königstein. 'For many years, Königstein as well as Freud had been on the list recommending them for professorships at the University of Vienna, a title which brought more patients and hence better income to its recipient. Königstein received the professorship that fall, while Freud ... was once again passed over.' Passed over, overlooked; one might wish not to be noticed by the evil eye, but not to be noticed at all can in its own way be a product of – and give rise to – envy. Hart (1949: 17) states, 'It has been my experience with eye patients that the resistance to any penetration of light into the cause of their guilt is unusually great. The eye is not only the organ punished for seeing the forbidden but it symbolises the rejection of insight. "I wish to remain blind to any further enlightenment" seems to be what they say.'

The evil eye works through a specific mechanism, that of draining the liquid – the life – out of the other. The *Jewish Encyclopaedia* (Blau, 1924) glosses it as follows, extending the evil eye from an expression solely of envy to encompass anger and resentment as well:

> A supposed power of bewitching or harming by spiteful looks, attributed to certain persons as a natural endowment...Simeon ben Yohai and the popular amora R. Johanan could, with a look, transform people into a heap of bones. According to R. Eliezer, Hannanniah, Mishael and Azariah, after they had been rescued from the fiery furnace, were killed by the many eyes that were directed at them in astonishment. 'When R. Eliezer ben Hyrcanus was shut out of the place of teaching, every spot upon which he turned his eye was burned up; even a grain of wheat upon which his glance fell was half burned while the other half remained untouched, and the pillars of the gathering-place of the scholars trembled'...According to Rab, out of 100 people 99 die through the evil eye...Children are especially susceptible to the influence of the evil eye. Because of their beauty they arouse the envy of the mothers of other children, who cast upon them their evil glances; but 'wise women' understand how to counteract the influence which such glances may exert. (Ibid.: 280–1)

The evil eye is a penetrating, destructive element that has to be defended against, particularly because of its effect on babies. How does it work? '(1) the evil eye contains the element of fire, and so spreads destruction; (2) the angry glance of a man's eye calls into being an evil angel who takes vengeance on the cause of wrath' (Noy, 1971: 997). The evil eye causes living beings to dry up, so babies vomit or have diarrhoea and mothers lose their milk; conversely, descendents of the Biblical figure Joseph – known as Joseph Ha-Tsaddik (Joseph the Righteous), who might also be 'Tsaddi' a fisherman – are immune because of their relationship with water. This is why, if one is to avoid the evil eye, one engages in an obscene gesture (sticking the right thumb in the left hand and the left thumb in the right hand) to put the eye to shame, and recites the formula: 'I, so and so, son of so and so, am of the seed of Joseph, whom the evil eye may not affect.'

There are various ways of averting the evil eye, especially in relation to children, the eye's primary object of hate. The best strategy is to lessen the likelihood of the envious glance in the first place, for example by veiling or covering a baby with a dirty rag or giving it an ugly name. Contemptuously dismissing the beauty of one's own child in the face of the admiration of others is an important technique, as is actually dirtying the child and making it ugly. 'A mother or father would sneer or gaze with feigned contempt at the handsome appearance of a child in order to avoid inviting envy' (Shrut, 1960: 205). A baby being taken out for the first time might be washed in the trough used for feeding pigs, and a child going to school (an invitation to bad spirits in general) might be covered in a dirty cloak. In some places, hair from a male donkey for a boy child and from a female donkey in the case of a girl child was placed in the child's clothing. Other ways of avoiding the evil eye included dropping excrement or material representing excrement (coal, garlic, ashes, old wood) in water and sprinkling the water around the room; someone affected by the evil eye might be given the water to drink. Shrut (1960), having provided a guide through these techniques, adds another instructive passage on Jewish practices. He describes a procedure involving putting nine burning coals or nine pieces of bread into water and seeing if any would float. If so, this would be taken as evidence of the presence of the evil eye. Some of the water would then have to be drunk and some of the coal or waterlogged bread would be smeared on the head and chest of the affected person, 'with the muttering of a special incantation and throwing the remainder of the water on the ground outside the house. Any possibly increased bowel activity was thus interpreted as a further expulsion of the evil substance and forces (and, psychoanalytically, physical rejection or de-incorporation of the bad parents)' (ibid.: 205).

The bracket in this quotation is psychoanalytically preordained, implying that what is at the source of the evil eye is the parents' own hostility to their child; the rituals and amulets of prevention enact a disgusted repudiation of the parents' own violence towards their children. After all, if one has to go to such lengths to ward off evil, disowning, ruining, uglifying the child under the guise of protecting it, how – psychoanalytically, at least – can this not be read as an expressive announcement of one's own wish to damage the apparently beautiful and longed-for thing? Once again we are in the realms of projection, but not just as a description of how it must be the case that the evil eye works as a mode of projective identification. It is rather a simpler yet more troubling projection that is in operation: the one who possesses the beautiful thing, whether it be an infant or a material object, or good fortune or health, is envious *of the thing itself* and hates it. This envy is projected outwards and located in the malevolent gaze of the other, but it is our own gaze that we need to be protected against. The paradigm here is simply put in Kleinian theory as utterly characteristic of paranoid-schizoid thinking: even the loving breast is hated by the infant, because it is so self-sufficient and because the infant depends on it yet cannot fully control it. The infant therefore envies the 'good' breast as well as the frustrating, 'bad' one. Paralleling this, the rituals attached to avoiding the evil eye suggest that the parent envies the infant too. Rather than projecting this envy into the child (though this happens, perhaps more than anywhere in Kleinian theory itself, which makes the child a highly developed hater from the start of life), it is projected into an external force – a demonic spirit, a person whose eyebrows meet, a witch, the mother of a less favoured child, even at times a holy man. All these casters of the evil eye are imagos for the parent's own hatred of the child.

Shabad (2001: 170) has something similar to say: 'To the extent that the newborn's physical separateness and individual life are narcissistic insults to the mother's temporary glory of being the creative source of a new beginning, the primary manifestation of the evil eye is to begrudge the child its independent life by binding it to herself.' Shabad understands the evil eye as a representation of the mother's wish to secure the child to herself for all time – that is, it expresses her envy at the child's burgeoning separateness, an envy that is often enacted as suffocating love. Here is a mention of a word that appears a great deal in the literature – fascination or 'fascinatio':

> The root meaning of 'evil eye' derives from the Latin fascinatio, to fasten one's eye on or to bind one substance to another. Precisely because a mother's coveting of the child's new beginning may be disguised by her sweetly doting over-involvement, the child may be hard pressed to mobilize the overt aggression needed for separation and individuation away from a vulnerable, fragile parent. The consequent inhibition of self-assertiveness and sense of impotence in being imprisoned within the mother's sphere of influence helps us understand why spite is often unconscious and perversely masochistic. (Shabad, 2004: 664)

The affective content of the evil eye is linked to the mother's resistance to losing her child due to the child's growing independence; through protective 'sweetly doting over-involvement' the child is blocked from asserting her or himself as separate. More strongly, perhaps, 'the flip side of the malefic look, the mother's admiring gleam itself, insofar as it casts a seductively possessive spell on the child's developmental essence, also is a crucial aspect of the evil eye that eventually leads to perverse spite' (ibid.). Shabad goes on to suggest that whereas true admiration of another allows that other to breathe and be separate, and so in an important way it 'keeps its distance', the sorts of obsessive protection linked with engulfing love that one sees in the response to the evil eye smells strongly of reaction formation. Just as over-politeness signifies scornfulness, so obsessive love emits envy.

The reference to 'fascinatio' connects with a second major strategy for dealing with the evil eye. This relies on the possibility of distracting the eye by making it focus on something else. And what can be more distracting than the object of fascination itself, at least according to psychoanalysis, the phallus? Indeed, the mixture of phallocentrism, lewdness, disgust and obscenity that surrounds the evil eye speaks volumes of the links between eroticism and malevolent hatred. Echoing the Lacanian perspective described earlier, Bonomi (2010) argues that what is at stake in the evil eye is a representation of the gaze as material and disembodied: a real thing that can attach itself to its object and damage it. 'Before knowing that we are visible', he writes (ibid.: 111), 'we *feel* ourselves as visible, that is, we experience ourselves as the object of a gaze that is located outside us, independently from the fact that someone really is looking at us. We also feel ourselves seen when we are alone and nobody is looking at us. Besides being universal in childhood, this kind of experience reemerges later on in life in situations of enhanced vulnerability and in many pathological states. The gaze is mainly experienced as located behind us, disembodied and anonymous, although it can sometimes be interpreted as the gaze of a known person (especially of the father) or, in case of autoscopy, as one's own gaze (in this rare and extreme case, I see myself from outside).'

It is hard to read this passage without thinking of the psychoanalyst's gaze and of how it is experienced by the patient. Bonomi here identifies a universal objectifying gaze of this kind, imagined by all of us (it is 'universal in childhood') and retaining its power as a mesmerising force. On the whole, the body protects us from the power of such gazes, because it is fantasised as a non-transparent shelter upon which the gaze bounces, and that can deceive the looker or at least hide our innermost secrets from those who wish to pry into them. But there are deficiencies in this protective device: our own eyes, looking out from the body, also allow light in; they reveal the inside too fully, they too often give us away. And then there are the failures of bodily autonomy, ranging from everyday to psychopathological, in which the boundaries of the body-ego break down and the disembodied stare gets through, entering – and poisoning, it seems – the soul. The evil eye appears as 'the most diffused version of the disembodied gaze' (Bonomi, 2010: 114). Bonomi points out how shame operates here, as a response to the exposure of the secret self, and how this links with coverings over the body's nudity in order to keep the shame-inducing gaze of others at bay. But the sexual body is also fascinating, and so some kinds of display might also have a protective value. Bonomi makes some of the links:

> In ancient times, the most common defense against the evil eye was a representation of an erect penis. If we leave psychoanalytic common wisdom aside, the association between the eye and the phallus might appear obscure. In order to understand it, we have to consider that both have the power to hypnotize. Thanks to its charm, the phallus was perceived to be as powerful as the eye, and therefore it could be used to resist (as a jewel on the forehead) the power of the gaze. In ancient Rome, the phallus-shaped amulet used to ward off the evil eye was called a fascinum. Besides representing a clue of the hypnotizing effect of the phallus, the name reveals charm, fascination as the battlefield between Eros and Thanatos. The magic phallus is in fact supposed to neutralize the impending death by fascinating the disembodied gaze, that is, by binding it (from the Latin verb fascio, fasciare, to bind). (Bonomi, 2010: 115)

It was no news to the early psychoanalysts that there is an association between the eye and castration anxiety. Freud (1919) comments on this in relation to the eye-stealing Sandman of Hoffman's tale; Coleman (1939: 311) states, 'To rub the eye has a masturbatory significance and blindness or loss of the eye are substitutes for castration. Looking has frequently a magical meaning. The snake, basilisk or hypnotist charm by means of the eye.' Flügel (1924) is equally belligerent in his sexual interpretations of the 'polyphallic' protections against the evil eye that are found in many cultures. 'The eye is well known as a phallic symbol', he writes (ibid.: 188), 'and Abraham has recently shown that a "fixed stare" in women may have the meaning of an erect penis... Now, in view of the fact that nearly all the most potent amulets to ward off this influence are phallic symbols, it is clear... that the principal and original injury that is feared from the evil eye is itself castration.' Servadio (1939) proposed that the fear of the evil eye corresponds to the fear aroused in children at seeing the genitals of adults, which may be so great as to have traumatic effects, giving rise to inner conflicts and a devastating sense of guilt. 'Connected with the fear at seeing the genitals of others is the need to hide the genitals; fear of "being seen" is castration fear, because the sight of the member may incite to amputation' (ibid.: 564). There is thus an intrinsic relationship between gaze, envy, phallic erection, castration anxiety and death. Hart (1949: 7) pronounces, 'As the eye is both a penetrative and receptive organ, it can be used in both sexes to represent a male or a female genital.' He goes on, 'The murderous glance of the Medusa with its terrifying head of serpents represents both the castration horror and polyphallic compensation associated with the female genital.'

It is Geza Róheim (1952) who provides the most extensive psychoanalytically oriented documentation of the extent of these various 'fascinations' in different cultures. Having surveyed various manifestations of the evil eye and methods of averting it to be found across cultures, including the associations with drying up and the protective uglifying of children described earlier, Róheim attends to the use of sexual imagery to divert the evil eye away from its purported victim. One thing of note, as Hart also suggests, is that the protective devices are not only phallic. Another is that there is a connection between these sexual images and another strong association of the evil eye, with food, which in turn suggests how strong the trope of envious devouring might be:

> Now let us examine the main trends in counter-magic used against
> the evil eye. The spitting method used by mothers and midwives is
> interesting, for it reveals that they themselves are identified with
> the evil one and they are now spitting the child out, instead of
> devouring him. The main theme of counter magic is phallic. In Latin
> fascinum means both the evil eye and the penis as averter of the
> evil eye ... The fascinum was attached to the triumphal chariot of
> the emperor to ward off envy and the evil eye ... Greeks and Romans
> called the middle finger shameless because it symbolized the penis,
> but also the healer because pointing with it averted the evil. The
> gesture called 'fig' with the thumb stuck out between two fingers
> really symbolizes the union of the male and female sex organ as
> both the Greek and the Latin fica mean the vulva. (Róheim, 1952:
> 358–9)

Round stones with holes in them are used in healing rituals against the effects of the evil eye, in which water is passed through them and then drunk. Róheim (ibid.: 361) argues that 'all these holes and rings symbolize the witches' vagina. The fluid poured through the hole is therefore an imitation of coitus but on a pregenital level (milk, urine) or more precisely coitus with the witch-mother or the witch-mother's intercourse with herself.' In summary (ibid.: 362): 'Counter magic against the evil eye is essentially Libido against Aggression turned inward (Destrudo). The main form, however, is the fascinum. This represents several latent contents, (a) A denial of castration anxiety (the Gorgons biting mouth, the vagina dentata), (b) exhibitionism as a denial of voyeurism and (c) the symbolic representation of masturbation. And finally it means this "I am now an adult, not a child with body destruction phantasies and corresponding talio anxieties."[1]

One tries to avoid the evil eye, covering over what is beautiful, acting lewd, hiding what is precious away from everyone's gaze. These strategies are advisable, but one wonders about the limits of their worth. After all, one thing psychoanalysis attests to is the impossibility of concealment. Perhaps all that can be done is to note that the gaze is something that we cannot control; it is hard to duck or avoid it, and if it is true that there is a universal fantasy of a disembodied gaze out there – an all-seeing eye, as religious and dystopian imagery would have it – then there is truly no escape. Alerted to their nakedness by eating the apple of their desire, Adam and Eve cover themselves and try to hide from God. Rashi is very clear on what the issue is here: it is not the nakedness, but the feeling attached to it. He glosses God's question 'Where art thou?' (Genesis 3, 9) as 'Whence has the knowledge come to you what shame there is in standing naked?' The shame can only come from an awareness of being looked at and seen through; Adam and Eve are ashamed of their nakedness before God (there being no-one else around). What is this nakedness? It is obviously sexual, but more explicitly it is *knowledge* that they now have, acquired by eating from the tree of the knowledge of good and evil. They become self-aware, they become reflexive subjects; they are capable, for example, of hiding and lying. They cannot escape the disembodied gaze and the judgement that awaits them, because it is everywhere; but it is not this that makes them fearful so much as their shame, the knowledge of what they have done and what they are about, their self-transparency. Body and mind are permeable to sight; the gaze moves back and forth, the angels weep, their tears comforting and poisoning at one and the same time. We experience ourselves as watched over, which can be persecutory or comforting, or more likely both. Our permeability arises because there is no absolute distinction between inside and out, no total barrier of skin or clothing or anything else that can stop us being entered, read, understood and judged. If there is no external force to do this to us, we do it to ourselves: we are haunted by the shameful consequences of past actions, however encrypted they might be.

Haunting eyes

The evil eye is an example of destructiveness operating at a distance. No contact is necessary, not even a conscious intention or attempt at communication, just a devouring glance that inserts something in the other and consequently poisons it from within, drying up its liquid, sucking out its inside. Undoubtedly this falls under the heading of projective identification, but it is also one mechanism of haunting, in which what comes from outside possesses the subject. Perhaps the most resonant example, however, comes not from the anthropological literature but from one of the founding texts of postcolonialism, Fanon's (1952) *Black Skin, White Masks*. The central chapter's violent opening haunts Fanon's whole book and everything that has come since:

> 'Dirty nigger!' Or simply, 'Look, a Negro!'

> I came into the world imbued with the will to find a meaning in things, my spirit filled with the desire to attain to the source of the world, and then I found that I was an object in the midst of other objects. (Fanon, 1952: 109)

And a few pages later:

> 'Look, a Negro!' It was an external stimulus that flicked over me as I passed by. I made a tight smile.
> 'Look, a Negro!' It was true, it amused me.
> 'Look, a Negro!' The circle was drawing a bit tighter. I made no secret of my amusement.
> 'Mama, see the Negro! I'm frightened.' Frightened! Frightened! Now they were beginning to be afraid of me. I made up my mind to laugh myself to tears, but laughter had become impossible. (Ibid.: 111–12)

There is a huge amount of literature on these passages and also on Fanon's rendering of the Lacanian mirror phase (ibid.: 161). Much of this draws attention to the difference between Fanon and Lacan, showing that whereas the culturally undifferentiated Lacanian mirror phase attributes a universal alienation to the adoption of the visual image as the 'truth' of the subject, Fanon offers a specifically racialised version. The black subject is fixed as an *object* ('I was an object in the midst of

other objects') and does not appropriate the fantasy of integrated subjectivity. It is all too clear that what has happened is that the black subject
has been constructed in the light of an external gaze – the 'mirror-as-
camera' as Khanna (2004: 187) puts it. She goes on, 'The psychoanalytic
ambiguities of the mirror stage are, in a sense, then, the flip side of the
colonial machinery that renders the colonized subject split, and visible
only when refracting a certain form of light. The modern colonized subject has, then, a different ontological makeup than that of the colonizer
rendered through the relationship of looking, and not seeing oneself as
a mask, but rather, one's gestalt as a mask, and one's mask as a self.' The
Lacanian subject looks in the mirror and sees its image reflected back to
it, and then appropriates that image as a source of comfort and a means
for making meaning out of what was previously fragmented experience.
The black subject, racialised through the racist gaze, sees itself in the
white mirror that removes the possibility of self-assertion and mastery
and instead creates further fragmentation. 'All around me the white
man, above the sky tears at its navel, the earth rasps under my feet,
and there is a white song, a white song. All this whiteness that burns
me' (Fanon, 1952: 114). Oliver (2004: 24) summarises, 'For Fanon... if
man is alienated because he is thrown into a world not of his own making, the black man is doubly alienated because he is thrown there as one
incapable of making meaning... The privilege of autonomy and creative
meaning making has been bought at a cost to those othered as inferior,
dependent, and incapable of making meaning.'

Colonial power is built on this capacity of the coloniser to remove the
source of subjecthood from the colonised; and this power is reflected
and institutionalised continuously by the gaze, resting on and marking the skin through the process that Fanon calls 'epidermalization'.
This particular kind of evil eye projects the abjected elements of the
white onto the skin of the black. In particular, the black is positioned as
sexual, aggressive, physical; and this legacy of slavery and colonialism
continues to inhabit the dynamic of mastery that poisons the racialised
subject. 'For Fanon', claims Oliver (2004: 51), 'values are secreted,
injected, born of the blood, amputated, and haemorrhaging; they are
analogous to bodily fluids. As such, they are dynamic and mobile; and
more important, they move from body to body and can infect whole
populations.' The classic evil eye drains the liquid out of bodies; this
one makes racism viral. Fanon himself comments,

> When one has grasped the mechanism described by Lacan, one can
> have no further doubt that the real Other for the white man is and

will continue to be the black man. And conversely. Only for the white man the Other is perceived on the level of the body image, absolutely as the not-self – that is, the unidentifiable, the unassimilable. (Fanon, 1952: 161)

This kind of libidinally inflected racialised passion is a necessary component of an account one might try to give of why colonialism and racism are such inflamed, so personally *felt*, structures.

Derek Hook (2012) also draws attention to the way in which Fanon's notion of epidermalization 'prioritizes the visual register, providing an understanding not just of the stark visibility of race but of the effects of the "racial gaze"' (ibid.: 114). These authors and others emphasise how the white gaze constructs the black subject from the outside, through the operations of bodily oppression and the kind of look that pins the denigrated other to the ground. The gaze is both destructive and admiring; or rather it is full both of hate and of desire, and as such is marked by the kind of envy with which we have been dealing throughout this chapter. The white subject *needs* the black in order to define itself; and it desires the black as the repository of those necessary things – above all, sexuality – which it has repudiated out of anxiety and self-loathing. It is in this very particular sense that racism links haunting and the evil eye. The contemporary 'post-colonial' world continues to act out all the old tropes of colonialism and racism, without cease, it seems, with much of the energy it has ever had, repeating the violence of the past in a circuit that seems impossible to break. And the evil eye is one of the mechanisms through which this enactment occurs. It is fuelled by envy, projected onto the other, infiltrating the othered subject with its hatred; demanding that the racialised subject lives a life governed by evasive methods, thinking mostly of self-protection from an all-encompassing gaze. Maybe this is exaggerated; but it does not seem to be significantly so, whatever the passage of time since Fanon's first awareness of how 'Look, a Negro!' might make laughter impossible, might, that is, damage the chances of becoming a living human subject. All this is simply to say that whilst the evil eye might seem quaint, a piece of folklore, we still need to see how it is used to sustain an economy of the gaze in which some people have the power to subject others to their will.

5
Telepathy

Faking it

Psychoanalysis and telepathy are unexpected yet obvious twins. Alongside the undoubted rationalism of psychoanalysis, or perhaps as an underside to it, there is a different set of origins, associations and practices. Psychoanalysis would always be marked by its contact with the irrational because it could never contest and try to control it without being influenced by it, any more than it could speak about sexuality without being sexualised. But some of the sense of non-rational strangeness that characterises psychoanalysis arises from the specific historical circumstances in which it was formed. In this respect, the nineteenth-century interest in the occult that was also part of the heritage of psychoanalysis has continued to resonate, carrying something through to the twenty-first century as a hidden contagion from the apparently 'unseemly' elements of modernity itself. In Britain, for example, the Society for Psychical Research, in which the psychoanalyst Joan Riviere's uncle, Arthur Verall, was a significant figure, created interest in Freud's work in the early years of the twentieth century. This was partly because of the apparent similarity between the Society's concern with trance states and spiritualism and the Freudian account of hysteria. Frederic Myers, one of the founders of the Society, reviewed Breuer and Freud's (1895) *Studies on Hysteria* for its *Proceedings* in 1897 and Freud himself became a corresponding member in 1912 (Hinshelwood, 1995), publishing his paper 'A Note on the Unconscious in Psycho-Analysis' in the Society's *Proceedings* of that year (Freud, 1912a). Occultism was a big thing, dragging along with it a lurid mix of concerns ranging from Mesmerism, suggestion and mediumship, to fraud and fakery and – especially after the First World War – ghostly communications and intense, ungrievable loss.

Freud wrote a fair amount about the occult and about telepathy in particular. However, as has often been pointed out, something odd happened to this writing. It inhabited a peculiar sphere of indeterminacy in which what was written surfaced in an indistinct way, to be read but perhaps not to be taken completely seriously. Introducing Freud's (1921) paper on 'Psycho-Analysis and Telepathy', the editors of the *Standard Edition* explain,

> This was the first of Freud's papers on telepathy, and it was never published in his lifetime, though the greater part of the material in it was included in various forms in his later published papers on the subject. His next paper to be written, and the first to be published, is the one immediately following this in the present volume, on the somewhat different topic of 'Dreams and Telepathy'. Soon after this he wrote a short note on 'The Occult Significance of Dreams'. This was apparently designed for inclusion in *The Interpretation of Dreams* and it was actually first printed as part of an appendix in Volume III of the Gesammelte Schriften edition of that work, but was not included in any of its later editions. Finally, there was the lecture... on 'Dreams and Occultism' in the *New Introductory Lectures*. (Strachey, 1921: 176)

This pattern of writings that did not quite appear but infiltrated themselves into later pieces, is exacerbated by the presence of apparently spoken pieces that were actually never delivered, but pretended that they had been. Derrida (1988), in what has become a seminal exploration of psychoanalysis and telepathy, works this seam fully:

> The fake lecture of 1921, 'Psycho-Analysis and Telepathy', supposedly written for a meeting of the International Association, which did not take place, he never gave it, and it seems that Jones, with Eitingon, dissuaded him from presenting it at the following congress... The fake lecture of 1922, 'Dreams and Telepathy', was never given, as it was supposed to be, to the Society of Vienna, only published in *Imago*. The third fake lecture, 'Dreams and Occultism' (30th lecture, the second of the *New Introductory Lectures*), was of course never given... (Derrida, 1988: 508)

It takes rather little psychoanalytic acuity to understand this as ambivalence, but on whose part? On the one hand, some of Freud's colleagues, Ernest Jones in particular, were anxious that psychoanalysis would be damaged if it was tainted by too much contact with occult phenomena. On the other hand, telepathy and other forms of occultism were common currency amongst several analysts of the first generation. Roger Luckhurst (2002: 269–70) notes, 'More often than not... psychoanalysis and psychical research were entwined. James Strachey, it transpires, was led to Freud via a footnoted reference in the work of Frederic Myers. Ernest Jones, too, the strongest opponent of any occultist leanings within psychoanalysis, had begun his career reading William James and Myers.' Moreover, 'Of the close circle, Sandor Ferenczi's first paper in 1899 was on mediumship, as was Jung's doctoral thesis in 1902. Together Ferenczi and Jung sought to convince Freud to "conquer the field of occultism." ... By 1913, Freud visited séances, but one obvious fake led him to ask Ferenczi to withdraw his testimonial. Ferenczi gave a lecture on thought-transference to the Viennese Psychoanalytical Association in November 1913, and his correspondence is littered with references to the topic' (ibid.: 272–3). The Jones–Ferenczi axis was the one on which Freud's interest in telepathy ranged. Jones repeatedly discouraged him and used his position as official biographer in the 1950s to write the history of psychoanalysis' engagement with occultism as one of the vagaries of Freud's genius, not to be taken seriously. Ferenczi, by contrast, was responsible for Freud's 'conversion' to belief in telepathy in the 1920s. Freud himself, in an instructive and famous letter to Jones in 1926, cleverly managed to play both sides of this game. In this letter, he announces that having always being favourably disposed towards telepathy without being convinced of it, 'personal experience through tests, which I undertook with Ferenczi and my daughter, have attained such convincing power over me that diplomatic considerations had to be relinquished' (Freud, 1926: 597). But understanding Jones' squeamishness about the occult and the trouble it could cause for psychoanalysis, he did not want to push things too far. If anyone asks about it, he says, 'just answer calmly that my acceptance of telepathy is my own affair, like my Judaism and my passion for smoking, etc., and that the subject of telepathy is not related to psychoanalysis' (ibid).

The ambivalence looks real here, both within the institution of psychoanalysis and in Freud's mind. *Institutionally*, the issues range from the 'diplomatic' need to distance psychoanalysis from the suspicion of quackery and also, as Luckhurst (2002) has shown, to ensure that psychoanalysis was understood as having a distinct vision that would explain occult phenomena without ceding ground to other psychological approaches. But Freud's comment reveals more than this: 'my acceptance of telepathy is my own affair, like my Judaism and my passion for smoking'. Telepathy, smoking and Judaism; an odd triptych, each part perhaps disreputable, each of them 'my own affair' and therefore private. Freud says they are only accidentally connected to psychoanalysis, but surely we know better? If something is a person's 'own affair', then it relates precisely to what psychoanalysis deals with; after all, Freud's dreams, very much his own affair, are the main subject of his book *The Interpretation of Dreams* and are consequently amongst the foundation stones of the psychoanalytic canon. In the psychoanalytic consulting room too, the focus is on the patient's random and often trivial free associations, slips and dream fragments and moments of private concern. Supposedly irrelevant, personal issues are exactly what lie at the heart of psychoanalysis; without Freud's 'own affair' there would be no psychoanalysis at all. Freud's disavowal, therefore, does not work and perhaps was never really meant to do so. What we are learning here is that something pervades psychoanalysis just as psychoanalysis pervades Western culture; and this something is a little bit at odds with the orthodoxy, a little bit poisonous perhaps (as is smoke), certainly more than a little bit confusing.

Telepathy, smoking and Judaism: perhaps these are all ghosts of one kind or another. They are all obscure, they all act secretly and are hard to observe, yet clearly have effects. From the point of view of Western culture, there is also something slightly sordid or at least questionable about each one. For instance, if the foundations of psychoanalysis have something occult about them, they also have a lot that is Jewish. This has been heavily and extensively mined and will be returned to again in Chapter 6, but it is clear that it forms an uncanny background to psychoanalysis, somehow understood (unconsciously or consciously) as not quite reputable yet also inescapable. It governs a good deal of the historical and maybe some current antagonism towards psychoanalysis – its 'Jewish science' opprobrium – and has had reverberations within psychoanalysis itself, from the early ambiguity of Jung's relationship to the new movement, through the controversies and debasements of Nazi psychotherapy and postwar German psychoanalysis, to contemporary recrudescences of antisemitism in some intellectual and institutional settings (Frosh, 2005, 2012b). It is no private matter: the Jewishness of its origins continues to haunt psychoanalysis as another unlaid ghost, bursting out from time to time, sometimes celebrated but at other times abjected, especially when psychoanalysis is called to account for the antisemitism in its history. As something spectral within psychoanalysis, Jewishness can never be dispensed with.

Smoking is harder to classify, but even if it is only recently that smoking has become an embarrassment, Freud knew it to be a poisonous activity, and it certainly is transmitted through the air. It was probably no accident that the first great psychoanalytic novel, Italo Svevo's *Zeno's Conscience* (1923), centres on a man who cannot give up smoking, despite possessing a great capacity for free association, storytelling and rationalisation. In his immensely entertaining and bitter history of the early analytic movement, Wilhelm Stekel (1926) describes the first meeting of Freud's 'Wednesday Society' (the antecedent of the Vienna Psychoanalytic Society) in 1902. Smoke and smoking dominate his recollections of the occasion:

> Freud initiated a specific ritual which continued for many years. We arrived there after the evening meal. There were cigars on the table to which most of the participants helped themselves generously. In the beginning Freud smoked almost uninterruptedly. He smoked a small English pipe for which he had sacrificed his beloved Trabuko cigars, only to return to Trabukos again at a later stage. I have rarely seen a man smoke so much. (He had also given me an English pipe and English tobacco. Smoking must have been a complex of the master. From what he told me, I had the impression that he had 'oversmoked' himself. So he had to quit smoking for a few days.) (Stekel, 1926: 102)

Stekel was so impressed by all this that he wrote out the conversation about smoking that ensued and published it in the *Prager Tagblattes* newspaper. Naming himself the 'Tireless' and Freud the 'Master', Stekel concludes this dramatisation (which focused on creativity and on women) with a short interchange on smoking as poison. Freud, it seems, denied that smoking was damaging – or denied it in relation to his own smoking, which he claimed to be 'moderate' (though Stekel has already noted how Freud's smoking was 'uninterrupted'). Stekel himself introduces the idea of the last smoke ('tomorrow you'll quit') – an endless deferral of the reality principle under the guise of taking action, which is what Svevo takes up in his novel. The last smoke apparently renounces pleasure whilst continuing to engage in it in an eternal present of unkept promises:

> THE TIRELESS [STEKEL]: The master is right. Smoking produces a slight narcosis. But we medical doctors have to admit that it can become a dangerous poison as well.

THE MASTER [FREUD]: In large quantities smoking becomes dangerous to men. But what harm could moderate smoking do? I always
become distrustful when I hear that a patient died from smoking
too much. You very often find other causes hidden behind it.
Most often a combination with alcoholism, which seems to be
particularly noxious.

THE TIRELESS: I actually smoke very little. Five cigars a day, and
always after a meal. And I also believe that I could quit at any
moment. Indeed – after a particularly bad cigar I say to myself:
tomorrow, you'll quit. I have deceived myself for many years
with the idea that this cigar was the last one. The worn-out
consolation of all sinners! Big or small.

THE MASTER: You're not a smoker. You don't understand. I was not
allowed to smoke for two years. It was horrible. It felt like a
good friend had died and I had to mourn him from morning
to evening. Now I even have the same feelings for my pipe. She
is a good friend of mine, my counsellor, my comfort, my guide,
who smoothes my way. (Stekel, 1926: 104)

As an orally addictive phenomenon, smoking indexes the earliest
phases of infantile development that haunt adulthood. Given our
knowledge of Freud's own oral cancer, it also suggests a specifically
psychoanalytic torment: that what we desire most is most likely to
destroy us. Reading Stekel's dramatisation in the light of Freud's later
illness produces a shudder that is perhaps more than just knowledge
after-the-event. It is also an instance of an awareness of the future that
haunts the present, of that which will come to be already being visible
in what is. Commenting on Freud's (1900) 'specimen dream' of Irma's
injection, in which Freud looks down his patient Irma's throat to find
infected tubes, Salomon Resnick (1987) offers a reversion to what might
be called a 'pre-Freudian' account of dreams in terms of their 'premonitory' quality. In this reading, the discovery of diseased organs in Irma's
mouth is to be taken not just as a symbolisation of sexuality, but as an
anticipation of Freud's *own* future illness, the cancer of the mouth that
was to cause him so much agony and distort his speech. Resnick (ibid.:
119n8) comments that Freud is looking, ' "without knowing it", for an
anticipated memory of his own future. "Freud's cancer" is already speaking in the present, or in any case his worries and "tissular" fantasies are
being summoned in his transference with Irma, a transference that he
was later to call "countertransference".'

The double of 'The "Uncanny"' returns here: the deathly reminder of what already exists in the future. Freud knew of the link between cancer and smoking, and sees in the tubes of the patient in his dream his own destroyed tissues and deathly wishes. Writing to Jones in 1923 after the removal of a growth on his jaw, he acknowledged: 'Smoking is accused as the etiology of this tissue-rebellion' (Gay, 1988: 419). The invasion of tissue by smoke, the clouding of air by particles that carry poison, is already a theme in early psychoanalysis, reaching backwards and forwards across time. Add to this the more recent awareness of passive smoking, in which people who do not smoke are affected by those who do, and a model for wordless transpersonal communication of disturbance emerges, tied in with unconscious deathly impulses. And finally, there is a strangely emotive twist. When his beloved daughter Anna was away in 1922, Freud wrote to Lou Andreas Salomé about his feelings. He had long been sorry for Anna, he said, 'for still being at home with us old folks'. However, 'if she really were to go away, I should feel myself as deprived as I do now, and as I should do if I had to give up smoking!' (Freud, 1922b: 113). Given how intensely connected he was to Anna, and she to him, and perhaps – if this can be hazarded – affected by a slightly poisonous anxiety about the effect of having been her analyst, this says a lot about how what is not necessarily good for us is unavoidably inhaled, and can become an unconquerable addiction. *'She is a good friend of mine, my counsellor, my comfort, my guide, who smoothes my way'* (Stekel, 1926: 104): this could be Freud's paean to his daughter, his nurse and confidante, who took over speaking in public for him when he could no longer do it as a consequence of his cancer. But it is not praise for Anna; it is a homage to his pipe.

Assimilating and vomiting telepathy

The third element in the triptych, telepathy, also passes unseen between people. Freud was adamant that psychoanalysis had little to learn from telepathy and the occult in general, but rather it could be used to throw light *on* such phenomena. Yet his assertions in that regard read as 'protesting too much'; and it is apparent that just as he tries his hardest to draw a line between the activities and beliefs of occultists and those of psychoanalysts, so he opens up a channel through which they communicate with one another. A telepathic channel, one might say, because it is secret and not easily visible. The starting point for this is Freud's averred doubt over the reality of telepathic phenomena. All his examples are of *failed* telepathic acts, some of which nevertheless have clear psychodynamic meaning. For himself, when it comes to telepathic communications and premonitions, nothing happens, though even here he leaves something dangling:

> Like every human being, I have had presentiments and experienced trouble, but the two failed to coincide with one another, so that nothing followed the presentiments, and the trouble came upon me unannounced. During the days when I was living alone in a foreign city – I was a young man at the time – I quite often heard my name suddenly called by an unmistakable and beloved voice; I then noted down the exact moment of the hallucination and made anxious enquiries of those at home about what had happened at that time. Nothing had happened. To balance this, there was a later occasion when I went on working with my patients without any disturbance or foreboding while one of my children was in danger of bleeding to death. Nor have I ever been able to regard any of the presentiments reported to me by patients as veridical. I must however confess that in the last few years I have had a few remarkable experiences which might easily have been explained on the hypothesis of telepathic thought-transference. (Freud, 1901b: 261)

Freud acknowledges the existence both of presentiments and of trouble; the problem is, they do not relate to one another, presentiments do not necessarily lead to trouble, and trouble is not accompanied by any presentiment of it occurring. But Freud does not leave it at that; he drops hints that there is something more at stake for him than simply pouring scorn on superstitions – although his final sentence, on his 'remarkable experiences', was not added until 1924, showing how his views changed (and incidentally paralleling a softening in his attitude towards his Jewish identity that also occurred during his later life). Luckhurst (2002: 270) comments, 'Freud stated, "I must confess that I am one of those unworthy people in whose presence spirits suspend their activity and the supernatural vanishes away." This is untrue, both of Freud and of his institution. Even this denial gives itself away, in Freud's awareness of telepathic messages from phantasms of the living and in his reference to the Spiritualist argument that the presence of sceptics disturbs the spirits. Freud knows not to know; a perfect instance of disavowal.' Not only does Freud show knowledge of spiritualism, but he also leaves open a door to it by mentioning his own 'remarkable experiences' that might indeed be explained by the 'hypothesis' of telepathic thought-transference. This language of explanation and hypothesis is the scientific language upon which Freud draws all the time, which suggests that by the 1920s he was willing to address telepathy as a potential equal, a hypothesis that could in principle be true. But he then covers over this trace of belief by providing a series of apparently occult presentiments or telepathic events that he explains through rationalistic means. Or almost rationalistic: the characteristic of all the explanations is that they rely on acceptance of unconscious processes that without belief in *psychoanalysis* might seem just as occult as any other way of explaining them. Freud himself puts the situation charmingly:

> The differences between myself and the superstitious person are two: first, he projects outwards a motivation which I look for within; secondly, he interprets chance as due to an event, while I trace it back to a thought. But what is hidden from him corresponds to what is unconscious for me, and the compulsion not to let chance count as chance but to interpret it is common to both of us. (Freud, 1901b: 257)

The ' "superstitious person" – "Freud" ' couplet is an important axis for psychoanalysis. However, given how impossible it is to find the central material object of psychoanalysis, the unconscious, how it can only be recognised by its effects, is this so different from belief in spirits? That is to say, are we dealing with what is in the 'mystical' frame one superstition stacked up against another, and in the 'scientific' frame one hypothesis competing on equal grounds with another similarly unprovable hypothesis?

Freud gives a complicated example of a woman who describes an experience of déjà vu that she had had when 12 years old. The then girl had been visiting friends and had found herself convinced that their house was one she had been in before, even though the evidence was strongly against this. Freud establishes that at that time the friends she was visiting had a gravely ill brother, and the girl herself had a brother who had only just recovered from a life-threatening illness. This leads him to the interpretation of the experience:

> She found an analogous situation in the home of her friends, whose only brother was in danger of dying soon, as in fact he did shortly after. She ought to have remembered consciously that she herself had lived through this situation a few months before: instead of remembering it – which was prevented by repression – she transferred her

feeling of remembering something to her surroundings, the garden and the house, and fell a victim to the 'fausse reconnaissance' of having seen all this exactly the same once before. From the fact that repression occurred we may conclude that her former expectation of her brother's death had not been far removed from a wishful phantasy. She would then have been the only child. In her later neurosis she suffered most severely from a fear of losing her parents, behind which, as usual, analysis was able to reveal the unconscious wish with the same content. (Freud, 1901b: 267)

This explanation seems so obvious and compelling that one needs to be actively reminded that it is only so because of the pervasiveness of psychoanalytic explanation itself, its saturation of Western culture. It is only once one is schooled in psychoanalysis that it becomes more plausible to attribute the déjà vu experience to the unconscious processes of repression and displacement than to some kind of immaterial communication between potential worlds, or some other such 'superstitious' explanation. That is, psychoanalysis' own mystical elements, its forceful and yet bizarre beliefs, its requirement to suspend the usual scientific requirements in favour of an unequivocal acceptance of invisible unconscious forces, is in itself a kind of occultism in which communications occur without any obvious means of support. Something channels these communications so that they can pass across time and space in ways that continued to trouble Freud throughout his psychoanalytic career. In his late seventies, in his *New Introductory Lecture* on 'Dreams and Occultism', Freud asserts his right to doubt his own doubt: 'If one regards oneself as a sceptic, it is a good plan to have occasional doubts about one's scepticism too. It may be that I too have a secret inclination towards the miraculous which thus goes half way to meet the creation of occult facts' (Freud, 1933: 53). To the putative listener who responds, 'Here's another case of a man who has done honest work as a scientist all through his life and has grown feeble-minded, pious and credulous in his old age,' Freud replies, 'At least I have not become pious, and I hope not credulous... But I am incapable of currying favour and I must urge you to have kindlier thoughts on the objective possibility of thought-transference and at the same time of telepathy as well' (ibid.: 54). It is perhaps not so much that Freud changed his mind in his old age, but that he became less worried about placing psychoanalysis and occultism on the same ground, and more ready to note the parallels between them. Derrida (1988: 523) comments, 'So psychoanalysis... resembles an adventure of modern rationality set on swallowing *and* simultaneously rejecting the foreign body named Telepathy, for assimilating and vomiting it without being able to make up its mind to do one or the other.'

Freud's push-me-pull-you attraction towards and repulsion from telepathy was very striking. In his 1921 paper, he sought to differentiate analysts from occultists on the grounds that the latter engage in wishful fantasies whilst the former are scientists, *materialists* even. 'Analysts are at bottom incorrigible mechanists and materialists', he wrote (ibid.: 179), 'even though they seek to avoid robbing the mind and spirit of their still unrecognized characteristics. So, too, they embark on the investigation of occult phenomena only because they expect in that way finally to exclude the wishes of mankind from material reality.' They are therefore at odds with occultists, despite the fact that there might be some 'reciprocal sympathy' between the two groups because 'They have both experienced the same contemptuous and arrogant treatment by official science' (ibid.). 'To this day', he states, disingenuously, 'psychoanalysis is regarded as savouring of mysticism, and its unconscious is looked upon as one of the things between heaven and earth which philosophy refuses to dream of' (ibid.). Unlike occultists, however, psychoanalysts are not only inheritors of the mantle of science, but are also flexible, willing to shift their beliefs in the light of new data, and consequently best placed to puncture the effectively religious states of mind of their opponents. (On this, it is worth recalling Stekel (1926: 107): 'Freud has a character trait that has done him great harm and has slowed down the development of analysis, and yes, even taken it in the wrong direction: *He is unable to accept that he erred!* He isolates himself from all corrections of his established viewpoints.') This is also why telepathy has very little to teach psychoanalysts, especially in relation to dreams, whereas 'psycho-analysis may do something to advance the study of telepathy, in so far as, by the help of its interpretations, many of the puzzling characteristics of telepathic phenomena may be rendered more intelligible to us' (Freud, 1922a: 219).

This sounds formidable, except that Freud leaves a door open for the existence of genuine telepathic events. The end of the previous sentence from 'Dreams and Telepathy' (1922a: 219) reads 'other, still doubtful, phenomena may for the first time definitely be ascertained to be of a telepathic nature'. There is, therefore, at least in principle, some room for manoeuvre: some occurrences which people think are 'doubtful' will not be explained psychoanalytically but will assert their existence as genuinely of a telepathic nature. By 1933, Freud is even clearer (ibid.: 36): 'Of these conjectures no doubt the most probable is that there is a real core of yet unrecognized facts in occultism round which cheating and phantasy have spun a veil which it is hard to pierce.' And if one wants a practical demonstration of mundane ambivalence, of asserting and denying something at the same time, here he is removing the term 'alleged' from telepathy and, in the same passage, retreating from the consequences of so doing. 'Permit me now, for the purpose of what I have to tell you, to omit the cautious little word "alleged" and to proceed as though I believed in the objective reality of the phenomenon of telepathy. But bear firmly in mind that that is not the case and that I have committed myself to no conviction.' Is it real or not; can one live with it or will it take one over; how much occultism can psychoanalysis tolerate?

What might be the genuinely telepathic elements that coexist with psychoanalysis and that cannot be converted into a psychoanalytic narrative but perhaps, if we can jump ahead a little, might share with psychoanalysis in the things that philosophy refuses to dream of? Could there be a mechanism that is both psychoanalytic and telepathic, describing communication across space, outside the medium of words – outside, that is, the symbolic dimension that we usually take to be the mode in which psychoanalysis itself operates? Can things that stand outside language really be transmitted and received? Before 'tele' became an abbreviation for 'television', it was a prefix that meant 'distant'. 'Telepathy': communication direct from one mind to another, but also experience or affliction over a distance. Psychoanalysis: examination of minds, but also something contagious, in which what is apparently 'inside' one person is somehow understood, perhaps even felt, by another. And perhaps in this contagion is exactly one of the things we look to explain in haunting – how certain fantasies spread from one person to another, across cultures and societies, infecting us all along the way:

> The word 'telepathy' was invented and first used by Frederic Myers in 1882...Freud's definition, which involves bringing together the concepts of telepathy and thought-transference, is very close to Myers': telepathy and thought-transference, says Freud, concern the idea 'that mental processes in one person – ideas, emotional states, conative impulses – can be transferred to another person without employing the familiar methods of communication by means of words and signs.'...It is also clear, however, that in historical terms the word 'telepathy' is part of an explosion of forms of communication and possibilities of representation. Telepathy...is indissociably

bound up with other forms of telemedia and teleculture whose emergence also belongs to the nineteenth century. (Royle, 1995: 368)

Eliza Slavet (2009: 147) comments, 'The new reality of hearing the actual voice of a person who was physically miles away made it not unreasonable to expect that one could at least sense the thoughts of a person who was only feet away.' But more than that, she points to the mystical background in which much of psychoanalysis is mired. Whilst Freud created a practice of speech that seemed to strive towards clarity and discrimination, 'he suggests that pre- or extra-linguistic forms of transmission, such as heredity or telepathy, are always in the background, silently and subtly controlling the more palpable transmissions such as writing and talking. Precisely because they are ungraspable, heredity and telepathy may be more potent; unlike that which is sensorially apprehended or physically graspable, such phenomena "seize" the psyche, compelling the imagination to conjure mysteries beyond belief' (ibid.: 133). Amongst other things, it is instructive to see this harnessing of heredity and telepathy together, how each of them is a speculative (at the time) medium through which something is transmitted with no visible means of support, yet with apparently undeniable impact.

This leads to the thought that something in telepathy might be more powerful than words, more basic or fundamental. Translated into the language of psychoanalysis, this must be a reference to unconscious communication, to the way we can indeed be 'seized' by what comes from elsewhere, bewildered to find ourselves lost to ourselves, seemingly under the control of another mind that just happens to be co-located with our own. Slavet links telepathy with heredity as things that stand in the background; we can see neither, yet may be 'silently and subtly' influenced by them. In this linkage we have the division between horizontal and vertical transmission: the former occurs between people, the latter across generations. That which binds us to one another is matched by that which binds us to those who came before and those who go after; perhaps in every case there is something cryptic being transmitted, and possibly they are the same thing. Royle (1995) is on a similar track here, but he sees the encryption as being that of telepathy *within* psychoanalysis. He writes (ibid. 364), 'What is implied by this proposition that a theory of telepathy and a theory of the unconscious "can be neither confused nor dissociated" is a logic of the crypt or parasite, a logic according to which "telepathy" becomes a kind of foreign body within psychoanalysis.' This has the truth in it of Derrida's location of telepathy as an indigestible substance, exactly *resistant* to assimilation or vomiting out. But perhaps psychoanalysis need not be so troubled by the infectious presence of telepathy so close to it. If it is the case that 'something' always leaks out of the unconscious and finds itself a place in the mind of the other, then maybe the spiritual and material oppositions are not so useful, and what can be thought about instead is what might be termed the 'inmixing of subjects', the way people somehow seem always to get inside one another's heads.

Communicating and transferring

Communication at a distance is precisely what happens. Whatever goes on in the patient is picked up by the analyst; conversely, the patient responds to the analyst's nuances. Something passes between them alongside, at variance with, or without words; conventionally, this is the transference-countertransference exchange. Freud (1919: 234) calls this 'telepathy', defining it as 'mental processes leaping from one of these characters to another – by what we should call telepathy – so that the one possesses knowledge, feelings and experience in common with the other'. It is the intersubjective aspect of psychoanalysis that makes it so much in thrall to a version of telepathy, or at least of 'thought-transference'. The German words make the connection very clear: *Gedankenübertragung* for thought-transference, which Freud states is 'so close to telepathy [*Telepathie*] and can indeed without much violence be regarded as the same thing' (1933: 39); *Übertragung* for transference itself. The issue is, how can the practice of psychoanalysis be based on the interpretation of unconscious communications if it is not the case that the unconscious communicates? And if it does communicate, how can the unconscious be a space of complete repression, characterised by the impossibility of conscious access? If there is a crypt and what is hidden in it is locked away, encrypted and coded, made unavailable, then how can it also be that everyone knows that it is there, or at least that the analyst feels it to be so, that it is hidden yet transferred, that some message comes from 'beyond the grave', the entombed unknown?

For Campbell and Pile (2010), telepathy and psychoanalysis go hand in hand because telepathy expresses a truth of unconscious life: it is secretive *and* expressive, hidden *and* revealed:

> On one side, there appears to be an unconscious that is communicative and open; yet, on the other, it is sullen and uncommunicative. In dreams, slips of the tongue, works of art, religion, city life, Freud

sees evidence of a repressed material escaping into representation, yet the unconscious is meant to be a container capable of keeping thoughts imprisoned so that they can do no harm. Somewhere in the midst of a notion of a repressed unconscious, Freud must hold onto both an idea that repression can be evaded and that the unconscious can communicate. (Campbell and Pile, 2010: 408)

Telepathy is consequently bound to repression as a necessary coupling. There has to be a way in which what is not available to speech is nevertheless carried across the intersubjective gap, so that one person can at least guess at what is happening in another. Of course, at its most restrictive this might simply mean that the analyst observes and listens and pieces together the story that patients are 'really' telling behind the fragments of a story that they *believe* they are telling. There is no particular magic involved in such a process, just intelligent people using their powers of reasoning to work out what must (at least according to psychoanalytic theory) be going on 'in' the unconscious of patients for their talk to make sense. This is certainly consistent with the 'detective story' model of psychoanalytic therapy that Freud deploys, in which the task of the analyst is portrayed as hunting out clues from the slips and dreams of the patient until the background unconscious wish or repressed traumatic memory is brought to light. However, even in Freud's writings another element can be found, having to do with the analyst's receptivity to unconscious communications from the patient and the difficulties that these communications involve. The proposal that an analyst must be attuned to the patient's unconscious communications, must 'withhold all conscious influences from his capacity to attend, and give himself over completely to his "unconscious memory"' (Freud, 1912b: 112), suggests that analytic understanding is not just a matter of reasoning from patients' signs, but of becoming exposed in a direct way to the affective and maybe also conceptual contents of what is supposedly repressed. This is why, Campbell and Pile (2010: 418) state, 'telepathy is arguably not the opposite of repression, merely the means by which it enigmatically returns, becomes undone and is transported. In these terms, telepathy is in every sense a symptom of the repressed: like the hysterical symptom, it carries and transports what cannot be consciously spoken or represented; and yet, unlike hysteria, telepathy is a symptom that is given over, or taken up by the other.'

Freud takes seriously the telepathic claim that direct communication across an unspoken abyss can be achieved, but he reads it, as one would expect, as mediated by an unconscious that he never ceases to regard as material – however elusive it is to the observing eye. In his 'lecture' on 'Dreams and Occultism' (1933: 31–56) he gives some entertaining examples of failed telepathy and fortune-telling, which he nevertheless sees as having occult and psychoanalytic relevance, being instances of thought-transference. One concerns a childless woman of 43 who had many years before been assured by a fortune-teller that she would have two children by the age of 32. In fact, she did not have the promised children, but somehow this had not stopped her from being impressed by the prophecy. Freud is also impressed, but for other reasons:

> You will say that this is a stupid and incomprehensible story and ask why I have told it you. I should be entirely of your opinion if – and this is the salient point – analysis had not made it possible to arrive at an interpretation of the prophecy which is convincing precisely from the explanation it affords of the details. For the two numbers [2 and 32] find their place in the life of my patient's *mother*. She had married late – not till she was over thirty, and in the family they had often dwelt on the fact of the success with which she had hastened to make up for lost time. Her two first children (with our patient the elder) had been born with the shortest possible interval between them, in a single calendar year; and she had in fact two children by the time she was 32. What Monsieur le Professeur had said to my patient meant therefore: 'Take comfort from the fact of being so young. You'll have the same destiny as your mother, who also had to wait a long time for children, and you'll have two children by the time you're 32.' But to have the same destiny as her mother, to put herself in her mother's place, to take her place with her father – that had been the strongest wish of her youth, the wish on account of whose non-fulfilment she was just beginning to fall ill. The prophecy promised her that the wish would still be fulfilled in spite of everything; how could she fail to feel friendly to the prophet? (Freud, 1933: 40–1)

The most significant point here, in Freud's mind, is that the fortune-teller ('Monsieur le Professeur') could not have known anything of the woman's unconscious wish or actual family history when he made his prediction. However, he somehow spoke to it, providing details that symbolically expressed exactly what the woman was seeking from him – an (Oedipal) assurance that she would imitate and supplant her mother. For Freud, this could only mean that somehow the woman's unconscious desire had been communicated to the fortune-teller. 'Either the story as it was told me is untrue', he writes (ibid.: 41) 'and the events occurred otherwise, or thought-transference exists as a real phenomenon.' On the basis of this and other cases, Freud opts for the latter option: thought-transference is real, but it is not an occult phenomenon, it has to do with the unconscious.

This is what matters. For Freud, the unconscious is a material fact, which means that appealing to it as the mediator of unintended, apparently magical communication is to provide an explanation of that communication – even if to non-believers it might seem simply to replace one mystical account with another. In his vision, the unconscious is a kind of invisible telephone line, perhaps buried in the ground so that the way it links a speaker with a receiver is not visible, but nevertheless is actually there. Here is Freud explicitly drawing this exact analogy:

> The telepathic process is supposed to consist in a mental act in one person instigating the same mental act in another person. What lies between these two mental acts may easily be a physical process into which the mental one is transformed at one end and which is transformed back once more into the same mental one at the other end. The analogy with other transformations, such as occur in speaking and hearing by telephone, would then be unmistakable. And only think if one could get hold of this physical equivalent of the psychical act! It would seem to me that psycho-analysis, by inserting the unconscious between what is physical and what was previously called 'psychical', has paved the way for the assumption of such processes as telepathy. (Freud, 1933: 55)

The unconscious as a telephone line is alert to the transmissions coming from one person and capable of translating these enigmatic transmissions into something that can be understood. Freud goes so far as to think that this 'direct psychical transference' might be the 'original, archaic method of communication between individuals' (ibid.). Usually, it remains in the background, displaced by more subtle and explicit means of communication – speech, mainly. But at times it comes through; for instance 'in passionately excited mobs' and, one assumes from the context, where what is being communicated is a repressed idea. 'If there is such a thing as telepathy as a real process', Freud concludes (ibid.), 'we may suspect that, in spite of its being so hard to demonstrate, it is quite a common phenomenon.'

Transformations and translations, *Gedankenübertragung* (thought-transference) and *Übertragung* (transference). Psychoanalysis places these things right at the centre of its experience. 'Through transference, and through his discussions of telepathy, Freud would continue to evoke the possibility of unconscious communication between individuals, and to evoke a non-repressive unconscious co-existing with a repressive unconscious' (Campbell and Pile, 2010: 408). Luckhurst references another powerful analytic source for this argument:

> In 1926, Helene Deutsch published 'Occult Processes occurring during Psychoanalysis', which suggested that 'during psychoanalysis the psychic contact between analyst and analysand is so intimate, and the psychic processes which unfold themselves in that situation are so manifold, that the analytic situation may well include all the conditions which facilitate the occurrence of such phenomena.' These effects are 'probably connected with transference' and 'seem to indicate the existence of an essential relationship between analytic intuition and the telepathic process.' (Luckhurst, 2002: 275)

Whatever is going on in psychoanalysis when one person picks up the unconscious impulses of another can be thought of in terms of a telepathic exchange. The analyst is wired up, is sensitised to the unconscious messages of the other, is a decoding machine, a receiver and translator. Transference always seems like a mystery: how can it happen that this ridiculous situation in which one person simply lies on a couch and talks, and the other occasionally comments, can become so highly charged? The answer is: because there is something between them, something in the air, something that crosses the borders, something that disrupts the taken-for-granted separateness of each one of us from all others.

Inmixing of subjectivities

The dream of progress remains, but is undermined – or perhaps underpinned – by a 'regressive' longing for what cannot be understood, a mystical gap that has been filled in various ways including (on its negative pole) violence, nationalist mythologies and religious fundamentalism. Since Derrida's (1988) mimetic account of Freud and telepathy, we have become fully aware of just how what is being referenced here is a traumatic, repressed underside of psychoanalysis itself. Derrida in fact turns things around to argue that the *non*-existence of telepathy is what requires explanation, the suggestion that there would be a part of the subject that is wholly unknowable to others, remaining incommunicado and impossible to read:

> The truth, which I have always difficulty getting used to, that non-telepathy is possible. Always difficult to imagine that one can think something to oneself, deep down inside, without being surprised by the other, without the other being immediately informed, as easily as if it had a giant screen in it, at the time of the talkies, with remote control for changing channels and fiddling with the colours, the speech dubbed with large letters in order to avoid any misunderstanding. (Derrida, 1988: 504)

Derrida calls the possibility of 'non-telepathy' a truth, as if there really could be such an absolutely private self-communication. He plays on the idea that it is surprising to come across this truth, as if it is commonsensical to assume that one might be in open communication with others, that others can always read one's mind and that there is no private space in which to hide. As Freud put it in the 'Dora' case (1905: 76–7), 'He that has eyes to see and ears to hear may convince himself that no mortal can keep a secret. If his lips are silent, he chatters with his finger-tips; betrayal oozes out of him at every pore. And thus the task of making conscious the most hidden recesses of the mind is one which it is quite possible to accomplish.'

'Betrayal' is the way Freud thinks about it, a secret that oozes out, that cannot be kept un-telepathised. You only have to look and listen in order to know what is in the deepest recesses of the other's mind. The unconscious hides and reveals at the same time; in most instances, the only person who cannot see what is happening is the one whose unconscious is doing the betraying. Dora does not know that her play with her purse reveals her masturbatory fantasies, but Freud knows it straight away, and not just because he is a psychoanalyst – anyone with eyes and ears could see it. This chimes with the common view of the unconscious, that it is a trickster that deliberately gives us away to each other. However, the situation is more complex and more open than that. As we have seen, even Freud acknowledges that there might be processes of unconscious-to-unconscious communication that seem telepathic, and that this could be a good thing – not a betrayal, but a means by which important ideas might be communicated, within and outside of psychoanalysis. More generally, the question of whether intersubjectivity is possible is one that hangs over psychoanalysis and raises vital issues in its wake. Can the other be known? Is it right to strive to know the other? Is this a process whereby 'recognition' is bestowed, thus creating the other as a subject in her or his own right, or is the impulse to inhabit the other's mind a form of colonialism, of appropriation of the other's being to make it our own? What are the ethics of intersubjectivity, and what are the possibilities?

There are two pulls, in somewhat opposite directions. One stresses the necessary interrelation of different subjectivities as they encounter each other, encouraging an openness of each human subject to others. This does not necessarily mean the disappearance of each subject in the other, though more mystical ideologues might like to see it that way. Winnicott is a central source here, with his irritatingly ubiquitous statement on interdependence (1975: 99): 'There is no such thing as a baby... if you show me a baby you certainly show me also someone caring for the baby, or at least a pram with someone's eyes and ears glued to it. One sees a "nursing couple".' Whilst this might seem an overly concrete and normative way of considering the earliest relationships of life, it succinctly makes the point that humans are social beings, born into relationships of mutual dependency, and that the way these relationships work out (or are 'worked through') is a powerful influence on the psychological make-up of every one of us. It is not that we are born separate and then have to forge links with others, though people often think of things that way. It is rather that we are born in the context of intimate, dependent relationships and the nature of these relationships is crucial in determining what our emotional lives will be like.

Winnicott's (1971) ideas about transitional phenomena are drawn on heavily by those wishing to claim that there is a fundamental capacity for intersubjective exchange, at least in the analytic situation. The trick here is to hold in tension the individual subjectivity of patient and analyst with an appreciation of the area of their mixing together – the 'third', in current terminology. In a much quoted paper on the intersubjective third, Thomas Ogden (2004) links this with the process of projective identification, showing amongst other things how much Kleinian thinking has permeated the world of American psychoanalysis. He is interested in how projective identification 'has the effect of profoundly subverting the experience of analyst and analysand as separate subjects' (ibid.: 189). Ogden's fuller account of it has something of a mystical tinge, but what he is trying to articulate is how analysis involves giving up something about one's separateness in order to experience a new type of relational way of being, which can then allow the patient and the analyst to separate out again, as changed 'subjects'. Ogden writes:

> Projective identification can be thought of as involving a central paradox: the individuals engaged in this form of relatedness unconsciously subjugate themselves to a mutually generated intersubjective third for the purpose of freeing themselves from the limits of whom they had been to that point. In projective identification, analyst and analysand are both limited and enriched; each is stifled and vitalized. The new intersubjective entity that is created, the subjugating analytic third, becomes a vehicle through which thoughts may be thought, feelings may be felt, sensations may be experienced, which to that point had existed only as potential experiences for each of the individuals participating in this psychological-interpersonal process. In order for psychological growth to occur, there must be a superseding of the subjugating third and the establishment of a new and more generative dialectic of oneness and twoness, similarity and difference, individual subjectivity and intersubjectivity. (Ogden, 2004: 189–90)

Analysis works when the 'third' of the analytic relationship, which Ogden calls a 'new intersubjective entity', allows both analyst and patient to think new thoughts and feel new feelings. This on its own is not enough, however. The patient and analyst must also become able to let go of the third ('there must be a superseding of the subjugating third') without destroying or denying it. They must be able to hold it in play whilst also returning to their individual subjective positions. The resonance of Winnicott is very strong in this material, from the idea that it is only a separate individual who can be 'used' by the subject (as in Winnicott, 1969) to Ogden's claim that it is possible to offer an 'accurate and empathic understanding and interpretation of the transference-countertransference' (Ogden, 2004: 191). In all this, Ogden is holding open the prospect of a mode of being in which one can absorb oneself in the other and then come away from that absorption refreshed and changed, but still alive. This demands a considerable degree of generosity on each subject's part, a willingness to merge with the other and then let go. It is also precipitously dangerous: how much does one have to trust others in order to engage with them in this way, and how can such trust be won? We surely all know that this level of dependence opens up extreme degrees of vulnerability; we were, after all, infants once.

Knowing others so intimately can be a way of taking them over – a point not lost on Winnicott ('One should be able to make a positive

statement of the healthy use of non-communication in the establish-
ment of the feeling of real [*sic*]' (Winnicott, 1963: 184)). This is why
resistance to fully knowing another might be an anticolonial act: 'recognising the individuality' of the other, as Ogden (2004: 191) might have
it. For Judith Butler (2005), such resistance is crucial for the avoidance
of what she calls 'ethical violence'. This does not preclude understanding or recognising the other; it rather makes the *refusal* of telepathic
understanding the basis for such recognition:

> By not pursuing satisfaction and by letting the question remain open,
> even enduring, we let the other live, since life might be understood
> as precisely that which exceeds any account we may try to give of it.
> (Butler, 2005: 42)

For Butler, recognising the other means being aware of the limits of
recognition, which is an ethical act because it 'lets the other live' without forcing her or him to be whole and knowable, without imposing
a kind of narrative integrity that 'may be preferring the seamless-
ness of the story to something we might tentatively call the truth
of the person, a truth that, to a certain degree...might well become
more clear in moments of interruption, stoppage, open-endedness –
in enigmatic articulations that cannot easily be translated into narrative form' (ibid.: 64). This tentative truth is something that can only
be glimpsed, never known; it revolves around an interruption that is
always present, from well before the subject exists. However, the situation is very complex. We let the other exist in order not to engage in
ethical violence. But the other is already split by the presence of the
unconscious. In Butler's account it is specifically the entry of otherness
into the psyche that means it can never be owned by any subject. She
draws vividly on Laplanche (1999) in articulating this idea. Because the
unconscious is the domain of uninterpretability, founded in response
to the untranslated messages of the other, it operates as a site of continued incoherence within the subject, yet also as a site of truth; this
truth being that the subject is always open to otherness, formed in
its image. The agency of the subject is generated by the other's enigmatic embrace. What Butler (2005: 75) calls the 'sociality at the basis of
the "I"' is an obvious foundation for an ethical relationship with the
other: 'I find that my very formation implicates the other in me, that
my own foreignness to myself is, paradoxically, the source of my ethical connection with others' (ibid.: 84). Insisting on one's own integral
identity is a way of doing violence to the self; obliterating the opacity of
the other through knowing too well, through, for example, a thirst for

absolutely transparent 'communication', also amounts to a mode of violence in which the disturbingly interrupted nature of social subjectivity is overlooked.

In dialogue with this, Bracha Ettinger's (2006) adumbration of the 'matrixial borderspace' embodying compassion and responsibility, mentioned in the previous chapter, has considerable resonance. 'Primary compassion and empathy', she asserts (ibid.: 119), 'are interconnected to "hypnotic" and "telepathic" transfer of waves and frequencies, and to trans-inscription and cross-inscription of psychic-mental traces – all matrixial supports for the more articulated and more conscious attitudes of respect, admiration, sorrow, awe, forgiveness, trust and gratitude, and finally the more mature compassion and full empathy, and all contributing to the creative process and to art as *transcryptum*.' Unpacking Ettinger's language is notoriously hard, though the surfacing of telepathy and crypts in this quotation is obviously no accident. Perhaps what is more important at this point is to let the 'hypnotic' and 'telepathic' tendencies of her prose roam across the landscape of uncertainty between and within subjects. Ettinger has developed the notion of 'metramorphosis' to refer to the way borders can be crossed without being removed entirely – an image with obvious political associations but here suggesting that it might be possible to be connected to the other without colonisation taking place. 'Co-habitation' is Butler's (2011) name for this, though Ettinger retains the notion of 'hospitality' even though it has connotations of one subject *owning* the space to which the other is granted access, rather than having something truly shared. In any event, what is key to Ettinger's proposal is the way in which 'I' and 'non-I' are always linked in the matrixial, and that out of and through this linkage comes the connectedness inherent in the telepathic phenomena with which we have been dealing:

> Unexpected empathic induction and transmission, unconscious semi-telepathic and semi-hypnotic influences appearing as intuition and inspiration are revealed in different ways in different individuals (analyst and analysand) along matrixial threads where traces of initiation-in-jointness and initiation-by-jointness are cross-inscripted and trans-inscripted. (Ettinger, 2006: 120)

Whether this is a poetic conjuring up of an aspirational ethical position or a precise fingering of a universal human capacity for connection-in-difference is perhaps open to debate. But Ettinger certainly conveys something of the cloudy mix of what might be thought of as a profound 'in-between' state in which things that are usually kept apart flow together, and knowledge of them is shared.

Overall, there is a paradox at work here. The subject is interrupted and opaque, and knowing fully any subject – whether self or other – is impossible, which might seem to imply that a truly private space can exist. This is the surprise that Derrida imagines Freud to feel. However, precisely this opacity-to-oneself means that one is not 'in control' of such a private space, that here is no privileged knowledge of it available to the subject. Because of this lack of control, leakages of communication always occur. Something is passed from one to the other, over distance, without either interlocutor being clear about what is happening. Opacity is about knowledge, but not about understanding: that is, we may not be able to interpret the communications from self or other, but we are nevertheless subjected to them, in the mode of Laplanche's (1999) enigmatic messages. They travel, these communications, without any obvious means of support.

There is, finally, something threatening about the degree of intersubjective interpenetration assumed by telepathy and thought-transference. Another's unconscious communications come directly into us; can we resist them, will we be overwhelmed by them, will we hold onto our own sanity? Herbert Rosenfeld (1971) describes how projective identification operates and in particular what it might mean to someone to become lost in another. He shows how projective identification can be a way in which the patient attempts to enter into and omnipotently control the analyst. This means not only that the ego-other boundary has been obscured, producing anxieties about loss of self, but also that the patient sees the analyst as having been infected with her or his own madness. Rosenfeld writes (ibid.: 122), 'The analyst is then perceived as having become mad, which arouses extreme anxiety as the patient is afraid that the analyst will retaliate and force the madness back into the patient, depriving him entirely of his sanity. At such times the patient is in danger of disintegration.' This is perhaps the worst type of projective identification, getting rid of the envious destructiveness in the mind at the expense of the mind itself. Perhaps it is also a salutary warning about what happens when the inmixing assumed in psychoanalysis goes too far, when we come face to face with the madness that is intrinsic to encrypted minds, to extreme mental states. At this point, the sanctuary we all seek from invasion by hostile forces might break down, and only the firmest and most independent thinkers can hold their own. Can we survive such a thing? The Talmud tells a famous story about a loss of separateness and the

chances of recovering, under the heading of what happens when one
enters Paradise and comes face to face with the Throne of Glory:

> The Rabbis taught: Four sages entered Paradise. They were Ben Azzai,
> Ben Zoma, Acher [Elisha ben Avuya, called Acher – the other one –
> because of what happened to him] and Rabbi Akiva...Ben Azzai
> gazed at the Divine Presence and died. Regarding him the verse states,
> 'Precious in the eyes of God is the death of His pious ones' (Psalms
> 116:15). Ben Zoma gazed and was harmed [he lost his sanity]. Regard-
> ing him the verse states, 'Did you find honey? Eat only as much as
> you need, lest you be overfilled and vomit it up' (Proverbs 25:16).
> Acher cut down the plantings [he became a heretic]. Rabbi Akiva
> entered in peace and left in peace. (Talmud, Chagigah 14b)

Entering in peace and leaving in peace is possible, but only if you are
Rabbi Akiva, one of the great saints of Judaism. Otherwise, even for
sages, it is immensely dangerous to lose oneself in this way: you die,
go mad or abandon your beliefs. It may seem bathetic to apply this to
the psychoanalytic situation, but if we think about what it means for
people to 'unconsciously subjugate themselves to a mutually generated
intersubjective third', as Ogden puts it, perhaps the anxiety becomes
clear. How precarious might our boundaries be even without this kind
of unconscious subjugation, and how hard might it be to recover them
once we have let them go? Perhaps the lament for Ben Zoma is the one
to take to heart as a warning: 'Did you find honey? Eat only as much
as you need, lest you be overfilled and vomit it up.' If we are truly in
telepathic communication with others, if their unconscious transmissions mesh willy-nilly with our own, we may find out more than we
ever wanted to know.

6
Transmission

The history of a trauma

Discussing transference, which is principally a phenomenon occurring in the clinic between a patient and an analyst, Eliza Slavet notes that it demonstrates how the present becomes filled up with the remnants of the past. These remnants are alive and active, giving them haunting power, the function, once again, of ghosts:

> There is a sense that transference is the key to psychoanalysis, to the invocations of the past which overwhelm the present. The individual herself becomes a sort of test tube where the present and the past, the living and the ghosts, are mixed together, creating potentially explosive reactions... Freud attempted to name these invisible forces – they were ghostly transmissions from the past that took up residence in the individual's psyche and found a home in the unconscious. But in naming these forces, psychoanalysis might also heighten their effects. (Slavet, 2009: 131)

This last point needs to be remembered: as psychoanalysis articulates the ghostly remainders, so it brings them into the light and allows them to act more openly. It makes them potentially workable with, but also exposes them to, the (evil) eye. What troubles people about psychoanalysis could be its failure to politely hide the things it finds to be of value but that so often have sordid elements and associations. In doing this, it makes a stand against the wish to eradicate the past, a wish that was powerfully identified by Adorno and Horkheimer (1947) and that was explicitly linked by them to an envious attack on the dead. Adorno and Horkheimer also make a significant connection with that bubbling undercurrent of psychoanalysis, its 'forgotten' Jewish past. 'In reality', they write (ibid.: 216), 'the dead suffer a fate which the Jews in olden days considered the worst possible curse: they are expunged from the memory of those who live on.' These are precisely the conditions under which haunting occurs.

Slavet (2009) continues her analysis by pointing to the explicit overlaps in Freud's work between transference, telepathy and other forms of transmission. She notes that these overlaps take linguistic, historical and cultural forms:

> *Linguistic* because Freud uses the same root word – *Übertragung* – to refer to transference, telepathic thought-transference, and intergenerational transmission. *Historical* because Freud's meditations on these three forms of transmission were concurrent. In the very same letters in which he confronts the problems and questions of transference and the inheritance of memory, he also considers the possibilities of telepathy and prophecy. *Conceptual* because the images and anxieties are interwoven, repeated, and transformed: Explosive chemical reactions, telephones, foreign bodies, and alien guests haunt Freud's writing not only on these three forms of transmission but also on the unconscious and its symptoms. (Slavet, 2009: 141)

Intergenerational transmission (*Übertragung*), telepathic thought-transference (*Gedankenübertragung*) and transference (*Übertragung*) all have the same linguistic and cultural root; psychoanalysis is consequently saturated with the idea of unconscious transmission from the past to the present, from one generation to another, and from one person to another. That is to say, haunting is something that happens continually, in all different directions. What we are left with here is a network of connections around vertical and horizontal transmission, and a proposed mechanism for theorising this.

It is the intergenerational element that is the primary concern of Freud's late social texts, and particularly *Moses and Monotheism*, which was written in the 1930s. Jacqueline Rose (2007: 84) makes the first important link here. 'We could say', she writes, 'that the question of his Jewish identity propels Freud towards the idea of "transgenerational haunting", a concept forged by the Hungarian émigré analysts Maria Torok and Nicolas Abraham, significantly in the aftermath of this historical moment, as they tried to understand the silent persistence of the Holocaust in the minds of second-generation Jews.' Certainly the issue of Jewish identity is at the centre of much of Freud's thinking in the period in which he wrote *Moses and Monotheism*, precisely the period of the gathering storm of Nazism. But for the moment it is another track that is suggested by this concatenation of transference and transgenerational haunting, namely the question of what happens to traumatic experiences. As Rose notes, the origins of Abraham and Torok's theorisation of cryptography is the question of how the Holocaust persists in the mind. This has continued to be a major issue for those working with second-generation survivors and also, more tentatively and at times apologetically, the children of perpetrators. It is not just the Holocaust, of course, though this is the key modern trauma for Jews and for intellectuals trying to make sense of the triumph of barbarism; it is all trauma in every place that it appears, in all acts of personal violence and political oppression, of colonialism and genocide, of sexual and racial hatred, of the occlusion of historical wrongs and the persistence of their return. *Transference* occurs in the consulting room as something in the personal relationship between patient and analyst. But transference (*Übertragung*) is also transmission; it is the past breaking into the present to force it into its own shape; it is the present chained to the past, not knowing what puppet master is pulling the strings. 'Freud's conceptualizations of transference and inheritance', writes Slavet (2009: 135), 'are not so much "sequences" but constant processes of transmission, unpredictably moving back and forth between individuals, generations and genera. There is compression of time: The past overwhelms the present, even as the present pushes toward the future and calls upon an absent past, present only insofar as it can be imagined.'

This is clearly in some way an account of the history of trauma as it becomes personalised and reproduced from one generation to the next. We have already encountered cryptography in Abraham and Torok's (1976) account of the Wolf Man and in Derrida's (1986) meditation on their discovery. 'The very thing that provokes the worst suffering must be kept alive,' Derrida states (ibid.: xxxv), putting his finger on a recurrent problem in comprehending intergenerational transmission as well as personal psychic suffering. Why should it be that so much of one generation's life is spent managing the difficulties of the previous one? Is there really something hidden that gets encrypted and encapsulated and passed down whole, never really broken into and dispersed but instead sitting there as a kind of lump of burdensome secrecy, creating disturbance, troubling the well-being of each generation? As the Bible says (Exodus 20, 5), 'visiting the iniquity of the fathers upon the children unto the third and fourth generation'? We will come back to the specifics of this question about fathers and children, but the issue is whether there is an unconscious form of transmission – a real haunting – that is embedded in the notion of transference and that inescapably both lies at the heart of trauma and also of the inheritance of identity. To put it differently, perhaps Freud is right in thinking that identity and haunting go together, and if so then we might have to see all identity construction as a mode of traumatic possession. Haunting is then the *norm*, not the pathological exception: the present is always filled out by the past, each generation by those that have come before.

Gabriele Schwab (2010) provides an insight into traumatic inheritance in the case of the children of perpetrators, in this instance postwar generations of Germans. She draws on Abraham and Torok but stresses not so much the hiddenness of the encrypted secret, as the way it leaks:

> Traumatic silences and gaps in language are, if not mutilations and distortions of the signifying process, ambivalent attempts to conceal. But indirectly, they express trauma otherwise shrouded in secrecy or relegated to the unconscious. Cryptographic writing can breathe traces of the transgenerational memory of something never experienced firsthand by the one carrying the secret. It is the children or descendants, Abraham insists, who will be haunted by what is buried in this tomb, even if they do not know of its existence or contents and even if the history that produced the ghost is shrouded in silence. Often the tomb is a familial one, organized around family secrets shared by parents and perhaps grandparents but fearfully guarded from the children. It is through the unconscious transmission of disavowed familial dynamics that one generation affects another generation's unconscious. (Schwab, 2010: 4)

The 'unconscious transmission of disavowed familial dynamics' seems here to be not so much hidden, but rather the observable 'return of the repressed' – ways in which the silences of the first generation haunt the later ones, puzzling them and calling out for some kind of solution. It is as if these silences become gaps in experience or in identity, impossible moments of lack that produce an urgent need to find out, a compulsion to try to create narrative wholeness or closure. Under other circumstances, one might see this kind of seeking as a defensive manoeuvre, undertaken to make it possible to live with uncertainty. Here, however, it seems that the later generations are so close to the 'traumatic silences and gaps in language' that they impact on them in ways that cannot be denied, and as a consequence something has to be done about it. One hopes. Schwab suggests that the children of perpetrators are forced to take action:

> Children of a traumatized parental generation, I argue, become avid readers of silences and memory traces hidden in a face that is frozen in grief, a forced smile that does not feel quite right, an apparently unmotivated flare-up of rage, or chronic depression. Like photography, traumatized bodies reveal their own optical unconscious. It is this unconscious that second-generation children absorb. (Schwab, 2010: 14)

This can have dramatic consequences, in Schwab's view, as the hidden past continues to infect the present, mystifying it at the same time as announcing that something is terribly wrong. The melancholic object, as we saw in Chapter 3, retains its power because it is not recognised or mourned; it is there as a present absence, as something that is not supposed to exist yet in fact does so, casting its baleful shadow over the living as well as the dead. When there is shame attached, perhaps the process is even more potent. 'Silencing these violent and shameful histories', writes Schwab (ibid.: 49), 'casts them outside the continuity of psychic life but, unintegrated and unassimilated, they eat away at this continuity from within. Lives become shadow lives, simulacra of a hollowed-out normality.' It is hard to recover from such a position. Silence surrounds the subject yet also speaks through the gaps and fragments of language; Schwab (ibid.: 54) lists 'metaphor, metonymy, homophony, homonymy, puns, semantic ambiguities, malapropisms, anagrams, and rebus and similar figures that all combine concealment and revelation'. This explosion of silence and speech is much the same as what happens in the routine practice of psychoanalysis, where the patient secretes meaning in the very act of denying it. Yet here, in this politically charged intergenerational site, it has existential status.

In a keynote address to the International Psychoanalytic Association Congress of 2007, Werner Bohleber (2007) offered a subtle and open account of the history of collective remembrance in postwar Germany, tracing the difficulties, lies and silences within and between the generations. His paper was given great piquancy by its geographical location: the first International Psychoanalytic Association Congress in Berlin, and only the second in Germany, since the Second World War. Much of the piece is concerned with theories of memory and trauma, but the final section deals with the issue that Schwab also raises – the search by later generations of Germans for some kind of filling-in of the gaps in their understanding. They knew something was wrong, but could not lay their hands on it. They were not helped in this by the refusals of their parents, which amounted to a rewriting of history in which the perpetrator generation denied its participation in Nazism and turned itself 'into the victims of Hitler and a small group of fanatical followers and culprits' (Bohleber, 2007: 345). As Bohleber points out, this field was extensively examined in Mitscherlich and Mitscherlich's (1975) *The Inability to Mourn*, which uses the language of melancholia to examine postwar German societal pathologies and enactments. Bohleber comments (2007: 345), 'The apologetic victim-consciousness that members of the perpetrating generation retroactively created for themselves was fuelled from both sources – the defensive repudiation of guilt and the traumatic experiences themselves.'

It is the effect of these processes of denial on the children of the perpetrators that interests Bohleber in his presentation. 'The silence concerning their own participation and gaps in family biographies had produced a hazy and partly distorted sense of reality in the children,' he writes (ibid.: 345–6). 'The parents' repudiated self-reflection also frequently prevented a critical engagement with national socialist ideals and moral concepts to which they had subscribed. Many assured themselves of their validity through a narcissistic functionalization of their children, in whom any different kind of attitude was fiercely attacked.' This left members of the later generation with few options other than either to remain silent and buy into their parents' defences, or to oppose them fully, often with violence, but still without analysing or coming to terms with what was occurring within their own family relationships. Even as German society gradually officially recognised its complicity in the Holocaust, Bohleber claims, the second generation could not rid itself of its attachments to the 'fathers' who had actually committed the crimes or compromised with them. The split identification with these fathers – idealisation and denigration – blocked movement forward: Bohleber argues that the children's impulse towards truth-seeking was constantly opposed by defences against finding anything out, leading to complicity with the parents' denial of guilt. Bohleber eventually concludes, soberly, 'in many cases, clarification and reconstruction has only so far been possible in a very fragmentary way, since the parents' silence could not be broken or the children instigated the clarification too late rather than within their parents' lifetimes' (ibid.: 348). At the end of his address, Bohleber asserts that the new 'third generation' 'takes its own more independent view of the events and the family involvements' (ibid.). This may be the case, but what is perhaps most striking in this piece is its commentary on the way in which the first generation's secrecy colonises the next generation, which can only act it out in acceptance or violent repudiation, or both. It is clear, one should note, that a great deal of reconciliation and mourning work has gone on in German society over the long period since the end of the Third Reich; but it is equally clear that something continues to trouble its citizens, and that this breaks out from time to time to mark the culture as one still harbouring its silences and its ghosts.

In this environment, some observations by Cathy Caruth about the question of survival from trauma provide a link with the broader issues of transmission. Caruth (1995) examines Freud's (1920) *Beyond the Pleasure Principle* for its engagement with the question of traumatic return, specifically the literalness of the traumatic dream. As many analysts have noted, it is this literalness that is perhaps the hallmark of trauma: the traumatic event is not symbolised but, as the Lacanians might say, remains in the Real. This means that it is inaccessible but also that it keeps coming back, disrupting everything, a threatening hollow at the heart of whatever is held dear. It ceases therefore to be *history* at all, in the sense that it is never properly represented; it is rather an unrecognised past that saturates the present, with both individual and social-historical significance. 'The traumatized, we might say, carry an impossible history within them, or they become themselves the symptom of a history that they cannot entirely possess' (Caruth, 1995: 5).

Caruth goes on to emphasise the time lag in trauma, the way it is marked by a prevailing belatedness or 'latency': 'The historical power of the trauma is not just that the experience is repeated after its forgetting, but that it is only in and through its inherent forgetting that it is first experienced at all' (ibid.: 8). The inherently unsymbolisable nature of trauma is what is being described here, giving it its backward temporality. There is an event, and it is traumatic to the extent that it is not recognised as such but becomes repressed and silenced. It is inaccessible, yet it continues to operate; the psyche wrestles with it and unconsciously identifies with it. When it occurs, its significance passes the subject by; but later, it cannot be avoided, it keeps cropping up, and yet is nowhere to be found. If one thinks about this schematically, it becomes clear that what is being described is some kind of crisis that creates the structure within which later events take place. The backwards referentiality, the becoming-real that is only possible because an original act has been occluded and foreclosed, is exactly what makes society function. This is perhaps one of the things that Freud (1913) was getting at with his idea of the killing of the primal father: a repressed secret is necessary for the founding of society. Seeing psychoanalysis as a therapeutic social intervention, Freud aims to draw attention to this secret and bring it into the light of reason. As Rose (2007: 78) puts it in relation to the later text, *Moses and Monotheism*, Freud wanted 'the Jewish people, and through them all people, to imagine the unimaginable – to contemplate the possibility that the most binding social ties are forged through an act of violence'. What kind of violence would this be? Freud's (1913: 157) answer is characteristic of someone steeped in concerns with authority, power and betrayal (he was writing at the time of his break-up with Jung): 'It seems to me a most surprising discovery that the problems of social psychology, too, should prove soluble on the basis of one single concrete point – man's relation to his father.'

The cultural inheritance of paternal violence

The question here is how transmission occurs, how each generation lives its life not just in the light and shadow of its predecessors, but also as a function of its own hidden past. From Laplanche (1999) we have the idea of an untranslatable message that is passed down from parent to child, something exciting and troublesome that the infant takes in but can do nothing with. Laplanche sees this as a mode of sexual seduction. From the trauma theories we have another dimension: that what is too terrible to symbolise becomes encrypted, hidden away in a place where it is inaccessible, but from where it continues manifesting itself, leaking out and perhaps eventually taking the subject over. This is a personal and relational issue, but also a sociohistorical one; whole cultures are driven this way, re-enacting the founding violence that lies at their source. And according to Freud at least, much of this violence is of the paternal variety.

Although Freud's major exploration of the 'primal father' in *Totem and Taboo* used the general 'civilised-savage' dichotomy adopted by colonialist anthropology, by the time the Nazis came he was addressing in detail his lifelong interest in the Biblical figure of Moses and, through that, the more specific question of Jewish identity. Echoing his view of the content of the 'original' trauma, Freud's motif in relation to his use of Biblical sources was that of a covering-over, in which he sees them as embodying evidence of an act of violence, even of a crime. He writes that the texts concerning Moses show evidence of their being 'mutilated and amplified' in the interests of orthodox readings, yet still preserve their 'otherwiseness' (Felman, 1982) in 'noticeable gaps, disturbing repetitions and obvious contradictions' (Freud, 1939: 43). These are, according to Freud (ibid.), 'indications which reveal things to us which it was not intended to communicate. In its implications', he writes, 'the distortion of a text resembles a murder: the difficulty is not in perpetrating the deed, but in getting rid of its traces.' Whether in subtle distortions or visible undercurrents of dispute, religious texts commonly reveal the uncertainties and ambivalences that go into their construction, but are then repressed ('murdered') to produce an acceptable mode of orthodoxy. Tracing these traces, exploring where they lead, is thus a way to unpick the official story that a community might tell about itself. As in the psychoanalytic encounter, when this happens what is often revealed is an undercurrent of disowned things, of secrets one might not usually want to know, yet that are there all the time, pressing for release.

Whilst Freud's focus is on the story of Moses, this is not the obvious location for paternal violence in the Bible. The primary father, at least for the Jews, was Abraham rather than Moses, and the Ur-story is that of the 'Binding of Isaac' (Genesis 22). This has already been touched on and a variant reading given of it, that of the 'compassion' of the son for his father. What is more familiar and more persistent in its resonance, however, is its violence. The narrative runs as follows. Abraham has just about put all his complex affairs in order and seems to be settled in the land of the Philistines. He has had two children in his old age. One of them, Ishmael, born of a maidservant, has been sent into the wilderness; the other one, Isaac, the child of Abraham's wife Sarah, is to be his successor, through whom God's promise of future fertility is to be fulfilled. Out of nowhere ('after these things') God speaks to Abraham and demands that he take Isaac to Mount Moriah, three days' journey away, and offer him up there as a burnt offering. Abraham does this without question, and Isaac complies. When they are on the mountain alone together, Abraham binds Isaac tightly to a pile of wood (hence the name 'binding' or 'Akedah' for this event) and takes a knife to slay him. At that moment, an angel intervenes, commanding (verse 12), 'Abraham, Abraham, lay not your hand on the lad, nor do anything to him.' Abraham desists and then has his attention drawn by the angel to a ram caught in a thicket by its horns. He releases Isaac and sacrifices the ram instead, for which reason Jews use a ram's horn as a shofar or trumpet on Rosh Hashanah, the New Year.

This story, which is absolutely central to Jewish readings of Abraham as a man of ideal and unbounded faith, is also important in a different version for Moslems. The Akedah is iconic in Western culture too, and not only because Christianity treated it as a forerunner of the Golgotha story, claiming the actual sacrifice and resurrection of Jesus as superior to the aborted sacrifice of Isaac. For Kierkegaard (quoted in Zornberg,

2009: 169), 'There were countless generations who knew the story of Abraham by heart, word for word, but how many did it render sleepless?' The horror and disturbance of the piece troubles, it seems, much of the world's dreams. Wilfred Owen made it into one of the greatest poems of the First World War, the 'Parable of the Old Man and the Young' (1918). In his case, however, the ending was expressively, and as will be seen in some ways accurately, different:

> When lo! an angel called him out of heaven,
> Saying, Lay not thy hand upon the lad,
> Neither do anything to him. Behold,
> A ram, caught in a thicket by its horns;
> Offer the Ram of Pride instead of him.
> But the old man would not so, but slew his son,
> And half the seed of Europe, one by one. (Owen, 1918: 61)

Despite these broad cultural resonances, one does not need to move outside Judaism for the significance of the Akedah as a template for intergenerational transmission of trauma and identity. Religiously, it is crucial in marking the confirmation of God's covenant with Abraham. Abraham passes this final 'test' of his faith, the tenth such test, and God rewards him in a way that resounds down history: 'in blessing I will bless thee, and in multiplying I will multiply thy seed as the stars of the heaven, and as the sand which is upon the sea-shore' (Genesis 22, 16ff). But there is a more sombre resonance of the Akedah too, as the paradigmatic example of how to face the final test of one's existence, which at times of extreme duress has been the model for action by Jews whose lives were threatened. Shalom Spiegel (1967), in his comprehensive account of the Akedah in Jewish history, documents in great detail instances in which the readiness of Abraham to sacrifice his son was concretely re-enacted by Jewish communities suffering extreme persecution, notably in Roman and Crusader times – events that are recollected in prayers and lamentations that entered the Jewish canon. For example, Spiegel offers liturgical material from the time of the Crusades that uses the Akedah as a motif, often implicitly or explicitly posing a direct question: why when God was moved to save one person, did He do nothing when so many were murdered?

> Once at the Akedah of one on Mount Moriah, the Lord shook the world to its base! ... O heavens, why did you not go black, O stars, why did you not withdraw your light, O sun and moon, why did you

not darken in your sky? When in one day one thousand and one hundred pure souls were slain and slaughtered! Oh the spotless babes and sucklings, innocent of all sin, oh the innocent lives! Wilt thou hold thy peace in the face of these things, O Lord? (Spiegel, 1967: 20)

Spiegel points out how this material not only draws on the Akedah but also suggests that the generations faced by these massacres saw themselves as having undergone a greater trial than Abraham: 'Ask ye now, and see, was there ever such a holocaust as this *since the days of Adam?*' (ibid.: 19–20). Adam, not Abraham; that is, this tragedy was greater than that of the Akedah. But the model of Abraham's behaviour as the father who would actually have killed his son is exactly the model that some – perhaps many – took. Spiegel gives several examples, including one from Worms, where 800 Jews died in two days of destruction in 1096. The records describe how Meshullam, a respected member of the besieged community, took his son and called out, 'All ye great and small, hearken unto me. Here is my son whom God gave me and to whom my wife Zipporah gave birth *in her old age*, Isaac is the child's name; and now I shall offer him up *as Father Abraham offered up his son Isaac.*' Zipporah then intervened to try to stop the killing: 'O my lord, my lord, *do not lay thy hand upon the lad...*' But the father did not stop: '*And he bound his son Isaac, and picked up the knife to slay his son,* and recited the blessing appropriate for slaughter. And the lad replied, "Amen." And the father slew the lad' (ibid.: 24). Meshullam and his wife then ran out and were murdered. Amongst the many striking things about this documentary record is the direct use of the exact words from the Biblical account (italicised in the quotation); the Akedah becomes a template for the sacrifice of the son. Of course there is a difference in that the boy is killed by his father to prevent him falling into the hands of the mob; but it is also a religious act, a way in which the Jews of that time and place set themselves within the narrative trajectory of their traumatic history, starting with the first Jew of all, 'Father Abraham'. And it is also an accusation: 'Over such as these, wilt Thou hold Thy peace, O Lord?' (ibid.: 25).

There is a lot of complexity in the attitudes expressed in the material Spiegel presents, some of which are recapitulated in theological responses to the Holocaust. These attitudes range from a passionate indictment of God for not intervening to prevent slaughter, even though loss of *faith* never seems to be an issue, to using the Akedah as the precedent for sacrificing one's son if one has to – hence making the acts of the persecuted generation continuous with those of Abraham. The traditional interpretation, however, is at variance with many of these attitudes. For the classical rabbis, the Akedah should be read first as a test of Abraham's willingness to give up his most precious possession for the sake of God; and second as an injunction *against* child sacrifice. The rabbinic commentators insist that the Akedah demonstrates the *superiority* of Judaism in rejecting the child sacrifices that were common practice amongst the surrounding peoples of the time. This is no small feat and occurs not without struggle; and the rabbis repeatedly show sensitivity to it. Indeed, they go to great lengths to assert the superiority of animal over human sacrifice, resonating with the psychoanalytic idea of the superiority of the symbolic over the concrete. There is frequent reiteration in the rabbinic literature of the idea that in replacing the ram with Isaac, it is *as though* Isaac has been sacrificed. The ram symbolises Isaac and in this way converts a practice that has become abhorrent into one that is acceptable to God. Spiegel quotes several Talmudic examples on this, concluding (ibid.: 73) that, 'The Akedah story declared war on *the remnant of idolatry in Israel* and undertook to remove root and branch the whole long, terror-laden inheritance from idolatrous generations.'

This much is clear, yet there is evidence that even though the classical view is strong and dominant, traces remain of something else – a tradition that Isaac actually died and was brought back to life. First there is the ram itself, which was created on the world's first Sabbath eve in order to serve its purpose, and was too valuable to disappear as a whole burnt offering, despite the fact that this was exactly what happened to it. On the one hand, the ram was sacrificed and burnt to ashes; on the other, every bit of it was used for a holy purpose, from the tendons that would become the strings of King David's harp, to the skin that was worn by the Prophet Elijah, to its two horns, one of which was sounded at the Revelation on Mount Sinai and the other of which will sound in the days of the Messiah. How to manage this dilemma? By assuming that the ram was resurrected after it had been burnt. 'The ram Abraham offered up was indeed completely consumed as a burnt offering unto the Lord, but out of its very ashes it was restored anew, miraculously' (Spiegel, 1967: 40).

And if this could happen to the ram, then why not to Isaac himself? The obvious textual problem that Abraham was prohibited from harming his son is matched by another textual difficulty: what then did happen to Isaac? On the way to the mountain, the text states twice (verses 6 and 8): 'they went both of them together'. After the Akedah, however, it states (verse 19): 'So Abraham returned unto his young men.' In the next chapter, when Sarah dies, there is also no mention of Isaac; so what could have happened to him? Spiegel quotes various naturalistic explanations offered by the rabbis (he went by another route, he remained on Mount Moriah for three years until he reached the age of 40, and then he married Rebeccah). But some commentators suggested a more radical solution, which we encountered in Chapter 4: Isaac had actually been sacrificed, and just like the ram he was awaiting his return to life. 'And Isaac, where was he? The Holy One, blessed be He, brought him into the Garden of Eden, and there he stayed three years... R. Judah says: When the sword touched Isaac's throat his soul flew clean out of him. And when He let His voice be heard from between the two cherubim, "Lay not thy hand upon the lad," the lad's soul returned to his body. Then his father unbound him, and Isaac rose, knowing that in this way the dead would come back to life in the future; whereupon he began to recite, Blessed are thou O Lord who quickens the dead' (Spiegel, 1967: 30). We also know from the quotation given in Chapter 4 that some rabbis associated the phrase 'one bead of thy necklace' from the Song of Songs (4, 9) with the mark left by the knife on Isaac's neck; an alternative account is that even though Abraham did not slay his son with the knife, he left him to *burn*, reducing him to ashes. Spiegel points out that this would have happened if after restraining himself, Abraham genuinely did *nothing* to Isaac; as he had already bound him to the burning pyre, 'why, in a twinkling the whole pile went up in a blaze and the flames of fire had Isaac to themselves and "he was reduced to ashes" and dust' (Spiegel, 1967: 36). There are indeed many references to the 'ashes of Isaac' in rabbinic literature, for example to explain the custom of putting ashes on the head of a mourner, all of which attest to the continuing echoes of the idea that Isaac was actually sacrificed and then returned to life. The point here is not to reread the Akedah in opposition to the rabbis: over time, they had their way and symbolism (albeit in the material form of animal sacrifice) triumphed over the desire for human sacrifice. Nevertheless, this seems to have been a hard-won battle and one that perhaps had an ironic turn when later Jews found themselves enacting not the staying of Abraham's hand, but the sacrificial act.

There is a lot more that could be said about the Akedah, and indeed there is an immense religious and psychoanalytic literature on the topic. But this is enough for now. The key points are first the residue of paternal violence, and second the way this works through history. On the first, we have sufficient material to suggest that the subjugated narrative of Isaac's actual death survived. Not only has this been picked up in Christianity (which is presumably one reason why it was repressed by Jews), but it is also a genuine element in Jewish myth-making. More psychologically minded commentators also recognise that what is going on in the text is a very difficult and uncertain struggle between the impulse to protect and the impulse to murder. Aviva Zornberg (2009) notes that the early rabbinic commentators tell a story of Abraham's youth in which he destroys his father Terach's idols and is put in a furnace by the ruler Nimrod as a consequence. Abraham survives this, but his brother Haran, copying Abraham, does not. Zornberg argues that this is read by the rabbis as a filicide, the murder of his son by Terach, and that awareness of this as a flaw in paternity is something that haunts Abraham. For the rabbis, this mode of human sacrifice may have been what marked the idolatrous world that Abraham left; for Abraham in the story, the leaving of it was not yet absolutely secure. Zornberg comments:

> In all his apparently random wanderings, he is fated to reach that place. For what has been implanted in him – the father who kills his son – will have to undergo a *test*: something implicit in his past, an 'unthought known', will have to be unfolded, lived through in the present, so that it can finally assume its proper place in the past. (Zornberg, 2009: 193)

The test therefore is of whether Abraham can resolve the violence implicit in fatherhood. In a savage reversal of Freud that is also psychically accurate, the classical commentators understood a father's murderous envy of his sons. (They also, it seems, understood a son's complicity in this: as Isaac was, according to Rashi, 37 years old at the time of the Akedah, he must have participated willingly in the events being narrated.) Additionally, whilst it is true that as a consequence of the Akedah God's promise of protection to Abraham and his descendents is confirmed, there is also evidence that Abraham is punished for his willingness to revisit the trauma of paternal violence on his child. As scholars have often noted, the shock of the Akedah is such that Abraham's wife Sarah dies when she hears of it, and Abraham himself loses the capacity to talk to God or to his son, for he is never recorded as doing so again. Perhaps his sacrificial zeal is too much for him and his family, and for the interpreters of texts. This is a scandalous reading from the perspective of orthodoxy, but in tune with the psychoanalytic perspective that textual traces constantly flag up repressed secrets. The cryptologists know this: cryptographic writing allows hidden material to seep through so that it can be felt, if not easily acknowledged. This is true too for the intergenerational transmission of trauma, where it is the gaps and silences, the obvious bits that are missing from the narratives of lives, which lead younger generations to hunt for the truth or to repeat the trauma. Shwab's (2010: 4) premise, noted above, references this: 'Traumatic silences and gaps in language... express trauma otherwise shrouded in secrecy or relegated to the unconscious.'

The second point is about the historical continuity in the story. At times of extreme duress, of which there have been many, Jews have called upon the Akedah and identified themselves with it – or at least with the violent, subjugated version in which Isaac actually dies. Of course this has been to lament and also to avoid what seemed to be worse, the giving-over of children to the murderous mob and the certain death that would then follow anyway. But it is also a psychological and spiritual state of identification that is evoked when the Akedah is called upon in this way. The identification is specifically with the protagonists in the Akedah story, but also with the trauma of history itself, as if to say, 'we knew all along that we were likely to be called, and have prepared ourselves for this day. Now we are at one with what has gone before and with what will come later. We know exactly what is hidden in the crypt; the beast has broken forth, and is at our throats.'

Inheritance

It might seem relatively straightforward to account for the kinds of cultural transmission described here in terms of explicit mechanisms of communication and identification from parents to children, and also from material practices in the wider society influencing the perceptions and assumptions of each individual in relatively similar ways. If Jews choose to use the Akedah as a template for their response to suffering, it is because of the textual power of the original Biblical material and commentaries and the reiterated homilies that result in Abraham being taken as an identificatory model in Jewish culture. There is also a broader point that some fundamental challenges face every human subject and so it should not be surprising if a relatively restricted range of responses to them is uncovered. All humans have to deal with birth, hunger, separation, sex, loss and death, so it should be no surprise if they develop roughly similar fantasies and material practices to enable them to do so.

Freud accepts the force of this kind of environmental account of transmission. Addressing the claim that there is an 'archaic heritage' that passes automatically between generations, he considers the possibility that it is better explained by the biological tendency of each person to react in a similar way to the events of their lives. He notes

(1939: 98), 'The immediate and most certain answer is that it consists in certain [innate] dispositions such as are characteristic of all living organisms: in the capacity and tendency, that is, to enter particular lines of development and to react in a particular manner to certain excitations, impressions and stimuli... Now, since all human beings, at all events in their early days, have approximately the same experiences, they react to them, too, in a similar manner.' Freud, however, was nowhere near satisfied with such explanations. The passage just quoted concludes in favour of acceptance of the notion of an 'archaic heritage' in which there is inbuilt knowledge of certain events that have occurred in the history of civilisation in general and (in *Moses and Monotheism*, with its focus on the Jews) in the experience of a particular people. Freud (1939: 80) has already 'invited' his readers 'to take the step of supposing that something occurred in the life of the human species similar to what occurs in the life of individuals'. Now he becomes more assertive and definite:

> When we study the reactions to early traumas, we are quite often surprised to find that they are not strictly limited to what the subject himself has really experienced but diverge from it in a way which fits in much better with the model of a phylogenetic event and, in general, can only be explained by such an influence. The behaviour of neurotic children towards their parents in the Oedipus and castration complex abounds in such reactions, which seem unjustified in the individual case and only become intelligible phylogenetically – by their connection with the experience of earlier generations. (Freud, 1939: 99)

Freud here identifies what he regards as a key reason why the more obvious explanations of transmission are inadequate: that the reaction of the individual to a specific set of circumstances very often seems not to be linked clearly either to the nature of that circumstance or to 'what the subject himself has really experienced'. There is also an argument to *intensity*, in the sense that the degree of attachment to certain behaviours seems to Freud to be inexplicable if one only considers contemporaneous events and personal experiences. Religion is the clearest instance of this. Freud argues that it is insufficient to think that religion is perpetuated merely by being communicated by one generation to another. Given the irrationality of religious belief, such communications 'would be listened to, judged, and perhaps dismissed, like any other piece of information from outside; it would never attain the privilege of being liberated from the constraint of logical thought' (ibid.: 101).

Rather, the underpinnings of religious belief must lie in repressed material, shared across people so that it can 'bring the masses under its
spell' (ibid.). For Freud, only what is repressed can return with the force
required to ensure neurotic attachment to irrational ideas. Religion relies
on this for its sustenance and so do other unaccountable commitments
and madly held positions, including the most problematic forms of
social identity.

It is on the basis of arguments of this kind that Freud feels he cannot do without the assumption that something is passed down directly
through the generations, unmediated by experience and not explicable
by 'direct communication and of the influence of education' (ibid.). His
full statement of this demonstrates his complete awareness that he is
holding to a view that will itself seem irrational and that is at variance,
by the mid 1930s, with the collective view of evolution held in scientific
communities. But never mind, he thinks; the truth has to be maintained
even if no-one else sees it that way:

> When I spoke of the survival of a tradition among a people or of the
> formation of a people's character, I had mostly in mind an inherited
> tradition of this kind and not one transmitted by communication. Or
> at least I made no distinction between the two and was not clearly
> aware of my audacity in neglecting to do so. My position, no doubt,
> is made more difficult by the present attitude of biological science,
> which refuses to hear of the inheritance of acquired characters by
> succeeding generations. I must, however, in all modesty confess that
> nevertheless I cannot do without this factor in biological evolution.
> (Freud, 1939: 99–100)

'In all modesty' means that Freud is confident that his view of evolution is accurate, whatever the scientific evidence might suggest –
an attitude that did not endear him to his many critics. His view of
what is passed down is very precise and concrete: the 'inherited tradition' to which he refers comprises 'not only dispositions but also
subject-matter – memory-traces of the experience of earlier generations'
(ibid.: 99). In summary, 'We must finally make up our minds to adopt
the hypothesis that the psychical precipitates of the primaeval period
became inherited property which, in each fresh generation, called not
for acquisition but only for awakening' (ibid.: 132).

Freud's account of what the detailed content of these archaic memories might be is well known and needs little elaboration here, though it
is worth stressing the centrality of the father to the whole story. Briefly,

in *Totem and Taboo* (Freud, 1913), he argues that civilisation is set in motion when an original 'primal father' who possesses all the women in his troop or 'horde', is murdered and then eaten by his sons. Because they felt not only hate for their father, but also love, the murder haunts them and encourages them, out of guilt and remorse, to set the father up as a 'totem' and to incorporate his terror within them. As with the development of the individual's superego, what had been an external authority was incorporated internally as a sense of guilt, more powerful and unassailable for all that. In addition, to prevent a repetition of the primal situation, the brothers, under the shadow of the totem, imposed certain rules on themselves to regulate their relations and restrain their passions. 'The dead father became stronger than the living one had been,' asserts Freud (1913: 143). 'What had up to then been prevented by his actual existence was thenceforward prohibited by the sons themselves, in accordance with the psychological procedure so familiar to us in psycho-analyses under the name of "deferred obedience".' Freud uses this both as a 'just-so' story to account for the origins of civilisation and as a model for his notions of acquired inheritance: in every generation, the same ambivalence towards the primal father, the same sense of guilty and murderous envy, is present in every human subject. These intergenerational links are insufficiently explained by overt modes of social transmission; rather, there is an inherited disposition to repeat the traumatic original event, triggered into action by some experience in the actual life of the individual concerned.

In a manner reminiscent of his account of thought-transference, Freud assumes the existence of a mental mechanism that allows each individual unmediated access to another's unconscious, and through this he assumes that every generation opens up a communicational channel through which the original traumatic killing of the father is passed down. 'For psycho-analysis has shown us', he writes (ibid.: 159), 'that everyone possesses in his unconscious mental activity an apparatus which enables him to interpret other people's reactions, that is, to undo the distortions which other people have imposed on the expression of their feelings. An unconscious understanding such as this of all the customs, ceremonies and dogmas left behind by the original relation to the father may have made it possible for later generations to take over their heritage of emotion.'

By the time of *Moses and Monotheism*, written over twenty years later, the archaic heritage hypothesis has both hardened and been made more specific. Here the primal father is Moses, the murder of whom by the Hebrews is given more psychic force because it is a recapitulation of the original murder of the father of the primal horde. Freud argued that the Moses of the Exodus who liberated the band of slaves was an Egyptian monotheist; the impossible demands he then placed upon his new people led to them murdering him. However, the guilt attached to this percolated down through the generations. When a second Moses arose, the two stories were then amalgamated to give the Biblical myth. What is important in this wild account, deeply held by Freud but already known by him to be extravagantly speculative, is that the killing of Moses is the traumatic moment that fixes Jewish identity in place. Every Jew, no matter how assimilated or distanced from the specifics of the tradition, has inherited the psychic memory of the event, and it is this that pulls Jews together and away from others, as a chosen people eliciting envious antisemitism in the peoples around them, and never able to escape their destiny. More broadly still, as Caruth (1996: 18) notes, 'The indirect referentiality of history is also . . . at the core of Freud's understanding of the political shape of Jewish culture, in its repeated confrontation with anti-Semitism. For the murder of Moses, as Freud argues, is in fact a repetition of an earlier murder in the history of mankind, the murder of the primal father by his rebellious sons, which occurred in primeval history; and it is the unconscious repetition and acknowledgement of this fact that explains both Judaism and its Christian antagonists.'

Something unsettling arises from all this. It is perhaps attractive to postulate the existence of a secret route straight back to the origins of humankind, lodged within each one of us. It provides a simple basis for understanding what otherwise are disturbingly intense feelings and erratically self-destructive actions. More romantically, it offers an explanatory account of the pull towards identity that seems continually to call on people in the most unexpected way. Rose (2007: 84) makes a link between Freud's own Jewish identifications and his attempt in *Moses and Monotheism* to account for the perseverance of Jewishness even after Judaism and all the trappings of Jewish affiliation have apparently been abandoned. The relevant quote is from Freud's famous 1926 letter to the B'nai B'rith in Vienna, acknowledging the importance of that organisation in the formative years of psychoanalysis. Despite his lack of religious belief or attachment to Zionism and his resistance to what he calls 'feelings of national exaltation', he states: 'But there remained enough to make the attraction of Judaism and the Jews irresistible, many dark emotional powers all the stronger the less they could be expressed in words, as well as the clear consciousness of an inner identity, the familiarity of the same psychological structure' (Freud, 1961: 368). What are these 'dark emotional powers' and this 'clear consciousness of an inner identity' if not something passed down, something that has been attained painfully in previous generations and is now part of the unavoidable inheritance of every Jewish individual? Freud might, therefore, have been explaining his own psychic resonance with Jewishness when postulating this specific mechanism of transmission.

The idea that there might be a way of directly inheriting the outcomes of a primal event is part of the general notion of the possibility of 'inheritance of acquired characteristics' known as Lamarckianism. Freud's adoption of this view, like his belief in telepathy, was for Jones and others an embarrassing slip, though there is also some evidence that this need not be the case if one considers it in its full historical context. For Yosef Hayim Yerushalmi (1991), the continuity of Jewish identity is attested to by the pervasive Lamarckian assumptions in *Moses and Monotheism* – the idea that specific 'learned' characteristics can be passed down through the generations, so that all Jews share not just a sense of a past history but the actual memory trace of that history, embodied and internalised, and linking them with one another through a mysterious yet material bond. Yerushalmi may have had his own axe to grind, intent as he was on recovering Freud for Jewish tradition; certainly he is at odds with Edward Said (2003), for whom Freud's act in making Moses an Egyptian has the effect of asserting a brokenness within Jewish communal identity that traumatically disrupts any idea of the continuity of national history. But the question of how memory operates as an unending sore – how, if one can think of it this way, Jewish inheritance can be *melancholic* – does seem to have exercised Freud avidly. Lamarckianism expressively dramatises the complications here, because it both asserts the force of inheritance and contests its irremediability. Yerushalmi's reading sees Lamarckianism as a mechanism underpinning the immutability of Jewish identity. Slavet (2009), however, explains how Lamarckianism was respectable in the 1920s as a potentially *environmental* alternative to radical Darwinism. She argues that at the time Freud was writing *Moses and Monotheism*, the attraction of Lamarckianism was that it offered the prospect that changes in social conditions could produce long-lasting alterations in the characteristics of a people – so that the attributes of Jewishness, specifically, were not necessarily fixed for all time. For this reason, Lamarckianism lined up with Jews and Bolsheviks; neo-Darwinism with antisemitism and the Nazis:

> In the 1920s and '30s, many Jewish scientists turned to Lamarckism to counter racist anti-semitism, particularly as Weismannism [the

theory that inheritance occurs through the germ cells] was used more and more to support anti-semitic politics and policies. For Jews, Lamarckism seemed to support the idea that the negative characteristics and conditions associated with being Jewish were the result of malleable environmental conditions (specifically, centuries of anti-semitism) rather than of *a priori* differences perpetuated by hard-wired heredity... Thus, while Jews were often stereotypically associated with Bolshevism, they were often drawn to it partly by a shared logic of Lamarckian environmentalism supporting the idea that the inequities of the present were determined by historical conditions that could and should be changed in the future. (Slavet, 2009: 78)

Things could change, albeit not easily. The adoption of a Lamarckian framework allowed Freud both to emphasise supposedly historical events and a mode of biological or 'racial transmission'. Memories of real occurrences could be passed on from one generation to another, unconsciously fixing Jewishness as a shared cultural identity not dependent on beliefs or attitudes adopted by any particular person. Those 'dark emotional powers' binding Jews together are somehow transmitted across the ages, as well as having a tangible presence between people who otherwise have little to do with one another. Given the right circumstances – antisemitic Europe, for example – they come to the fore, pressing Jews into identification with one another and renewing their fantasies and archaic fears.

Despite all this, one has to wonder why Freud argued that primeval inheritance and Lamarckianism was a more satisfying explanation of the transmission of values, identities and complexes than would be either a more psychological account of primal fantasy (shared fantasies that people draw on when dealing with psychic challenges) or the simpler view that gives pre-eminence to cultural materials and specific intergenerational identifications. After all, as many authors have shown, Freud himself knew that important elements of Jewish identity were not automatically transmitted. Circumcision is the prime instance here: according to Freud it is central to male Jewish identity and cultural affinity, yet it has to be enacted in every single individual instance, for otherwise the psychic markings of circumcision do not appear (Slavet, 2009; Geller, 2007). Rosine Perelberg (2009) is only one of many modern commentators eager to demonstrate that the Lamarckian hypothesis is unnecessary even for Freud's account of the continuing influence of the 'murdered father', let alone for Jewish identity. Her alternative is a familiar one (ibid.: 722): 'Unconscious phantasies, primary repression and primary identification (with both parents . . .) suggest that the infant is born into a triangular structure that precedes him, and it is in the context of that structure that he will form his identifications. What is highlighted is the unconscious and the desire of the parents.' This essentially classical view of how each subject is born into a pre-existing structure is mixed with a Laplanchian image of how the (m)other's desire enters into the subject as an enigmatic kernel. It suggests a complex but nevertheless material mechanism whereby transmission occurs: the structure (the Lacanian symbolic) is already there, positioning each subject within it. The seductive, sexualised unconscious desire of the adult also pre-exists the child, and is formative of its unconscious life. Even without this relatively modern psychoanalytic lexicon, why could Freud not simply have said that each generation unconsciously passes on its fantasies and fears to the next?

There is too much psychoanalysis of Freud around in the world, understanding everything about his theory in terms of his personal foibles and fascinations. But maybe there is room for one more. Jacqueline Rose (2007) argues that the purpose of his Lamarckianism was to account for Jewish identity ('It is, we could say, through Jewishness or *for Jewishness* that Freud's Lamarckianism also survives' (ibid.: 84)) and that this has to be understood as a personal quest for Freud, divorced from questions of belief. By the 1930s, she thinks, Freud has moved from a kind of cultural therapeutics in which psychoanalytic rationalism can conquer social unreason, to a more limited ambition of explaining why and how groups stay together and identity is passed on, 'To understand why people, from generation to generation – with no solid ground and in the teeth of the most historically unsympathetic conditions – *hold on*' (ibid.: 83). As Rose hints, there is something very personal in all this. Freud was at pains at times to deny his Jewish heritage, or at least his knowledge and any residual religious attachment. In a famous letter of 1930 to A. A. Roback, he comments:

> It may interest you to know that my father did indeed come from a Chassidic background. He was 41 when I was born and had been estranged from his native environment for almost 20 years. My education was so un-Jewish that today I cannot even read your dedication, which is evidently written in Hebrew. In later life I have often regretted this lack in my education. (Freud, 1961: 394)

In other places, he was more forthcoming: 'I was born on May 6th 1856, at Freiberg in Moravia, a small town in what is now Czechoslovakia.

My parents were Jews, I have remained a Jew myself' (Freud, 1925: 14). But his general argument was that nothing was passed down to him from his Jewish heritage ('My education was so un-Jewish'). This left him with little alternative but to assume some kind of automatic transmission of Jewish identity – otherwise, how could he, so secular and atheistic, so ignorant of the Jewish tradition, have felt such a pull? The easy, Sartrean answer that it was due to antisemitism was partly true but insufficient to explain the 'dark emotional powers' mentioned earlier, so the mystic Lamarckian link was called into play. But we know that Freud's assertions of ignorance were duplicitous. Yerushalmi (1991) rather persuasively documents evidence suggesting not only that Freud's father remained knowledgeable about, and at least to some degree committed to, Judaism throughout his life (tempering Freud's assertion about his 'estrangement'), but also that Freud himself retained at least some knowledge of Judaism. The claim, for instance, that he barely even recognised Hebrew when he saw it seems unlikely, especially given the trouble that his father took to assemble a 'melitzah' (a compendium of Biblical quotations) in Hebrew to write into the flyleaf of his gift of the rebound family Bible on the occasion of Freud's thirty-fifth birthday (Yerushalmi, 1991: 71ff.). Freud himself, taught religion by the inspirational Samuel Hammerschlag, may have focused on Judaism's ethical principles, but is unlikely never to have come into contact with its forms or its language. Indeed, even though the Freud family 'spoke German and ignored such observances as kashrut and the Sabbath' once they had moved to Vienna when Freud was three years old, they still recognised some major Jewish holidays and some scholars claim that Freud would still have heard his father's 'adept... Hebrew recitation of the Passover service' (Klein, 1985: 42).

How can we put together Freud's denial of Jewish knowledge and direct inheritance from his father with the assertion of a general phylogenetic inheritance that is based on the murder of a *primal* father but in important ways bypasses the *actual* one? It is not necessary to be a psychoanalyst to know that Freud had an ambivalent relationship with his father Jacob. He tells us as much in several of the dreams he presents in *The Interpretation of Dreams*, a book that he also explicitly states to be 'a portion of my own self-analysis, my reaction to my father's death – that is to say, to the most important event, the most poignant loss, of a man's life' (Freud, 1900 [1908 Preface]: xxvi). Whatever his own abandonment of Hassidism, Jacob Freud clearly invested in his son's Jewish education and maintained a connection with him around Judaism into the 1890s. Yet Freud was both embarrassed by his father and lived in some anxiety that he had let him down, as well as having a fear of usurping or surpassing him. Perhaps it is not too wild a claim to suggest that the Lamarckian intuition, held by Freud against his own better instincts or at least his scientific knowledge, was a way of relieving himself from the burden of being his father's Jewish son. That is to say, there is a mode of inheritance being claimed here, a way of having a direct link back to Moses, which certainly 'explains' the way intense identifications and identity complexes can arise in the most surprising places. But the simpler model, whereby what is not worked through in one generation becomes a mystery and a task for the next, might actually be harder to acknowledge. It places each of us in personal relationships with our parents and also with the social world in which we live; it is full of messy and unwanted details about other people's lives; it forces us to face up to what we have and have not been given, and what we wanted and what we could never ask for or give back in return. Abstracting this into the far distant past makes it ghostly, which suggests that it should also make it harder to deal with. But this is not actually the case. The immediate, detailed encounter is harder to manage. The ghost that returns is not that of the primal father of prehistory, grabbing the women and slain by the sons. The ghost that haunts is not the lawgiver who cannot be tolerated and has to be destroyed. The ghosts are, for each and every one of us, Freud included, our own parents and intimates, with all of whom we struggle and whose legacy is never fully worked through. We are inhabited by them; that is explanation enough for the toughness and inscrutability of our identifications, the way we keep on with unmanageable stuff even though we wish we could leave it all untouched, or at least leave it all behind.

7
Forgiveness

The Dybbuk

There are a variety of ways in which one can enter into the being of another person. Spirit possession of many kinds operates across cultures and is also found in psychoanalysis; what can one say about projective identification, for example, other than that it is a mode of insertion, of possessing the other? All the talk we have had of the 'third' as a place for intersubjective merger, of the uncanny and of doubling, of thought-transmission and telepathy, of the matrixial and the evil eye and transference – all this is a reference to such possession. Some of it is benign and even therapeutic; some of it is malicious and poisonous. All of it challenges the idea that each subject is separate from every other one. It insists on the normality of haunting and suggests that those who are not in some way possessed are also not fully human. The boundaries between subjects are permeable, it seems. Obviously we are all social subjects, inhabited by the ghostly presence of others who have come before or are contemporaneous with us. Sometimes, however, it seems as though we are so full of otherness that we are barely subjects at all. And sometimes, as Freud (1920) reminds us when describing the death drive, we long for dissolution.

'What do they want from me? I am old and weak; my body needs rest, my soul thirsts for solitude,' says the Rebbe in S. An-sky's play *The Dybbuk* (1920: 34) as he faces his greatest trial. He does not only mean that he wants to be left alone; he means that he wants to *cease to be*; he means that he has no longer the strength to continue as a separate living being, required to respond, to keep things within their bounds, required to be a Master when he knows such mastery is only an illusion. When his assistant Mikhoel announces the arrival of Sender, whose daughter has become possessed, the Rebbe, who knows what is to come and what is going to be asked of him, wishes only to be excused the trial he fore-sees. What he states most clearly, however, is that in the face of this tragic event the whole 'imaginary' world of the 'I' is called into question; psychologically, he disappears:

> MIKHOEL: Rebbe! Sender of Brinitz is here...A terrible misfortune has befallen him. His daughter has been possessed by a dybbuk, may Heaven preserve us...He has brought her to you.
> REB AZRIEL: (*As if to himself*) To me? To me? How could he have come to me when the 'me' in me is no longer here?
> MIKHOEL: Rebbe, everyone in the world comes to you.
> REB AZRIEL: Everyone in the world...a blind world...blind sheep following a blind shepherd. It is only because they are blind that they come to me; if they weren't blind they would go to Him who alone can say 'I', to the only 'I' in the world. (An-sky, 1920: 33)

It is not solely the terrible strain of authority and mastery that is bearing down on the Rebbe here, as the demands of the whole world ('every-one in the world') suck him dry. It is partially, to use the Lacanian paradigm, that the immense effort of continually rebutting the position of Master in favour of that of Analyst causes him such agony. 'Every-one in the world' is a hysteric, clamouring for answers, forcing him to take up the position of the one who knows, of the one who can make miracles occur. Yet his own position is more self-conscious than that: he knows that in the end he knows nothing at all. He is not even sure of being the 'deputy' of the One who knows: 'The world says I am', he tells his assistant, 'but I don't know for sure' (ibid.: 33). He has no substance as a master; he is the last in a line of wonder-working rabbis, still with some power in the eyes of the world and – as becomes clear – in the celestial sphere evoked by the play, but in his own eyes he is nothing, a breath that fades away, a fleeting dream.

Responsibility calls, however, and with it a resolution to play the game of restoring the world of appearances back to its normal state. The Rebbe is brought to his senses through an appeal to his ancestors, especially his sainted grandfather:

> Do you know, Mikhoel, that my grandfather, the great Reb Velvele, used to exorcise a dybbuk without using spells or incantations: he simply raised his voice and gave one penetrating scream. In my hour of need I turn to him and he supports me. He won't abandon me now. (An-sky, 1920: 34)

A benevolent kind of haunting operates here, in which the Rebbe occupies the place of his grandfather and draws strength from him. He may feel the waning of his power and indeed of the power of the whole tradition in which he stands (Mikhoel reminds him, 'You are the last in a long line of holy men' [ibid.]), but whilst he can draw on that tradition and inhabit it, he still has some strength. Much as he would like to, Reb Azriel cannot abandon his position as the only one who can restore order to a fractured world.

The Dybbuk is a strange and powerful meditation on possession and on how welcome it can be. It has its own history as a ghostly haunting, of something from beyond the grave. Solomon Rappoport, the author, known by the time of the writing of the play as S. An-sky, had himself twisted and turned through varieties of Jewish affiliation, from talented Talmudic scholar to revolutionary secular socialist, to an ethnographer of his own people; from Yiddish to Russian and back to Yiddish. Between 1912 and 1914, An-sky directed the Jewish Ethnographic Expedition collecting folk stories in the Jewish Pale of Settlement, amongst which were several concerning dybbuks – dead souls that enter the bodies of living people and take them over. It was out of this research that *The Dybbuk* arose; but as has often been remarked, An-sky's dybbuk was no simple re-emergence of a Yiddish folk figure. For in the usual tale the dybbuk has one of two forms: either it is an evil spirit, preying on a sinful girl, or it is a lost soul seeking reincarnation and redemption. An-sky clearly knew the stories about reincarnation (one appears early in his play), but this is not the nature of his particular dybbuk. Nor is An-sky's dybbuk staging the possibility of its own redemption. Rather, what is produced is a love story in which the dybbuk is a welcomed partner, in which a marriage takes place that denies and scandalises the usual order of things. Roskies (1992: xxvii) asserts, 'whether in storybooks or in the field, whether an object of faith or subject to doubt, there was never a dybbuk who was in love with the woman he possessed. The victim was always chosen at random – by virtue of her maidenhead or, alternatively, because of her susceptibility to sin. No story before Ansky's had ever told of a dybbuk who was a lover in disguise.'

If An-sky's dybbuk resurrects a Jewish folklorist tradition and rethinks it in potentially modern terms as a tale of romantic love pitted against religious orthodoxy, it is with a number of complications that call into question that very opposition, as the story (described below) makes clear. But before getting to this, it is important to complete the point about the haunting nature of *The Dybbuk* itself. Gabriella Safran (2010) speculates that An-sky may have been fascinated by dybbuk stories because they echoed his use of the gramophone to record the stories and songs he heard on his ethnographic travels. 'The fantasy of conquering death was prominent in the early history of sound recording', she writes (ibid.: 221), 'and An-sky recorded the people of the shtetl sometimes willingly and sometimes against their will, preserving their voices so that they could be heard long after their death.' This naturalistic reading is, however, just one layer of the multiple ghostly resonances of *The Dybbuk*. An-sky never saw his play performed and indeed lost the manuscript to it when he fled Russia after the Bolshevik Revolution. The play was written in Russian, translated into Yiddish and Hebrew, then back into Yiddish; it was put on to enormous acclaim as well as critical controversy as part of the commemoration of An-sky's death in 1920, was revived several times and became the subject of the greatest Yiddish film of all time, Michał Waszyński's (1937) version, shot in Warsaw and on location in the village of Kazimierz. Ira Konigsberg captures the palimpsestic quality of all this:

> The Yiddish version became the source for the Hebrew version by the poet Hayyim Nahman Bialik published in 1918, which itself became the source for another Yiddish version by An-sky when he lost his original copy fleeing from Russia in the same year. If we consider the fact that most viewers will read the film through the titles on the screen, then in the United States, for example, we approach that part of the film that is directly taken from the play through the English, which is a translation of the Yiddish, which is a translation of the Hebrew, which is a translation of the Yiddish, which is a translation of the Russian. Like a dream, the film's power and significance reside in the images which we approach through the webs and layers of verbal associations. (Konigsberg, 1997: 23)

Each version is haunted by the previous ones. Watching the film, however, is the most haunting experience of all. Almost everything and everyone in it died soon after it was made and is kept alive only by the film itself. The Yiddish language and its speakers were decimated by the Holocaust; only a vestige remained, and whilst there is some revival of Yiddish in contemporary ultra-Orthodox Jewish communities it has departed as a language of secular Jewish culture. The world conjured up by the film had already largely gone by the 1930s; but the faces and voices were real enough, as many of them belonged to the actual inhabitants of Kazimierz, most of whom died in the Nazi terror. The lead couple in the film survived, ironically and accidentally, when they missed their ship back to Poland from New York because of delays in making another film; and many of the other professional actors also fled to America. But the dominant musical presence in *The Dybbuk*, the great cantor Gershon Sirota, was killed in the Warsaw Ghetto in 1943. Reading or watching the play, but particularly viewing the film, is thus itself an act of memory and resurrection, laced unbearably with the knowledge of what came next; haunted once again, that is, by the future more than by the past. 'What was to come' is the temporality of viewing; the viewer's body is itself inhabited by the dybbuk of those whose lives were cut short, and perhaps have nowhere to go.

Konigsberg addresses the circularity of this as follows:

> The destruction that was to follow had certainly been hinted at by past events of suffering and loss that helped shape the culture dramatized in the film. *The Dybbuk* places its own young lovers in the context of a history of Jewish pogroms by several times relating them to the bride and groom killed on their wedding day some two hundred years earlier during such a slaughter and buried in the village square. In the film, the spirit of a father remains unconsoled in the world of the dead because he has been deprived of a son in the world of the living to say Kaddish for him so that he will be remembered. *The Dybbuk* is a Kaddish, a prayer for the dead, that asks us to remember its dead. (Konigsberg, 1997: 25)

Even in its form, then, *The Dybbuk* is a ghostly resurrection, something blowing back from before the Nazi Holocaust, back too towards the period of wonders and miracles that many Jews took refuge in during the time of the Hassidim, back also to the Chmielnicki massacres of the seventeenth century. It consequently embodies a kind of possession that is hard to lay to rest, however fervently the Kaddish is recited. It is also a manifestation not only of the melancholic elements of destroyed cultures, returning again and again to trouble and distress the present, but of the call to restitution and reparation and possibly, though sometimes at extreme cost, to forgiveness.

Love and consolation

The basic structure of *The Dybbuk* is not really one in which romantic love opposes the mores of a traditional society, even though on the surface that is what seems to happen. Patriarchy is certainly involved, a point that has given rise to some feminist readings in which the possessed girl's refusal to comply with the wedding arranged for her is seen as a revolt against a paternal order that is set on managing her as an object of exchange. That is certainly one issue, though it has to be noted that whilst the pursuit of money seems to be the main purpose of her father's matchmaking, this is not so that he should benefit himself but so that *she* should be financially secure. But it is hard to read the play primarily as a feminist revolt when the girl is possessed (penetrated) by a male dybbuk, the soul of the yeshiva student Khonon, and when the central romance fulfils an agreement between two men – the fathers of both Leah (the girl) and Khonon, who have promised them to each other. Leah's apparent rebellion is a fulfilment of a masculine agreement that took no account of her wishes; and her refusal of her official bridegroom could therefore be understood as due to the existence of a more binding patriarchal contract that trumps that arrangement. It is also worth noting that there is no single wicked character who is worthy of punishment in the story: everyone suffers, and they do so because of a mistake, a kind of hubris, in which humans take on the responsibility for making a vow that can never be assured. Not for nothing do Jews renounce all such vows on the night of the Day of Atonement (the solemn 'Kol Nidre' prayer that begins the fast is actually a legal formula: 'Our vows shall not be valid vows, our prohibitions shall not be valid prohibitions, and all our oaths shall not be valid oaths'). The play announces that the attempt to control the future by making promises is unsupportable; but it also has effects. In fact, the vow is fulfilled, but not in the way the pledgers wished it to be.

The story is quite a complex one and is presented slightly differently in the play and the film. Nissen and Sender are devoted friends at the court of their Hassidic master during the festival of the Tabernacles; they do not appear together in the play, but the film has a prologue demonstrating their love for each other and marking the intensity of their oath, the way it draws their two souls together in an eternal bond. Their wives are both pregnant, and the men promise each other that if one should have a son and the other a daughter, the two children shall marry. In the film, the pledge is sealed by Nissen singing the Song of Songs, the great love poem in the Bible that is also interpreted as a love song between Israel and God. But here, in *The Dybbuk*, it clearly has a secular, erotic significance, binding Nissen and Sender together; when, therefore, it recurs later in the film as a love song between their children, it is the homosexual bond between the fathers that is renewed.

On the way home from the Rebbe, Nissen is drowned and so never sees the baby son born to him; Sender's wife dies in childbirth and he is left to bring up his daughter Leah alone, with the help only of her aunt. Over time, he becomes rich. Nissen's son Khonon grows up as a Talmud prodigy and then turns to the study of Jewish mysticism (Kabbalism); he arrives in the town of Brinitz, where Sender lives, and stays to study there. He becomes a regular dinner guest at Sender's house, and of course he and Leah immediately fall in love with each other. This should be no surprise, for it is in the nature of 'love at first sight' that it is always a recurrence of a previous love – that is the meaning of transference, embedded in traditional mythologies as the uncanny return of something earlier, perhaps even from an earlier life. Mladen Dolar (1996: 133), commenting on the romantic conceit of the idiom 'their eyes met', notes, 'The sudden recognition implies that *the first time is already repetition*, one realizes what one has always already known ... Seeing the beloved for the first time, one recognizes him/her as somebody one has always known.' This is exactly what happens between Khonon and Leah: as they look into each other's eyes over the Sabbath table, they recognise themselves as destined for one another, as already promised. Sender, however, is blind to this; wilfully so, as it turns out. He does not realise that Khonon is the son of his old friend and is therefore the one destined for his daughter. Instead, he arranges a marriage for her with the young son of a rich family – a feeble, frightened young man, by no means a rival to Khonon, but nevertheless the official bridegroom. Dabbling in Kabbalah and trying to summon the power of Satan to make him rich enough to displace this groom, Khonon dies.

Before the marriage ceremony, Leah visits the cemetery, ostensibly to invite her mother to her wedding. However, she actually invites Khonon. The film then offers one of its most famous sequences: a set of dances that the bride has with the sick, the poor and with a figure of death, whom she mistakes for Khonon. At the wedding (or before it in the play), she casts herself on the grave that stands in the middle of her village, the grave of a young couple murdered on their own wedding day by the Chmielnicki mob. When she looks up, she is speaking with the voice of Khonon: 'You have buried me! But I have returned to my promised bride and will not leave her!' (An-sky, 1920: 29). The Messenger – the closest representation of an analyst in the play – announces, 'A dybbuk has entered the body of the bride' (ibid.).

The final acts of the play centre on the dybbuk and Reb Azriel from Miropolye, the Hassidic sage at whose court Nissen and Sender had originally met. The dybbuk is brought to Reb Azriel, who first calls a Beth Din (a court of law) to hear the accusations against Sender by Nissen. This is when it comes out that there has been a promise between the two men and that the dybbuk is claiming his due, his always-intended bride. There is great subtlety in the narrative argument at this point, laced with the drama of a court hearing involving the dead and the living. Nissen's complaint is that when Sender rejected Khonon as a suitor for his daughter, the 'Powers of Darkness' took advantage of his despair: 'they spread a net for him and caught him and removed him from the world before his time. And his homeless soul drifted from place to place until it entered the soul of his intended bride as a dybbuk' (ibid.: 42). The peroration is crucial here, as it refers to the obliteration not just of one life but of all that has gone before it and could have come afterwards – the destruction of a lineage, of a tradition, a state of being, in the phrase we have met before, 'expunged from the memory of those who live on' (Adorno and Horkheimer, 1947: 216). The court is told:

> Nissen ben Rivke states that with his son's death he has been cut off from both worlds. Nothing remains of him, neither name nor memory; there is no one to succeed him and no one to recite the Kaddish on the anniversary of his death. His light has been extinguished forever, the crown of his head has plunged into an abyss. He therefore asks that the court sentence Sender, according to the laws of the holy Torah, for spilling the blood of Nissen's son and cutting off the family line forever. (An-sky, 1920: 42)

The imagery here is reminiscent of that of a very different piece of literature from almost exactly the same time that also invokes lost worlds, T. S. Eliot's *Waste Land*:

> Under the brown fog of a winter dawn
> A crowd flowed over London Bridge, so many,
> I had not thought death had undone so many. (Eliot, 1922: 65)

This crowd that flows, this line of ghosts, links past and future, filling the present out with its demands, accusations and laments. When nothing remains, when the line is terminated – whether by neglect or by war or Holocaust – the lost souls are left flowing endlessly, with nowhere to go to find rest. And this is not only something that happens to individuals: as the parallel between these texts suggests, it can overwhelm entire cultures.

The Rebbe actually finds that Sender is not guilty on the legal technicality that an oath made before something exists (in this case, the men's children) is not binding; but he also acknowledges that 'the pledge was accepted in the higher realms', and he accordingly fines Sender half his wealth, to be given to the poor, and places on him the responsibility to say Kaddish for Nissen and Khonon. However, the dead do not accept this and the dybbuk refuses to leave. This then forces the Rebbe into an excommunication ceremony; he invokes all his power whilst still pleading with the dybbuk to leave on its own accord, but it is only when the shofar, the ram's horn, is blown that the dybbuk gives in. The Rebbe then releases him from the excommunication and calls for the planned wedding to take place immediately. But whilst the whole party is out greeting the approved groom and his family, who have been called urgently to them, Leah wakes up to find the dybbuk leaving her, and enters into a desperate dialogue with this lost soul:

> LEAH: Your voice is as sweet to me as that of a violin on a silent night. Tell me who you are.
>
> KHONON'S VOICE: I have forgotten. It is only through your thoughts that I can remember who I am.
>
> LEAH: It's coming back to me now. My heart was drawn to a bright star. In the deep of night I shed sweet tears, and someone always appeared in my dreams. Was it you?
>
> KHONON'S VOICE: Yes...
>
> LEAH: Return to me, my bridegroom, my husband. I will carry you in my heart, and in the still of the night you will come to me in my dreams and together we will rock our unborn babies to sleep... (An-sky, 1920: 48)

In a heartbreaking moment of lament, she steps outside the magic circle that the Rebbe has drawn around her and unites with Khonon. She declares:

> I am enveloped in a blaze of light. My bridegroom, my destined one, I am united with you for all eternity. Together we will soar higher and higher, ever higher. (An-sky, 1920: 49)

The play ends with the formula on discovering a death, 'Blessed be the true Judge.'

It can perhaps be seen why this story perturbs the fabric of haunting so profoundly. In some ways it represents a reworking of folklore elements with a modernist sensibility: the dybbuk and his 'victim' are lovers, the true love they have for one another is more powerful even than the court of law and the powers of excommunication. Yet the source of their love is the love of their fathers for one another and the pledge they make to each other that is respected in the heavenly realm, despite the fact that the rabbinical court rules it invalid. That is, the bond forged in love is declared to have priority over the letter of the law; but this bond creates a kind of transgenerational trauma that can only be worked out through the bodies and souls of the children. To push this a little further, anachronistically perhaps but in a way suggested by the visual field of the prologue in the film: Sender and Nissen's homosexual attachment to one another cannot be spoken about. They are interrupted every time they try to tell their pledge to the Rebbe, and in the film they are quietened when they discuss it during the penitential service of Hoshana Rabba (the seventh day of Tabernacles). The voice of the cantor soars in a kind of rhapsodic, loving plea to God; but the hidden voices of the loving men are subdued. Neither of them return to relationships with their wives; the one dies, the other is left a widower. But the trauma of the repressed homosexual desire lives on, transfigured into the immediate recognition of one another by Khonon and Leah, and by the aversion against recognition of Khonon by Sender. Again in the film, it is when Sender hears Leah sing the Song of Songs to the tune inherited by Khonon from the father he never knew, that he realises who Khonon was; this love song is what has linked them, and it is what brings Nissen back from the dead to accuse his friend of betrayal.

This reading owes a lot to Butler's (1997) idea of melancholic gender identity, specifically the founding of heterosexuality (especially heterosexual masculinity) on the basis of an occlusion of homosexual desire. This melancholic attachment to the same-sexed other lives on as an unrecognised and unmourned object, constantly bleeding gender of its stability but also remaining as an unacknowledged possibility. The haunting in *The Dybbuk* references this quite precisely: the spontaneity and authenticity of the young men's love for each other is recognised in a bond that is held to be valid on high; but it can only be worked through tragically in the next generation, as something that drives the young lovers together with such force that neither excommunication nor death can keep them apart. It also produces a further form of premonitory mourning. Leah partly celebrates, partly laments the lack of a future: 'together we will rock our unborn babies to sleep'. Is this a mode of consolation, a final grieving forgiveness that by blocking the birth of real babies allows all the unreal, melancholic ones to come forth? Babies that cannot grow old, that cannot be lost, that cannot be murdered by Chmielnicki or the Nazis? Nissen and Sender's love for each other has become destructive; it cannot continue. Their children inherit this love as an encrypted pattern that drives them together to tragedy. The bride dances with death; the lover returns; he is driven out; they find each other once again in death, soaring 'higher and higher', which is a formula that, in Jewish mysticism, usually means approaching the Throne of God. They have no control over their destiny – this is the irony of seeing the dybbuk as a rebellion – but in fulfilling it, they also engage in a highly subversive act: they reclaim the unacknowledged and unmourned love of their fathers and they preserve it for all time. Dolar (1996: 142), thinking about the double, the death drive and the Real, comments, 'If love aims at the extimate – the intimate external kernel – it is also a protection against it, but a protection that is ambiguous and constantly failing. The other side of the extimate is the uncanny, the emergence of the object that brings about disintegration and becomes lethal.' That is certainly what we have encountered here: an external force that is the most intimate lover possible – the one that literally gets inside a person – but also brings about lethal disintegration.

Two partially opposed psychoanalytic and gendered readings of *The Dybbuk* have been very well articulated in the literature. For Konigsberg (1997), the thrust of the film is a maternal one. This may seem surprising at first, as mothers are so noticeably absent: the closest we get to one is when Leah invites her dead mother to her funeral, and in the film when a minstrel sings of the pride the mother will have in seeing her daughter as a bride. Indeed, there is very little explicit femininity in the play; even Leah, the main female character, disappears for a long time as a person, becoming merely the shell for the voice of her male demon. But there is a clue in the names. Whereas the Jewish convention is to call people by their patronyms, everyone in this play is referred to matronymically. Nissen is 'Nissen ben Rivke' (Nissen son of Rebeccah); Sender is 'ben Henya'; the Rebbe is Azriel the son of Hadas; Leah is 'the daughter of Hannah'. In Jewish practice, this is what one does when praying for a sick person: one calls on the name of the mother as the one who offers succour and nursing, who will remind God of the merciful element of His being. The play is marked by this maternal impulse, in which the troubles and sicknesses of all concerned will be gathered up in a movement of comfort and care.

Konigsberg, responding in part to the way the actual absence of mothers is counterposed to this maternal impulse, is attuned to how the lovers bind themselves together and seek unification, dissolution in one another. He sees *The Dybbuk* as demonstrating an attempt to draw together what has been sundered, coded as a search for the 'Shechinah', the feminine element of God that in particular shelters

His people during the time of disruption and exile. *'The Dybbuk'*, he writes (Konigsberg, 1997: 34), 'is concerned with this apparent imbalance between male and female, ... the action is driven by a need to fill the emptiness, close the gap, integrate the maternal with the paternal.' This calls specifically on a pre-Oedipal, maternal mode of unification, before sexual difference, in which the lovers are absorbed into one another not as separate desiring beings, but as one and the same. They embody, therefore, the narcissistic fantasy of absolute wholeness (and not the matrixial fantasy of separateness and togetherness at the same time):

> I am not claiming that each of the two lovers represents the male and female elements in the Godhead seeking a reunification but rather that they are two parts of a single whole seeking to come together, and that this unification is itself necessary to and prepares for the fusion, the sense of totality and oneness that we trace back to the child's earliest relationship with the mother. (Konigsberg, 1997: 35)

Reading this mystically as well as psychoanalytically, Konigsberg (ibid.: 37) suggests that 'Khonon and Leah's love relationship is the first step of unification, of the two parts forming one, of the loss of the independent and isolated self that leads to the ultimate breakdown between the self and the external world, that returns one to the primary and original fusion of the child with the mother intimated and sometimes almost replicated by the numinous and overwhelming loss of personal identity in the relationship with God.' They escape the world of differences by retreating into the world of oneness, and their capacity for forgiveness depends on this kind of mystical unifying fantasy, in which splits and contradictions are overcome. As the Rebbe says of his supplicants, 'if they weren't blind they would go to Him who alone can say "I", to the only "I" in the world' (An-sky, 1920: 33).

Writing from a Lacanian perspective, and with appreciation of Konigsberg's paper, Wolfe (2010) offers an alternative view. Noting the temptation to read the play as an example of *'Liebestod'* – the consummation of love in death so sought after by Romantic protagonists – he also makes the point touched on above, that the love of Khonon and Leah cannot be read as a spontaneous romantic outburst. Rather, it is a love foretold by the Symbolic order itself; it is a love that in adhering to a paternal bond, overwhelms the intentions of the play's later participants. Whereas a 'maternal' embrace of death would seem to imply a way of backing out of the Symbolic, refusing the law that determines how subjects are positioned in relation to one another, the dybbuk in fact acts in accordance with that Symbolic law by returning to claim his predestined bride. In this context, what is at stake is not the opposition between an oppressive social system and an attempt to find true love and fulfilment, but rather the *failure* of the social system to deliver on its promises. Nissen and Sender have made a patriarchal pledge; the pledge is left unfulfilled and it takes a ghost to put things right. Of course, there is also a turn of the screw: in the film, Nissen and Sender are warned against making vows concerning the unborn, and the ruling of the rabbinical court is that such promises are not binding. So it could be argued that Nissen and Sender were themselves challenging the Symbolic order, or the 'Big Other', by acting on their disowned passion for one another, dooming the next generation to a traumatic repetition. There is much to be said in favour of this reading, but it cannot escape the fact that, according to Reb Azriel, the representative both of mystical knowledge and of justice, 'the pledge was accepted in the higher realms' (An-sky, 1920: 43). A bond is a bond; the system of law and order relies on that being the case. The lovers do not disrupt this; rather, they make amends for the failure of the system to keep its word.

The Dybbuk's subtitle, *Between Two Worlds*, is of importance here. These are clearly the worlds of tradition and modernity and also heaven and earth, life and death. Nissen complains that because of Khonon's death he has no heirs and no-one to say Kaddish for him: 'Nothing remains of him, neither name nor memory' (ibid.: 42). Khonon as dybbuk, resisting expulsion from the girl's body, accuses the Rebbe, representing authority, of abandoning him: 'There is a heaven and there is an earth and there are worlds upon worlds in the universe, but nowhere is there a place for me' (ibid.: 36). The unborn babies of Leah's fantasy, the joining of souls at the end – all these attest to the movement 'between two worlds', the sense that there is no place that can hold the lovers, and also no-one who can be fully trusted. The play initially appears to set things right; the power of the Rebbe, backed by the shofar blast, is, after all, sufficient to drive out the dybbuk. But shortly afterwards, we are aware that there is no route back to this old world; or perhaps that there is a higher authority that is making its own plans. 'And when my strength finally failed me,' says Khonon (ibid.: 48), 'I left your body to enter your soul.' Wolfe (2010: 5) comments, 'we see here that the very intensity of Khonon's passion for his sublime Woman corresponds directly *to* this horror. Union with her is all that will *save* him amidst the traumatic dissolution of fixed Symbolic structures and identities.' Unlike what Wolfe terms the 'hysterical' approach to the play that reads the unification of the lovers as going beyond the Symbolic into 'undifferentiated Oneness', this Lacanian reading (drawing particularly on Žižek and Dolar, 2002) emphasises how 'the "eroticized ecstasy" of *Liebestod* constitutes... not a culmination of the death drive, nor a radical "hystericization" of Symbolic structures, nor a reconciliation of masculine with feminine principles, but indeed a means of buttressing and sustaining the existing phallic framework amidst the threat of disintegration, a *defensive* response to the Symbolic's own encroaching instability' (Wolfe, 2010: 12). Wolfe concludes in this vein (ibid.: 16), 'What "hysterical" approaches to this play would seem to minimize is the way in which the lovers' love is itself a conjuration of and submission to a potently existent Other in which one's mandate and destiny are inscribed: "I am her destined bridegroom." '

There is an additional element to consider here when invoking this Symbolic law that contains the apparently spontaneous yet actually predetermined, deathly love that is enacted by the possession in *The Dybbuk*. The dybbuk 'resolutely' (An-sky, 1920: 45) refuses to leave the girl's body even under the threat of excommunication until the shofar, the ram's horn, is blown – in fact, until seven are blown together. For Wolfe (2010: 11), this is because the 'dead' letter of the law needs the 'supplement' of the Real (the shofar) to bring it to life and give it potency. But we have met this shofar before. The ram's horn is chosen as the instrument of religious force, used as an awakening to penitence, because of the ram of the Akedah, which replaces Isaac as the sacrifice. We even know what happened to that ram: 'as to its horns, with the left one the Holy One, blessed be He, sounded the alarum at Mount Sinai; and with the right one, which is larger than the left, He will in future sound the alarum at the Ingathering of the Exiles in the Age to come' (Spiegel, 1967: 39). The shofar is therefore a call to repentance, a reminder of the covenant between Abraham and God, and a window into another world, a direct channel to the source of the Symbolic itself. It is also a reminder of violence, both the threatened sacrifice of his son by Abraham and the actual killing of the ram – 'He comes and in his eye / is the cold glint of murder', as Ruth Brin (1999) expresses it in her 'Poem by a Ram to God'. It is in these different ways a mark of the Real, in which what *lies behind* the Symbolic is allowed to break through as the strange voice that resonates across generational and sexual differences to make them all present at the same time. All Jews, living and to come, were supposedly present at the Revelation on Mount Sinai, when the shofar blew; similarly, the Ingathering involves the resurrection of the dead, so all will be present at that future time as well. Experienced in this way, the shofar destroys temporality and along with it the organised structures of law and Symbolic order. It announces judgement and awe, which is why the dybbuk flees from it; but it also supplants the natural order of things, creating a world in which everything is possible all at once – which is perhaps why it also allows the lovers to escape the bounds of their bodies and become united as souls. And finally, it has a maternal element, precisely what has been invoked in its absence by the play. The sound of the shofar is terrifying, but it is also all-embracing; it surrounds the people at Mount Sinai and will do so again 'at the Ingathering of the Exiles'. Through the sound of the shofar, the people will be *ingathered*, gathered together, taken up in a nurturing hold, brought out of their lonely graves where they are separate from one another, and united again with their source.

There is a powerfully 'matrixial' feel about this. Bracha Ettinger's (2006: 100) insight into the Akedah as an exemplary instance of *compassion*, quoted in Chapter 4, comes to mind again: 'This compassion is primary; it starts before, and always also beyond, any possibility of empathy that entails understanding, before any economy of exchange, before any cognition or recognition, before any reactive forgiveness or integrative reparation.' The Rebbe certainly has compassion on the dybbuk even as he drives it out; he says as much (An-sky, 1920: 36): 'Wandering soul! I cannot help but feel deep pity for you and will do everything in my power to release you from the angels of destruction.' It is in the womb that the infant is surrounded by sound, an auditory environment that supports it and, one can only guess, gradually differentiates out, perhaps in the separate-but-together way that Ettinger proposes. The total immersion in the sound of the shofar does something similar. It terrifies, for sure, as an announcement of the presence and power of God, of the Real that can destroy all Symbolic relations. However, it is also a return of sorts; it offers a total environment of compassionate holding, into which the lost soul flows, to be joined almost immediately by the other that has been promised to it.

Forgiveness

The Dybbuk is a counterintuitive instance of haunting. Both the content and form of the play and film compress time, so that one generation and the next are contemporaneous, trauma recurs and memories are projected inwards and outwards. The 1937 film stands on a precipice; within eight years, most of its presences became literally ghostly, wiped out in the cataclysm of the Holocaust. Their visual image remains; most hauntingly of all, the aural resonance of its musical soundtrack, dominated by Gershon Sirota's singing of the prayers, stays behind in its own all-embracing time warp. What we have in *The Dybbuk* is an instance of haunting as *witnessing*. Within the film this is expressed in the way the lovers live out the repressed traumatic bond between their fathers, putting right the social order's failure to meet the terms of their pledge. They reconstitute the Symbolic order that has missed its mark, and in so doing also reveal the haunting presence of a Real that causes this rift in the first place, that unsettles the Symbolic with its own pulsations of desire. Outside, in the mundane 'real' world, the play testifies to a historical moment in which tradition and modernity collide and create a palimpsest, a layering of beliefs and visions. The film, made twenty years later, *becomes* the ghost that haunts its viewers into future generations. One cannot watch it without shivering with memory, nostalgia and loss. There are other such archives, both Jewish and non-Jewish; in some ways they are the shared expression of melancholia in the face of communal destruction as well as colonialism. This particular one is no different, but it is especially resonant; *within eight years* everything had gone.

The dybbuk itself, however, is not a pernicious influence. Occupying the body of the girl, it promotes unification, forgiveness and resolution of the rift in the social that has caused such distress. In a way, it also closes off the intergenerational transmission of trauma – *there are no more babies*. Can we read this as an act of truncation or one of completion? That is, has the dybbuk destroyed something or, by repairing the rent in the Symbolic, brought it to its desired end? 'We will rock our unborn babies to sleep,' says Leah as her soul joins that of Khonon; this does not sound like a lament, but rather a celebration of a moment of rest and happiness. If giving birth to babies is a matter of investing in a future, then *The Dybbuk's* 'no future' is not one of repudiation or destructiveness, but of escape and final fulfilment. The problem is, as we know, that this did not actually work.

Can a ghost heal? The Kabbalistic account of the creation of the universe, touched on briefly at the end of Chapter 3, has been receiving renewed attention because of its mythologising of fragmentation and repair, indexed in the mythical construction of the 'breaking of the vessels'. In essence, this is a justification of the experience of exile, developed in the sixteenth century by the followers of Isaac Luria in large part as a response to the expulsion of the Jews from Spain. The existential question that this vast historical trauma produced was why the exile of the Jews should be deepened rather than, as many expected at the time, brought to an end. How could one reconcile messianic expectation with actual displacement, harassment and suffering? There are three parts to this version of the story of how the world comes to be the way that it is. Gershom Scholem (1969, 1971) provides detailed accounts of these three parts, which can only be highly simplified here. First is *zimzum*, the withdrawal of the *Eyn Sof*, the Eternal and never-ending light of God to make room for creation – and also, in Luria's thought, to find a way of purifying the Eyn Sof through the extrusion of the principle of judgement. Then there is the creation of the ten vessels or 'sefirot' into which the divine light was to be poured. The upper three vessels managed to contain the light that flowed into them, but the light struck the next six 'all at once and so was too strong to be held by the individual vessels; one after the other they broke, the pieces scattering and falling' (Scholem, 1971: 596). One further vessel (*Malkhut* – kingship) also cracked, but not to the same degree. Some of the light that had been in the vessels found its way back to its source, 'but the rest was hurled down with the vessels themselves' and from their shards arose the worlds of wickedness and baseness and of material things. Indeed, the whole universe sank as a result: 'The irresistible pressure of light in the vessels also caused every rank of worlds to descend from the place that had been assigned to it. The entire world process as we now know it, therefore, is at variance with its originally intended order and position. Nothing, neither the lights nor the vessels, remained in its proper place' (ibid.).

The final element after this 'breaking of the vessels' is *tikkun*, cosmic restoration. Scholem writes (ibid.: 597), 'All the subsequent processes of creation come about to restore this primal fault.' Most importantly:

The crucial point in the various Lurianic discussions of these developments is that although the *tikkun* of the broken vessels has almost been completed by the supernal lights and the processes stemming from their activity, certain concluding actions have been reserved for man. These are the ultimate aim of creation, and the completion of *tikkun*, which is synonymous with the redemption, depends on man's performing them. Herein lies the close connection between the doctrine of *tikkun* and the religious and contemplative activity of man, which must struggle and overcome not only the historic exile of the Jewish people but also the mystic exile of the *Shekhinah* [the feminine element of God], which was caused by the breaking of the vessels. (Scholem, 1971: 600)

The process here – breaking of vessels, deepening of suffering and exile, redemption through prayer and righteousness – is a familiar one, not that different from the account Melanie Klein gives of the workings of reparation in the depressive position. But this is not because psychoanalysis explains mysticism; it is rather because the structure of damage and repair is a widely distributed one, operating at the psychological and interpersonal level, and at the level of society and culture as a whole. The rabbis show an astute awareness of this. Asking how it could be that God 'miscalculated' and built vessels that would crack, they state (Vayikra Rabbah 7, 2): 'if a regular man uses broken containers, it is a disgrace for him, but the containers used by God are specifically broken ones, as it says, "God is close to those of a broken heart" (Psalms 34, 19).' History and the social, psychology and the unconscious combine in this regard. Faced with actual trauma and the return of the repressed, what can one do in good faith other than to seek to find ways of remedying it, of seeking to address the trauma and make it good? The dybbuk is a manifestation of that impulse, trailing its own damage behind it as it seeks to reconcile the souls that have fallen from their proper 'vessels'. Each moment of historical oppression also produces this impulse – along with the contrary one of repudiation and disgust.

In Chapter 3, there was mention of Judith Butler's use of Walter Benjamin's representation of his friend Scholem's account of the breaking of the vessels. This lineage is itself of significance: from the most illustrious scholar of Jewish mysticism through the most radical and searching materialist philosopher of the twentieth century, who died trying to escape the Nazis, to one of the most influential contemporary social critics, all of them deeply versed in European intellectual culture, all of them inescapably faced with their own Jewish identities. For Scholem this involved resurrecting the buried history of Jewish mysticism; for Benjamin it meant a profound engagement with Kafka and with the displacement of the Jewish intellectual; for Butler it includes both a return to Benjamin and the idea of the messianic as a political process of regenerating lost histories, and – more 'locally' – a commitment to justice in Israel-Palestine. In each case there is ambivalence about the possibility of renewal and forgiveness, or perhaps more accurately, there is comprehension of the complexity of this process. As noted earlier, Butler insists on the potential to be found in Benjamin for a messianic strand that does not represent a drawing together or final finding of the shards and lost light of the vessels. Actually preserving them in all their multiplicity might instead be the way towards a secular messianism in which all the occluded voices of the past can have their say. The sparks are distributed precisely so that they can be found every-where, in the other as well as in the subject. They can never be fully gathered together into one place; that is the point, the reason why the vessels broke in the first place, because sanctity can never be made into any single subject's possession. So holding something separate is impor-tant; but that still leaves open the question of the conditions under which one might realistically seek to bring about states of repair.

The Dybbuk recognises how a society in decline can desert its own symbolic promises. Or maybe one should think of it as showing how all social orders – all symbolic structures – are full of rifts and incom-pleteness, and what *The Dybbuk* dramatises is how painful it is when one comes face to face with these. The lovers strive to heal this rift by fulfilling a pledge that is recognised in the highest heights, by the source of power for the symbolic order in which they are placed. They thereby affirm the well-being of the Symbolic, its phallic potency, just when the impossible dilemmas of that potency are visible to all. Repairing the breach would involve a wedding between a dead groom and a living bride; it cannot be done without violence. The Rebbe tries to deal with this by trumping the authority of the One by the casuistry of the law, and thereby breaking the fathers' vow by applying to it the terms of the symbolic order itself. But this does not work, and what we are then exposed to is precisely a haunting by something that cannot be con-tained within the usual parameters of that order. Put more bleakly, *The Dybbuk* is a demonstration of how desperately we strive to maintain the appearance of symbolic order when experience demonstrates, time and again, that this order is teetering on the edge of collapse. And this is not fiction. Whilst the story of Khonon and Leah is an invented one, possi-ble only because ghostly things can be made to happen in the theatre and on film, *The Dybbuk* is a very material spirit, an actual visitation from beyond the grave. It not only 'brings to life' what once existed; it also fills out the present with the beings of those who have gone 'before their time'. It is a restless piece that holds the future responsible for what was to come.

What kind of forgiveness is possible when historical wrongs are done? There is a huge amount of literature on this, much of it building on the linked ideas of recognition and acknowledgement of injury (see Frosh, 2011b for an example). The general stance adopted in some of the most influential elements of such work is that subjects come into existence as a function of the recognition they achieve from others; and hence that social violence as a mode of obliteration of otherness has to be opposed by processes of witnessing and acknowledgement that reconstitute recognition. None of the protagonists in these discussions – Judith Butler and Jessica Benjamin, for example – minimise the complexity and difficulty of such processes of acknowledgement. Particularly in Butler's work, there is an emphasis on the 'invitation to violence' that comes from the exposure to the dependency and vulnerability of the other, which itself is partly a function of the subject's own dependency and vulnerability, built into the human condition. The mimicking of the tale of the broken vessels is no accident: we break things as an intrinsic, inescapable condition of being, because there is a way in which each subject has to test itself against externality in order to find its own boundaries. The 'invitation to murder' that Butler (2005) finds in Levinas instances this: an ethics that deserves the name comes from overcoming such an inclination, not from simply living out an in-built programme to be good. This is also referenced in the psychoanalytic, specifically Kleinian, idea that our capacity to be ethical subjects is measured by our ability to make good the damage we do. Butler (2009: 177) comments, 'For Klein, as well as for Levinas, the meaning of responsibility is bound up with an anxiety that remains open, that does not settle an ambivalence through disavowal, but rather gives rise to a certain ethical practice, itself experimental, that seeks to preserve life better than it destroys it.'

The focus on *injury* in many discussions of violence and reconciliation is a potentially problematic one, as it can escalate to a competition between injured subjects as to who has been more damaged, who 'deserves' victim status more than any others. It may be more productive to focus instead on *injuriousness*, the capacity – the temptation – present in each of us to do damage. This makes violence the constituting element of social and personal life, which in principle seems like a pessimistic move, a tragedy in the making, restoring to the centre of social theory a liberal consciousness that the best one can do is rein in the instincts; or – worse – a parody of social Darwinism that justifies violence on the basis of the 'natural' tendency for the strongest to win out. Such a move is far from the intention and moment of Butler's argument. 'To preserve life better than it destroys it' is the impetus of her thought and the action that follows from it. If the subject is constituted by and in violence, then whether or not it has suffered injury is no longer the point: the temptation to violence is in any case there. Acknowledgement of the violence one does arises from, as Butler (2009: 179) puts it, '[A]n understanding of the possibilities of one's own violent actions in relation to those lives to which one is bound, including those whom one never chose and never knew, and so those whose relation to me precedes the stipulation of contract.' Every one of us has injuriousness within us and is tempted to express that in relation to others with whom we have contact and on whom we are likely to be dependent. When we share a space, whether physical or psychical, we are likely to do harm. Recognition of this tendency to violence, this temptation to destroy everything, leads to recognition of the responsibility we have to struggle against the temptation and to acknowledge what we have done when the struggle fails.

The large amount of literature on post-Holocaust studies has been touched on briefly previously in this book; one could add to this a considerable range of work on truth and reconciliation commissions around the world, as well as on human rights and witnessing (for example, Potter, 2006). Jacqueline Rose's (2003) paper on 'Apathy and Accountability: The Challenge of South Africa's Truth and Reconciliation Commission to the Intellectual in the Modern World' is a classic literary exploration of this topic of what can be forgiven and what can never go away. But I want to finish this chapter on a different plane, returning to the mythological mode of haunting that seems constantly to exercise us, that seems never to be exorcised. Once again this has a Jewish scene, but it also has universalistic elements in trying to explore the temptation to violence and what might channel it elsewhere.

'The Temptation of Temptation'

Emmanuel Levinas' (1968) paper 'The Temptation of Temptation' is one of his 'Talmudic Readings'. The context of these readings was a series of annual gatherings of French Jewish intellectuals, the 'Colloques d'intellectuels juifs de langue française' in which he participated from the early 1960s. These readings of Talmudic texts show him working within the traditions of Talmudic commentary, ostensibly just translating and describing, yet also reading with a contemporary twist, aware of the times and their concerns. They are hermeneutic readings that function to open out texts, in many places uncovering a subversive side-reading or subjugated narrative that produces a troubled surprise in traditional readers, unable to deny the presence of these textual strands, yet having their assumptions disrupted. In this way, they are true to a certain tradition not just of Jewish reading, but of *psychoanalytic* reading, in which texts are treated not as transparent productions from the unconscious of a particular author (a once common, but illegitimate use of psychoanalysis in literary criticism), but rather as the site of a struggle that leaves behind traces.

Levinas' title, 'The Temptation of Temptation', is set up by him as a commentary on how 'Western man' strives to 'experience everything' (1968: 32). 'We cannot let life pass us by!' he declares, not without irony (ibid.: 33). 'We must enter history with all the traps it sets for the pure, supreme duty without which no feat has any value.' Levinas prefaces his analysis of his Talmudic text by developing a theme around the nature of Western philosophical knowledge, in terms of which he defines the temptation of temptation – basically, the wish to know something completely before one engages in it, prior to experience. The actual 'temptation of temptation' for him is this 'temptation of knowledge' (ibid.: 34). Such philosophical knowledge is often opposed by the intuitive understanding of 'faith', and Levinas indexes this. But he is more interested in exploring whether a certain kind of knowledge can be achieved that is not marked by separation of the ego from the thing it knows, but instead means 'going within oneself further than one's self'. Levinas' reading of the Talmudic passage addresses this, but it also sets up a much more profound question: could we refuse to enter history, could we opt instead for chaos?

'The Temptation of Temptation' deals with an especially provocative moment in the Talmud (Tractate Shabbat) where the Rabbis are debating the line from the Exodus 19, 17 reading, 'And they stopped at the foot of the mountain...' This refers to the moment of the Revelation at Mount Sinai; the Israelites are encamped there awaiting the word of God. The people declare their willingness to hear and obey the Torah Law, before they know exactly what will be in it. But how free was this acceptance?

> Rav Abdima bar Hama bar Hasa has said: This teaches us that the Holy One, Blessed be He, inclined the mountain over them like a tilted tub and that He said: If you accept the Torah, all is well, if not, here will be your grave. Rav Aha bar Jacob said: That is a great warning concerning the Torah. Raba said: They nonetheless accepted it in the time of Ahasuerus, for it is written (Esther 9: 27) 'The Jews acknowledged and accepted. They acknowledged what they accepted.'... Resh Lakish taught: What does the verse (Genesis 1: 31) mean: 'Evening came, then morning, it was the sixth day'? The definite article is not necessary. Answer: God had established a covenant with the works of the Beginning: If Israel accepts the Torah, you will continue to exist. If not, I will bring you back to chaos. (Levinas, 1968: 31)

Levinas proceeds with his analysis of this passage and the section that follows it in a suitably Talmudic way, by commenting on the text line by line. It is not possible to follow this in detail here, but some elements can nevertheless be pulled out. He deals first with the idea that the mountain hovered over the people, threatening to crush them – that they were literally 'beneath the mountain'. Levinas (ibid.: 37) notes that: 'The choice of the Jewish way of being, of the difficult freedom of being Jewish, would have been a choice between this way and death...The teaching which the Torah is, cannot come to the human being as a result of choice. That which must be received in order to make freedom of choice possible cannot have been chosen, unless after the fact. In the beginning was violence.' Choosing ethically requires the prior acceptance of an ethical framework; hence the tension between acceptance and chaos. The first choice is a forced one, from which no human subject can step back, because if they do they cease to be human, they cease to stand in any kind of ethical relationship with themselves or with others. From this perspective, reason, the prerogative of philosophy, might even be seen as depending on revelation; something comes first, before it is possible to make choices within it. This is clearly a problematic reading as it suggests that the absence of choice in the acceptance of the frame of the Torah places a limit to reason and philosophy, and instantiates violence (the threat, the 'great warning concerning the Torah') at the heart of religious and moral action. This is the relevance of the reference to the Book of Esther ('the time of Ahasuerus'): the people may have accepted the Torah at Sinai, but they do not fully acknowledge it until they are saved from a deeply murderous threat many generations later. 'The order thus founded extends, after the fact', writes Levinas (1968: 38), 'to the act of foundation. Reason, *once it comes into being*, includes its pre-history.'

What remains central to this discussion, however, is the relationship between freedom and violence, and it is this that is the focus of the next section, ending with 'If Israel accepts the Torah, you will continue to exist. If not, I will bring you back to chaos.' Levinas comments (1968: 40), 'The following passage in fact shows us that this anteriority of acceptance in relation to freedom does not merely express a human possibility but that the essence of the Real depends on it.' In more detail, this is how to read the apparent lack of free choice embedded in the threat, *existence or chaos*:

> The mountain turned upside down like a tub above the Israelites thus threatened the universe. God, therefore, did not create without concerning himself with the meaning of creation. Being has a meaning. The meaning of being, the meaning of creation, is to realise

the Torah. The world is here so that the ethical order has the possibility of being fulfilled. The act by which the Israelites accept the Torah is the act which gives meaning to reality. To refuse the Torah is to bring being back to nothingness... The unfortunate universe also had to accept its subordination to the ethical order, and Mount Sinai was for it the moment in which its 'to be' or 'not to be' was being decided. The refusal of the Israelites would have been the signal for the annihilation of the entire universe. (Levinas, 1968: 41)

Levinas goes on in his analysis to explore further the relationship between freely taking something on and being coerced to do so, and in particular how knowing something might depend on the fullest engagement of oneself in that thing. But we do not need to follow him through to the end of this, though the journey has great value. We also should remember that the audience for Levinas' presentation was a Jewish one, and that he was speaking and writing from within a hybrid secular-religious tradition that had plenty of interest in universalising, but little or none in speaking deeply about other sets of belief and other cultures. So, if it can do so, this very provincial and specific discourse has to speak metaphorically to others, not least those in postcolonial situations and far removed from any assumption that the Jewish Torah founds the world of ethics.

The mountain hovers over all of us; thinking about it as a 'tub' does not quite capture the degree of threat involved. We are not being offered a bath in a gentle container; we are being offered the choice between existence and chaos. One must take one's ghosts seriously, as we have noted previously in this book, and in particular show interest in the injustices that they complain about. The resonance of a founding violence, in which individuals and communities are threatened – 'accept this or else' – runs through subsequent generations and structures the world of living creatures. Those that visit from elsewhere as ghosts and dybbuks, revenants and doubles, do so when the social order either does not live up to its promise, or offers an opportunity for a historical (which means continuing) wrong to be put right. 'Being has a meaning,' Levinas asserts; this meaning is that of an ethical responsibility towards others that founds the human as a subject. 'The world is here so that the ethical order has the possibility of being fulfilled.' Without this ethical framing, there is nothing; when it fails, there is no rest, there is only constant suffering 'between two worlds'.

The psychology and philosophy of this are powerful enough, but the politics of it are also pronounced. Speaking mythologically and metaphorically, as perhaps one must when dealing with claims of such specificity and grandiosity, the survival of humanity depends on the construction of social orders that accept an ethical frame that does justice to the needs of others, finding space for everyone to be recognised as full subjects.

This also requires recognition of the violence that lies at the edges of the social order and therefore of the protective movement of acknowledgement and reparation required to keep the further visitation of that violence at bay. This is not a matter of 'free' choice, but it *is* a choice – it just happens, however, that the choice is between existence and chaos. 'If you accept, all is well, if not, here will be your grave.' There is plenty of evidence that this is a real choice; we often go for chaos and the grave. It is still an open question whether the other choice will ever be fully made, and the ghosts and dybbuks will be allowed to speak again in their own voices, and find their rest.

Conclusion

It is easy to get into a melancholic state of mind, in which a sense of indefinable loss predominates. On a certain day, at the age of 57, I finished reading Gabriella Safran's (2010) biography of An-sky, who had died at 57, and picked up W. G. Sebald's (2001) novel, *Austerlitz*. Sebald too died at the age of 57. I am not superstitious, but this coincidence was unnerving.

What passes runs through us, sometimes as a celebration, more often as reminder tinged with regret, occasionally as something we cannot bear. It is mostly the last of these kinds of remembrance that has been the subject of this book. It is also necessary to stress that it is what 'passes' rather than what is 'past' that I have been dealing with, opening out a space for the future to haunt us. It is perhaps precisely the collapse of time that is endemic to the experience of ghostliness; that which should have been dealt with remains unsettled, that which should be properly still to come is already with us now. Our steps are dogged by both past and future; we are never left alone. This is one of the major effects of reading the uncanny with Freud: that we become aware of how much our sense of being haunted by the past is actually a shivering realisation of what is to come. Something lurks in mirrors and windows, reflecting on our being in ways that are rarely comforting. This is also part of the utility of haunting, that it ensures that we cannot remain at ease with ourselves. It is a *reminder* as much as it is a *remainder*; what is left over and uncared for insists on justice and reparation. Freud emphasises the deathly here, both in the sense of drawing attention to ill-grieved and hence melancholic objects and also advancing a thesis that death shadows everything, that life itself is a 'detour' rather than the real thing. This may seem unduly pessimistic, but only in the sense that it is gloomier than the legitimate pessimism that the evidence of our experience requires of us. Freud was responding to violence, destructiveness and loss, as well as to the beginnings of his own ravaging illness. Looking back over the best part of a century since 'The "Uncanny"' and *Beyond the Pleasure Principle*, is it easy to say that he was wrong?

Psychoanalysis has its own experience of being haunted. Institutionally, it labours still with unresolved conflicts and repressed or at least mis-remembered histories. I have dealt with some of these elsewhere in relation to psychoanalysis' Jewish history (Frosh, 2005, 2012b) and have touched briefly on the colonialist elements of psychoanalysis' past in this book. My main interest here, however, has been in the leverage psychoanalysis gives us in understanding various kinds of ghostliness and experiences of possession, especially those that drag violence in their wake. I have tried not to get too overwhelmed by anxiety and depression and to draw comfort from the possibilities of awakening the dead and invigorating the living that lie in the notion of haunting itself. If a spirit haunts, then it is not fully lost; the opportunity for repair exists, for settling what needs to be settled and provoking change where that is what has to be done. As the various strands of what is termed 'psychosocial studies' remind us, this is a process involving a human subject that is a meeting point between social and psychological layers. Maybe the idea of the *psychic*, which nicely combines insinuations of the occult with the idea of fantasy and the mind, can even be defined in terms of this meeting point. The psychic is that space in which unconscious personal elements and unconscious social elements come together, to make us feel possessed and not in control of ourselves. After all, psychoanalysis attests to how the experience of being haunted, of being taken over by something that arrives unexplained from somewhere else, unbidden, often unwelcome, but sometimes consolatory, is the most obvious and routine experience of all. Unfortunately, we hide from it most of the time.

Considering the psychic in this way, as a meeting point for social and mental forces, raises a further issue about the mechanisms of haunting. The materiality of ghosts has been a theme in this book, but it is perhaps worth reiterating here that we are not dealing with something mystical when considering how messages can be transmitted without obvious intention or conscious action. What is evident in all the discussions about telepathic thought transference and intergenerational transmission of trauma and responsibility, is that there are external factors that play their part in ensuring that memories are not lost. This is to say that the symbolic structures of culture – material objects, relational practices, traditions, rituals, class divisions, racialisations, gender discrimination, media representations, literary heritages and so on and so forth, all with their counterpoints in other structures that are hidden, denied and delegitimised – are themselves modes of remembrance. We may each, individually, become blind to what goes on, be 'stupefied' in the sense of numbed by the damage done to us or by us or in our name. But this does not mean that these things cease to exist or that when they return they have come from some realm of the spirit. They are there already, either explicitly expressed in the culture (for example, as discriminatory practices or as artistic products or shared fantasies), or embedded in the gaps and omissions that become evident at moments of crisis (for instance, the hidden oppression that can flare up as apparently random rioting). When they appear, even in a new guise, it is always as a mode of return: things that are missing are never fully lost, any more than the repressed is ever completely silent.

Many of the authors surveyed in this book assert the significance of haunting as a social event and see it as a kind of call to action. I am happy to adopt this reading and to assume that when ghosts appear it is in order to tell us to do something. A relationship needs to be put right; a society needs to deal with those it has oppressed and continues to write out of history; a rebellion is necessary, a revolution is on its way. Psychoanalytically, something that keeps stirring us up has to be acknowledged and worked with, however drastic the changes this demands in our ongoing lives. Haunting is therefore the space not only of the meeting of personal and social, but of past and future. It is a message from the past of what the future will become if we do nothing about it; indeed, of what we each will become if we do not reflect and change. It is also a message from the future about what the past has produced and about what needs to be returned to and remade if its effects are to be ameliorated. When Freud invents the death drive, it is in recognition both of what he has seen (the First World War, above all) and of what he prophesises (ongoing destruction). His intellectual intervention here is a kind of therapeutic act, an attempt to lift us into awareness. Not that he was fully aware himself: as we have seen, there was plenty of smoke around obscuring his vision. Nevertheless, psychoanalysis has offered more opportunities than we might have expected to unpick the way things that appear lost still remain both as waste and as excess. It also makes an important and surprising assertion: haunting is *normal*, and without it we – and others around us – suffer. What is the 'depth' of the present if not that which is given to it from past and future, our memories and wishes, our regrets and joys and fears and hopes? Without these things, our experience is thin, cut off from the sources that feed it and give it resonance.

One of the achievements of psychoanalysis – but in this respect it is little different from many other moral systems – is to show precisely how dependent we are on our ghosts and phantasms to make ourselves alive. Psychoanalysis also specialises in getting under the skin of each subject. The gaze and the telepathic cut up the body in such a way that it is no longer possible to imagine ourselves as separate from others, and psychoanalysis builds on this in its own practice, acting on the assumption that communication is possible, however distorted it may often be. Indeed, communication is avoidable only with great effort and at great personal and social expense. We are getting used to the idea that we are all the time run through with messages that we cannot interpret – electronic signals that pick up our every movement but that we cannot see or hear. What is shown in the material I have drawn together here is that this is not a *metaphor* for human communication but is exactly what happens. We are inhabited continually by what comes from others; it infiltrates us and we ignore it only through impassioned patterns of denial. These lost communications then keep circulating, fading and reappearing with the times, but they never actually come to rest until we actively find them a home. And it is only when we bring these hauntings to consciousness that we become fully alive ourselves, in possession of our own histories as well as allowing scope for those of others.

This all sounds like an ethical and maybe a political imperative, in which what is being claimed is that we need our ghosts if we are to be human subjects. Thinking about it in this way, perhaps it requires a programme with its own manifesto. If we could articulate a manifesto for dealing sensitively with ghosts, what might it contain? Here are some suggestions:

1. We should not let well alone. It usually means that something is being covered up in the interests of the colonial powers. There is, after all, such a thing as history written by the victors.
2. We must listen out for murmurs, hints and quiet echoes. We should watch out for doubles and respect déjà vu. There are very few direct paths for a ghost to go down, especially if it is locked away in a crypt somewhere, behind thick walls and a keyless door. This means that communication is likely to be roundabout, enigmatic, elusive and transient. We must treasure this communication if it chooses to go through us and enjoy the shivering it causes.
3. We should avoid trying to bring history to a close. It never works; it just means that some people triumph over others. As well as being

a way to perpetuate domination, declarations of the end of history are an indication that something important is being avoided. History does not end, because everything is always in the process of return.

4. We must not assume that the sympathetic gaze is any easier to bear than the judgemental one. Sometimes judgement is necessary, though it is true that it is pleasanter when tempered with mercy. But sometimes tears of pity can be as acidic as hate, because they remind us of what is wrong or of what we have lost.

5. We should seek out ceremonies of reparation, rituals of recovery. We will note their insufficiency but acknowledge that engaging in them may be all we can do. We must understand that if a ghost keeps troubling us, it may mean that we have missed the point; but it may also mean that we are the only hope the ghost has left.

6. We must recognise that we are ghosts too. There is little distinction between the haunted and the one who haunts; the former turns into the latter soon enough. Perhaps our capacity to recognise ghosts is what determines the likelihood that we too will be recognised in our struggle to be heard and seen. It is not obvious that there is any other way to do it.

To close, here is a story collected by An-sky during his ethnographic expedition in the Pale of Settlement and reported by Safran (2010: 211): 'An old cantor, jealous of his successor, dies, possesses the young man, and forces him to sing the Yom Kippur service in his voice, with the old cantor's melodies.' I like this story. It is admirably irascible, shows an ordinary maliciousness and an appreciation of what one generation can do to the next. It is nicely ambivalent: we all need to escape the melodies of the past, to find our own voice; but the past has a hold over us too, and sometimes if it feels an injustice has been done, it is entitled to take us over. Perhaps the new cantor should not have stopped singing the old melodies; on the other hand, what right did the old cantor have to stop the new one developing his own tunes? Is it possible to return and move forward at the same time? Maybe this cantorial dybbuk has a point in reminding us that the past has agency, it is restless, and whilst we have our rights too, it will never let us forget that it needs to be heard.

References

Abraham, N. (1988) 'The Phantom of Hamlet or the Sixth Act: Preceded by the Intermission of "Truth"', *Diacritics*, 18, 2–19.

Abraham, N. and Torok, M. (1976) *The Wolf Man's Magic Word: A Cryptonomy*. Minneapolis, MN: University of Minnesota Press.

Adorno, T. and Horkheimer, M. (1947) *Dialectic of Enlightenment*. London: Verso, 1997.

An-sky, S. (1920) 'The Dybbuk', in S. An-sky, *The Dybbuk and Other Writings* (edited by D. Roskies). New York: Schocken, 1992.

Anzieu, D. (1986) *Freud's Self-Analysis*. International Psycho-Analytical Library, 118, 1–596. London: Hogarth Press and Institute of Psycho-Analysis.

Baraitser, L. (2012) 'Maternal Publics: Time, Relationality and the Public Sphere', in A. Gulerce (ed.), *Re(con)figuring Psychoanalysis: Critical Juxtapositions of the Philosophical, the Sociohistorical and the Political*. London: Palgrave Macmillan.

Bayly, S. and Baraitser, L. (2008) 'On Waiting for Something to Happen', *Subjectivity*, 24: 340–55.

Benjamin, J. (2009) 'The Politics of Apology and Other Forms of Acknowledgment: Denial in the Face of Atrocity', available at: http://backdoorbroadcasting. net/2009/10/psycho-political-resistance-in-israel-palestine (accessed 18 April 2012).

Benjamin, W. (1940) 'Theses on the Philosophy of History', in W. Benjamin, *Illuminations*. London: Pimlico, 1999.

Bhabha, H. (2004) *The Location of Culture*. London: Routledge.

Blau, L. (1924) 'Evil Eye', in *The Jewish Encyclopaedia*. New York: Funk and Wagnalls.

Bohleber, W. (2007) 'Remembrance, Trauma and Collective Memory: The Battle for Memory in Psychoanalysis', *International Journal of Psychoanalysis*, 88, 329–52.

Bollas, C. (1987) *The Shadow of the Object: Psychoanalysis of the Unthought Known*. London: Free Association Books.

Bonomi, C. (2010) 'Narcissism as Mastered Visibility: The Evil Eye and the Attack of the Disembodied Gaze', *International Forum for Psychoanalysis*, 19, 110–19.

Breuer, J. and Freud, S. (1895) 'Studies on Hysteria', *The Standard Edition of the Complete Psychological Works of Sigmund Freud, Volume 2 (1893–1895): Studies on Hysteria*.

Brickman, C. (2003) *Aboriginal Populations in the Mind*. New York: Columbia University Press.

Brin, R. (1999) 'Poem by a Ram to God', in R. Brin, *Harvest: Collected Poems and Prayers*. Duluth, MN: Holy Cow Press.

Brooks, P. (1982) 'Freud's Masterplot', in S. Felman (ed.), *Literature and Psychoanalysis: The Question of Reading: Otherwise*. Balitmore, MD: Johns Hopkins University Press.

Butler, J. (1997) *The Psychic Life of Power*. Stanford, CA: Stanford University Press.

Butler, J. (2005) *Giving an Account of Oneself*. New York: Fordham University Press.

Butler, J. (2009) *Frames of War*. London: Verso.

Butler, J. (2011) 'Is Judaism Zionism?', in E. Mendieta and J. Vanantwerpen (eds), *The Power of Religion in the Public Sphere*. New York: Columbia University Press.

Campbell, J. and Pile, S. (2010) 'Telepathy and its Vicissitudes: Freud, Thought Transference and the Hidden Lives of the (Repressed and Non-Repressed) Unconscious', *Subjectivity*, 3, 403–25.

Caruth, C. (1995) 'Introduction', in C. Caruth (ed.), *Trauma: Explorations in Memory*. Baltimore, MD: Johns Hopkins University Press.

Caruth, C. (1996) *Unclaimed Experience: Trauma, Narrative and History*. London: Johns Hopkins University Press.

Chasseguet-Smirgel, J. (1987) ' "Time's White Hair We Ruffle": Reflections on the Hamburg Congress', *International Review of Psycho-Analysis*, 14, 433–44.

Cixous, H. (1976) 'The Laugh of the Medusa', in E. Marks and I. de Courtivon (eds), *New French Feminisms*. Brighton: Harvester.

Coleman, S. (1939) 'The Myth of the Fairy Birth', *Psychoanalytic Review*, 26, 301–14.

Derrida, J. (1986) 'Fors: The Anglish Words of Nicolas Abraham and Maria Torok', Foreword to N. Abraham and M. Torok (1976) *The Wolf Man's Magic Word: A Cryptonomy*. Minneapolis, MN: University of Minnesota Press.

Derrida, J. (1988) 'Telepathy', in M. McQuillan (ed.), *Deconstruction: A Reader*. Edinburgh: Edinburgh University Press.

Derrida, J. (1996) *Archive Fever*. Chicago, IL: University of Chicago Press.

Dolar, M. (1996) 'At First Sight', in R. Salecl and S. Žižek (eds), *Gaze and Voice as Love Objects*. London: Duke.

Eliot, T. S. (1922) 'The Waste Land', in T. S. Eliot (1963), *Collected Poems 1909–1962*. London: Faber and Faber.

Ettinger, B. (2006) 'From Proto-Ethical Compassion to Responsibility: Besideness and the Three Primal Mother Phantasies of Not-Enoughness, Devouring and Abandonment', *Athena*, 2, 100–54.

Fanon, F. (1952) *Black Skin, White Masks*. London: Pluto Press, 1986.

Felman, S. (ed.) (1982) *Literature and Psychoanalysis: The Question of Reading: Otherwise*. Balitmore, MD: Johns Hopkins University Press.

Fenichel, O. (1937) 'The Scopophilic Instinct and Identification', *International Journal of Psychoanalysis*, 18, 6–34.

Flügel, J. (1924) 'Polyphallic Symbolism and the Castration Complex', *International Journal of Psychoanalysis*, 5, 155–96.

Freud, S. (1900) 'The Interpretation of Dreams', *The Standard Edition of the Complete Psychological Works of Sigmund Freud, Volume 4 (1900): The Interpretation of Dreams (First Part)*, ix–627.

Freud, S. (1901a) 'On Dreams', *The Standard Edition of the Complete Psychological Works of Sigmund Freud, Volume 5 (1900–1901): The Interpretation of Dreams (Second Part) and On Dreams*, 629–86.

Freud, S. (1901b) 'The Psychopathology of Everyday Life: Forgetting, Slips of the Tongue, Bungled Actions, Superstitions and Errors', *The Standard Edition of the Complete Psychological Works of Sigmund Freud, Volume 6 (1901): The Psychopathology of Everyday Life*, vii–296.

Freud, S. (1905) 'Fragment of an Analysis of a Case of Hysteria (1905 [1901])' *The Standard Edition of the Complete Psychological Works of Sigmund Freud, Volume 7 (1901–1905): A Case of Hysteria, Three Essays on Sexuality and Other Works*, 1–122.

Freud, S. (1909) 'Analysis of a Phobia in a Five-Year-Old Boy', *The Standard Edition of the Complete Psychological Works of Sigmund Freud, Volume 10 (1909): Two Case Histories ('Little Hans' and the 'Rat Man')*, 1–150.

Freud, S. (1910) 'The Psycho-Analytic View of Psychogenic Disturbance of Vision', *The Standard Edition of the Complete Psychological Works of Sigmund Freud, Volume 11 (1910): Five Lectures on Psycho-Analysis, Leonardo da Vinci and Other Works*, 209–18.

Freud, S. (1912a) 'A Note on the Unconscious in Psycho-Analysis', *The Standard Edition of the Complete Psychological Works of Sigmund Freud, Volume 12 (1911–1913): The Case of Schreber, Papers on Technique and Other Works*, 255–66.

Freud, S. (1912b) 'Recommendations to Physicians Practising Psycho-Analysis', *The Standard Edition of the Complete Psychological Works of Sigmund Freud, Volume 12 (1911–1913): The Case of Schreber, Papers on Technique and Other Works*, 109–20.

Freud, S. (1913) 'Totem and Taboo: Some Points of Agreement between the Mental Lives of Savages and Neurotics (1913 [1912–13])', *The Standard Edition of the Complete Psychological Works of Sigmund Freud, Volume 13 (1913–1914): Totem and Taboo and Other Works*, vii–162.

Freud, S. (1915) 'Repression', *The Standard Edition of the Complete Psychological Works of Sigmund Freud, Volume 14 (1914–1916): On the History of the Psycho-Analytic Movement, Papers on Metapsychology and Other Works*, 141–58.

Freud, S. (1917) 'Mourning and Melancholia', *The Standard Edition of the Complete Psychological Works of Sigmund Freud, Volume 14 (1914–1916): On the History of the Psycho-Analytic Movement, Papers on Metapsychology and Other Works*, 237–58.

Freud, S. (1919) 'The "Uncanny"', *The Standard Edition of the Complete Psychological Works of Sigmund Freud, Volume 17 (1917–1919): An Infantile Neurosis and Other Works*, 217–56.

Freud, S. (1920) 'Beyond the Pleasure Principle', *The Standard Edition of the Complete Psychological Works of Sigmund Freud, Volume 18 (1920–1922): Beyond the Pleasure Principle, Group Psychology and Other Works*, 1–64.

Freud, S. (1921) 'Psycho-Analysis and Telepathy', *The Standard Edition of the Complete Psychological Works of Sigmund Freud, Volume 18 (1920–1922): Beyond the Pleasure Principle, Group Psychology and Other Works*, 173–94.

Freud, S. (1922a) 'Dreams and Telepathy', *The Standard Edition of the Complete Psychological Works of Sigmund Freud, Volume 18 (1920–1922): Beyond the Pleasure Principle, Group Psychology and Other Works*, 195–220.

Freud, S. (1922b) 'Letter from Freud to Lou Andreas-Salomé, March 13, 1922', *The International Psycho-Analytical Library*, 89, 113–14.

Freud, S. (1925) 'The Resistances to Psycho-Analysis', *The Standard Edition of the Complete Psychological Works of Sigmund Freud, Volume 19 (1923–1925): The Ego and the Id and Other Works*, 211–24.

Freud, S. (1926) 'Letter from Sigmund Freud to Ernest Jones, March 7, 1926', *The Complete Correspondence of Sigmund Freud and Ernest Jones 1908–1939*, 596–7.

Freud, S. (1933) 'New Introductory Lectures on Psycho-Analysis', *The Standard Edition of the Complete Psychological Works of Sigmund Freud, Volume 22 (1932–1936): New Introductory Lectures on Psycho-Analysis and Other Works*, 1–182.

Freud, S. (1939) 'Moses and Monotheism', *The Standard Edition of the Complete Psychological Works of Sigmund Freud, Volume 23 (1937–1939): Moses and Monotheism, An Outline of Psycho-Analysis and Other Works*, 1–138.

Freud, S. (1961) *Letters of Sigmund Freud 1873–1939* (edited by E. Freud). London: Hogarth Press.

Frosh, S. (2002) *After Words: The Personal in Gender, Culture and Psychotherapy*. London: Palgrave Macmillan.

Frosh, S. (2005) *Hate and the Jewish Science: Anti-Semitism, Nazism and Psychoanalysis*. London: Palgrave Macmillan.

Frosh, S. (2010) 'Psychosocial Textuality: Religious Identities and Textual Constructions', *Subjectivity*, 3, 426–41.

Frosh, S. (2011a) 'Psychoanalysis, Antisemitism and the Miser', *New Formations*, 72, 94–106.

Frosh, S. (2011b) 'The Relational Ethics of Conflict and Identity', *Psychoanalysis, Culture and Society*, 16, 225–43.

Frosh, S. (2012a) 'Hauntings: Psychoanalysis and Ghostly Transmission', *American Imago*, 69, 241–64.

Frosh, S. (2012b) 'The Re-Enactment of Denial', in A. Gulerce (ed.), *Re(con)figuring Psychoanalysis: Critical Juxtapositions of the Philosophical, the Sociohistorical and the Political*. London: Palgrave Macmillan.

Gay, P. (1988) *Freud: A Life for Our Time*. London: Dent.

Geller, J. (2007) *On Freud's Jewish Body: Mitigating Circumcisions*. New York: Fordham University Press.

Gilman, S. (1993) *Freud, Race and Gender*. Princeton, NJ: Princeton University Press.

Gilroy, P. (2004) *After Empire: Melancholia or Convivial Culture?* London: Routledge.

Gordon, A. (1997) *Ghostly Matters: Haunting and the Sociological Imagination*. Minneapolis, MN: University of Minnesota Press.

Green, A. (1983) 'The Dead Mother', in A. Green, *On Private Madness*. London: Hogarth Press, 1986.

Hart, H. (1949) 'The Eye in Symbol and Symptom', *Psychoanalytic Review*, 36, 1–21.

Hinshelwood, R. (1995) 'Psychoanalysis in Britain: Points of Cultural Access, 1893–1918', *International Journal of Psychoanalysis*, 76, 135–51.

Hook, D. (2012) *A Critical Psychology of the Postcolonial: The Mind of Apartheid*. London: Routledge.

Kafka, F. (1961) *Parables and Paradoxes*. New York: Schocken.

Khanna, R. (2004) *Dark Continents: Psychoanalysis and Colonialism*. Durham, NC: Duke University Press.

Klein, D. (1985) *Jewish Origins of the Psychoanalytic Movement*. Chicago, IL: Chicago University Press.

Konigsberg, I. (1997) ' "The Only 'I' in the World": Religion, Psychoanalysis, and "The Dybbuk" ', *Cinema Journal*, 36, 22–42.

Kristeva, J. (1988) *Strangers to Ourselves*. London: Harvester Wheatsheaf.

Lacan, J. (1949) 'The Mirror Stage as Formative of the Function on the I as Revealed in the Psychoanalytic Experience', in J. Lacan, *Écrits: A Selection*. London: Tavistock, 1977.

Lacan, J. (1953) 'The Function and Field of Speech and Language in Psychoanalysis', in J. Lacan, *Écrits*. London: Tavistock, 1977.

Lacan, J. (1973) *The Four Fundamental Concepts of Psychoanalysis*. Harmondsworth: Penguin.

Lacan, J. (1975) *The Seminars of Jacques Lacan: Book 1 (1953–4)*. Cambridge: Cambridge University Press.

Laplanche, J. (1999) 'The Unfinished Copernican Revolution', in J. Laplanche, *Essays on Otherness*. London: Routledge.

Levinas, E. (1968) 'The Temptation of Temptation', in E. Levinas, *Nine Talmudic Readings*. Bloomington, IN: Indiana University Press, 1990.

Luckhurst, R. (2002) *The Invention of Telepathy*. Oxford: Oxford University Press.

Maciejewski, F. (2006) 'Freud, His Wife, and His "Wife"', *American Imago*, 63, 497–506.

Mahlendorf, U. (2000) 'A Structural and Intertextual Reading of Freud's "On Dreams"', *Psychoanalytic Quarterly*, 69, 369–95.

Mitscherlich, A. and Mitscherlich, M. (1975) *The Inability to Mourn*. New York: Grove Press.

Morrison, T. (1987) *Beloved*. London: Picador.

Nagel, T. (1974) 'What is it Like to Be a Bat?' *Philosophical Review*, 83, 435–50.

Noy, D. (1971) 'Evil Eye', in *Encyclopaedia Judaica*. Jerusalem: Keter.

Ogden, T. (2004) 'The Analytic Third: Implications for Psychoanalytic Theory and Technique', *Psychoanalytic Quarterly*, 73, 167–95.

Oliver, K. (2004) *The Colonization of Psychic Space*. Minneapolis, MN: University of Minnesota Press.

Owen, W. (1918) 'The Parable of the Old Man and the Young', in W. Owen, *The War Poems*. London: Chatto and Windus, 1994.

Palacios, M. (2013) 'Between Fantasy and Melancholia: Lack, Otherness and Violence', in L. Austed (ed.), *Nationalism and the Body Politic*. London: Karnac.

Perelberg, R. (2009) 'Murdered Father: Dead Father – Revisiting the Oedipus Complex', *International Journal of Psychoanalysis*, 90, 713–32.

Potter, N. (ed.) (2006) *Trauma, Truth and Reconciliation: Healing Damaged Relationships*. Oxford: Oxford University Press.

Resnick, S. (1987) *The Theatre of the Dream*. London: Tavistock.

Robinson, A. (2004) 'The Politics of Lack', *British Journal of Politics and International Relations*, 6, 259–69.

Róheim, G. (1952) 'The Evil Eye', *American Imago*, 9, 351–63.

Rose, J. (2003) 'Apathy and Accountability: The Challenge of South Africa's Truth and Reconciliation Commission to the Intellectual in the Modern World', in J. Rose, *On Not Being Able to Sleep*. London: Verso.

Rose, J. (2007) *The Last Resistance*. London: Verso.

Rosenbaum, M. and Silbermann, A. (1930s) *Pentateuch with Rashi's Commentary: Genesis*. New York: Hebrew Publishing Company.

Rosenfeld, H. (1971) 'Contribution to the Psychopathology of Psychotic States', in E. Spillius (ed.), *Melanie Klein Today: Volume 1, Mainly Theory*. London: Routledge, 1988.

Roskies, D. (1992) 'Introduction', in S. An-sky, *The Dybbuk and Other Writings* (edited by D. Roskies). New York: Schocken, 1992.

Royle, N. (1995) 'The Remains of Psychoanalysis (I): Telepathy', in M. McQuillan (ed.), *Deconstruction: A Reader*. Edinburgh: Edinburgh University Press.

Safran, G. (2010) *Wandering Soul*. New York: Harvard University Press.

Said, E. (2003) *Freud and the Non-European*. London: Verso.

Scholem, G. (1941) *Major Trends in Jewish Mysticism*. New York: Schocken.

Scholem, G. (1969) *On the Kabbalah and its Symbolism*. New York: Schocken.

Scholem, G. (1971) 'Kabbalah', *Encyclopaedia Judaica*. Jerusalem: Keter.

Schwab, G. (2010) *Haunting Legacies: Violent Histories and Transgenerational Trauma*. New York: Columbia University Press.

Sebald, W. (2001) *Austerlitz*. London: Penguin.

Servadio, E. (1939) 'The Fear of the Evil Eye', *Psychoanalytic Review*, 26, 550–67.

Seshadri-Crooks, K. (2000) *Desiring Whiteness: A Lacanian Analysis of Race.* London: Routledge.

Shabad, P. (2001) *Despair and the Return of Hope.* Northvale, NJ: Jason Aronson.

Shabad, P. (2004) 'Perverse Spite', *Psychoanalytic Psychology*, 21, 662–7.

Shrut, S. D. (1960) 'Coping with the "Evil Eye" or Early Rabbinical Attempts at Psychotherapy', *American Imago*, 17, 201–13.

Slavet, E. (2009) *Racial Fever: Freud and the Jewish Question.* New York: Fordham.

Spiegel, S. (1967) *The Last Trial.* Woodstock: Jewish Lights Publishing, 1993.

Stavrakakis, Y. (2007) *The Lacanian Left.* Albany, NY: State University of New York Press.

Steiner, J. (2006) 'Seeing and Being Seen: Narcissistic Pride and Narcissistic Humiliation', *International Journal of Psychoanalysis*, 87, 939–51.

Stekel, W. (1926) 'On the History of the Analytical Movement', *Psychoanalysis and History*, 7, 99–130 (2005).

Strachey, J. (1921) Editor's Note to 'Psycho-Analysis and Telepathy'. *The Standard Edition of the Complete Psychological Works of Sigmund Freud, Volume 18 (1920–1922): Beyond the Pleasure Principle, Group Psychology and Other Works*, 173–94.

Svevo, I. (1923) *Zeno's Conscience.* Harmondsworth: Penguin, 2002.

Waszyński, M. (1937) *The Dybbuk.* New York: Bel Canto Society, 2005 (film).

Winnicott, D. W. (1956) 'On Transference', *International Journal of Psychoanalysis*, 37, 386–8.

Winnicott, D. W. (1963) 'Communicating and Not Communicating Leading to a Study of Certain Opposites', in D. Winnicott (1965), *The Maturational Processes and the Facilitating Environment.* London: Hogarth Press.

Winnicott, D. W. (1969) 'The Use of an Object', *International Journal of Psychoanalysis*, 50, 711–16.

Winnicott, D. W. (1971) *Playing and Reality.* London: Tavistock Publications.

Winnicott, D. W. (1975) *Through Paediatrics to Psycho-Analysis.* London: Hogarth Press.

Wolfe, G. (2010) 'Love and Desire "Between Two Deaths": Žižek avec An-sky', *International Journal of Žižek Studies*, 3, 1–22.

Yerushalmi, Y. H. (1991) *Freud's Moses.* New Haven, CT: Yale University Press.

Žižek, S. (1990) 'East European Republics of Gilead', *New Left Review*, 183, 50–62.

Žižek, S. (1991) *Looking Awry.* Cambridge, MA: MIT Press.

Žižek, S. (1996) ' "I Hear You with My Eyes": or, the "Invisible Master" ', in R. Salecl and S. Žižek (eds), *Gaze and Voice as Love Objects.* London: Duke.

Žižek, S. (2000) 'Melancholy and the Act', *Critical Inquiry*, 26, 657–81.

Žižek, S. (2005) 'Neighbors and Other Monsters: A Plea for Ethical Violence', in S. Žižek, E. Santner and K. Reinhard (eds), *The Neighbor: Three Inquiries in Political Theology.* Chicago, IL: University of Chicago Press.

Žižek, S. (2006a) *How to Read Lacan.* London: Granta.

Žižek, S. (2006b) *The Parallax View.* Cambridge, MA: MIT Press.

Žižek, S. (2011) *Living in the End Times.* London: Verso.

Žižek, S. and Dolar, M. (2002) *Opera's Second Death.* London: Routledge.

Zornberg, A. (2009) *The Murmuring Deep: Reflections on the Biblical Unconscious.* New York: Schocken.

Index